Politics and the Environment

Risk and the role of government and industry

D0165285

Politics and the Environment

Risk and the role of government and industry

Michael Howes

London • Sterling, VA

First published by Earthscan in the UK and USA in 2005

ISBN: 1-84407-212-6

For a full list of publications please contact:

Earthscan
8–12 Camden High Street
London, NW1 OJH, UK
Tel: +44 (0)20 7387 8558
Fax: +44 (0)20 7387 8998
Email: earthinfo@earthscan.co.uk
Web: www.earthscan.co.uk

22883 Quicksilver Drive, Sterling, VA 20166-2012, USA

Earthscan is an imprint of James & James (Science Publishers) Ltd
and publishes in association with the International Institute for
Environment and Development

A catalogue record for this book is available from the British Library

Library of Congress Cataloguing-in-Publication Data

Howes, Michael.
 Politics and the environment: risk and the role of government and industry/
 Michael Howes.
    p. cm.
 Includes bibliographical references and index.
 ISBN 1-84407-212-6 (pbk.)
  1. Environmental risk assessment. 2. Environmental policy. I. Title.

GE145.H69 2005
333.72–dc22
                                                            2004030220

Printed on elemental chlorine-free paper

Typeset in 11/13 pt Minion by Midland Typesetters, Maryborough, Victoria
Printed by CMO Image Printing Enterprise, Singapore

Contents

List of figures and tables

List of abbreviations and acronyms

ACF	Australian Conservation Foundation
ACTU	Australian Council of Trade Unions
AGPS	Australian Government Publishing Service
AMC	Australian Manufacturing Council
ANZECC	Australian and New Zealand Environment and Conservation Council
APEC	Asia Pacific Economic Community
BATNEEC	Best Available Technology Not Entailing Excessive Cost (UK)
BCA	Business Council of Australia
BHP	Broken Hill Proprietary Company (Australia)
BPEM	Best Practice Environmental Management
BPEO	Best Practicable Environmental Option (UK)
CAA	Clean Air Act (USA)
CEPA	Commonwealth Environment Protection Agency (Australia)
CEQ	Council on Environmental Quality (USA)
CFCs	Chlorinated fluorocarbons
CHOGM	Commonwealth Heads of Government Meeting
CIA	Central Intelligence Agency (USA)
CO	Carbon monoxide
CO_2	Carbon dioxide
CSIRO	Commonwealth Scientific and Industrial Research Organisation (Australia)
DASETT	Department of Arts, Sport, Environment, Territories and Tourism (Australia)
DDT	Dichlorodiphenyltrichloroethane
DEH	Department of Environment and Heritage (Australia)
EIA	Environmental Impact Assessment
EIS	Environmental Impact Statement
EMAS	Eco-Management and Audit Scheme (EU)
EPA	Environmental Protection Agency (USA)
EPBC	Environment Protection and Biodiversity Conservation Act (Australia)

EPHC	Environment Protection and Heritage Council (Australia)
ESD	Ecologically Sustainable Development (Australia)
EU	European Union
G8	Group of 8 (wealthiest countries in the world)
GDP	Gross domestic product
HCFCs	Hydrochlorofluorocarbons
HEC	Hydro-Electric Commission, Tasmania (Australia)
HMSO	Her Majesty's Stationery Office (UK)
ICESD	Intergovernmental Committee on Ecologically Sustainable Development (Australia)
IGAE	Intergovernmental Agreement on the Environment (Australia)
IMF	International Monetary Fund
IPC	Integrated Pollution Control
IPCC	Intergovernmental Panel on Climate Change (United Nations)
IPPC	Integrated Pollution Prevention and Control
ISO	International Standards Organisation
ITV	Independent Television (UK)
IUCN	International Union for the Conservation of Nature
MP	Member of Parliament
NAPA	National Academy of Public Administration (USA)
NBH	North Broken Hill Company (Australia)
NCE	National Commission on the Environment (USA)
NCEP	National Commission for Employment Policy (USA)
NEPA	National Environmental Policy Act (USA)
NEPC	National Environment Protection Council (Australia)
NGOs	Non-government organisations
NO_2	Nitrogen dioxide
NO_x	Oxides of nitrogen
NPI	National Pollutant Inventory (Australia)
NRDC	Natural Resources Defence Council (USA)
O_2	Oxygen
O_3	Ozone
OECD	Organisation for Economic Cooperation and Development
OMB	Office of Management and Budget (USA)
PCSD	President's Council on Sustainable Development (USA)
PM	Prime minister
ppm	Parts per million
PPP	Pollution Prevention Pays
PVC	Polyvinylchloride
QCC	Queensland Conservation Council (Australia)
QEPA	Queensland Environment Protection Agency (Australia)

R&D	Research and development
RCEP	Royal Commission on Environmental Pollution (UK)
Rio+5	United Nations General Assembly nineteenth special session (on the Rio Earth Summit and implementation of Agenda 21), New York, USA, 23–28 June 1997
Rio+10	United Nations World Summit on Sustainable Development, Johannesburg, South Africa, 26 August–4 September 2002
RMIT	Royal Melbourne Institute of Technology (Australia)
SARA	Superfund Amendment and Reauthorization Act (USA)
SIPs	State Implementation Plans (USA)
SO_2	Sulphur dioxide
TRI	Toxics Release Inventory (USA)
TV	Television
TWS	The Wilderness Society (Australia)
UK	United Kingdom
UK EA	United Kingdom Environment Agency
UN	United Nations
UNEP	United Nations Environment Program
US	United States (of America)
US EPA	United States Environmental Protection Agency
USA	United States of America
USSR	United Soviet States of Russia
UTG	United Tasmania Group (Australia)
UV	Ultraviolet (radiation)
VCR	Video cassette recorder
WCED	World Commission on Environment and Development
WEF	World Economic Forum
WTO	World Trade Organisation
WWF	World Wide Fund for Nature
WWII	World War II

Dedicated to the memory of Timothy William Howes

Preface

Does government try to do too much or too little with regards to the environment? Since the late 1970s there have been many attempts to reduce the size of the state in countries like the USA and Australia. Many European states, on the other hand, have tried to maintain a larger public sector, while the UK has sought to find a 'Third Way' by engaging in public–private partnerships. This book taps into this debate because it has a major impact on the ability of society to respond to environmental risks. The purpose is twofold. First, to contribute to an important public issue about how much and what kind of government society needs. Second, to make public more than a decade of research into environmental governance across three continents combined with many years of experience with industry, community groups and government organisations.

A lot of the facts in the area of environmental governance are disputed, so I have tried to build a composite picture by triangulating different sources of information from academia, government, business, non-government organisations and community groups, international organisations, the media and private think-tanks. The bedrock of this research is the list of 460 items presented in the bibliography, including reports, books, articles, conference and briefing papers, letters, media releases and sundry archival material. I have supplemented these with my own interviews, surveys and discussions with key stakeholders, as well as my experience as an industrial chemist and technical manager in the manufacturing sector, a member of several environmental non-government organisations and a participant in reviews of government institutions.

This book represents an accumulation of research and experience over many years. The ideas have been evolving over time and some have appeared in embryonic form in previous papers of mine. An earlier version of the strategy that appears in Figure 1.3 appeared in Howes (1998a). A draft of the section on Australian ESD policy that appears in Chapter 6 was published in Howes (2000). Chapter 5 is based in part on Howes (2001a & 2002a). The four methods for analysing the effectiveness of environment agencies in Chapter 8 were developed from Howes (1998b), these include: meeting the goals set; tracking selected indicators of environmental quality; enforcement and overcoming resistance; and redirecting the flow of resources through society and the environment.

There are many challenges in producing a volume of this kind. First, addressing such a profound subject as the survival of the planet requires some means by which to distil the topic into a more manageable task. This is why I have focused on industry and national environment protection institutions in three countries over the last few decades. What is learnt from this comparison, however, will obviously have broader implications. Then there is the problem of making sense of the topic so that the reader will have some context by which to judge the significance of the information. To this end I have avoided technical jargon wherever possible and provided a theoretical framework that fits with the empirical data to make its meaning plain. Finally, by the time this book goes to press it will already be a history of what has happened, rather than what is happening, yet it still provides useful lessons that could inform future decisions.

Acknowledgments

I would very much like to acknowledge the organisations and individuals who have helped me to create this volume. First, is the essential and ongoing support of Griffith University, in particular the Australian School of Environmental Studies and the Centre for Governance and Public Policy. Together they have provided me with the funding, resources and time necessary to complete this project. The research assistants funded by Griffith were of particular help, so many thanks go to Daniel Franks (who proofread the second draft), Sarah Walker, Samantha LaRocca and Elliott Orr. Part of the funding for the work on which this book is based came from a Griffith University Research Development Grant and an earlier small grant from the Commonwealth Department of Environment.

Much of the first stage of research was undertaken with a great deal of help from the University of Adelaide. Two people deserve special mention: Professor Doug McEachern (formerly with the Department of Politics, Adelaide and currently Pro-Vice Chancellor at the University of Western Australia) and Associate Professor Tim Doyle (Department of Geography and Environmental Studies, Adelaide). Doug and Tim, more than anyone, got the project started and saw me through some tough times.

I was also very fortunate to be able to spend extended periods of time at the University of California at Berkeley and University College London, which proved helpful bases from which to conduct much of the overseas research. The theoretical approach that I have adopted was very much influenced by the Centre for Cultural Research into Risk at Charles Sturt University and the two years I spent there allowed me to complete a large part of the puzzle.

I would particularly like to thank those people who helped me at the Commonwealth Department of Environment, the National Environment Protection Council, the Environment Protection and Heritage Council, the Queensland Environment Protection Agency, the Tasmanian Greens, the Wilderness Society, the US Environmental Protection Agency, INFOTERRA, the US National Environment Protection Institute, the World Bank and the UK Environment Agency.

Of course this volume would not be possible without the support of Allen

& Unwin. My thanks to Elizabeth Weiss for approving the proposal, supervising the project and making lots of useful suggestions. Thanks also to the three anonymous expert reviewers who made many constructive suggestions on the first draft, to Jeanmarie Morosin's editing and to Erica Wagner, who encouraged me to submit a proposal in the first place. Thanks also to Earthscan for agreeing to co-publish the book.

Last but not least I would like to thank all those friends and family members who have given me endless amounts of personal support over many years, particularly Kerry Argent for her endless patience, support and proofreading.

INTRODUCTION

The state, environmentalists and industry

It was the best of times, it was the worst of times, it was the age of wisdom, it was the age of foolishness, it was the epoch of belief, it was the epoch of incredulity, it was the season of Light, it was the season of Darkness, it was the spring of hope, it was the winter of despair, we had everything before us, we had nothing before us . . .

Charles Dickens, *A Tale of Two Cities* (1859)

Are we experiencing the best of times or the worst of times? What lies before us and what should national government do about it? These questions have been much debated by critics from all sides of politics and they lie at the core of this book. We certainly live at a point in history where our actions can have profound consequences for the future of the entire planet, which makes the issue of more than academic interest! On the 'worst of times' side we face serious risks, such as those posed by major industrial accidents and global environmental degradation. On the 'best of times' side, new technological developments promise a multitude of potential benefits and many people have achieved a standard of living that would have been unimaginable only a few generations ago. To complicate matters, the benefits are so unevenly distributed that mass poverty and disease remain persistent in many parts of the world. Further, the industries that are the main source of benefits systematically create the very risks that threaten our future. These issues have led to a growing expectation that government should be able to do more despite current pressure to 'downsize' the public sector. How can we make sense of these paradoxes? This book addresses these issues using a three-way comparative analysis of national environmental governance and its impact on industry in the USA, UK and Australia. The choice of this particular approach will be explained first, followed by a brief explanation of three key political players (the state, industry and the environment movement) and an overview of the forthcoming chapters.

Why look at environmental risks?

Environmental risks provide a pivotal set of case studies because they entail serious ecological, social, economic and political consequences. When things go wrong, ecosystems can be devastated, many people might die, large transnational firms could face bankruptcy and governments may lose office (see Chapter 1). Further, the use or misuse of technology plays a key role in both creating these risks and developing responses. The purpose, however, is not to drive the reader to despair with yet another catalogue of depressing facts. Instead, the objective is to face the issues head-on, critically but constructively review what has been done and identify potential avenues for improvement.

Why look at industry?

This book is about change: understanding the historical changes of modernisation that delivered so many benefits but also created serious environmental risks; examining the changes made by national governments in response to those risks; and proposing further changes to put us on a more sustainable branch of development. These are such broad themes that the focus needs to be narrowed in order to produce a manageable research task and a more concise/readable book. Industrial development, spurred on by the spread of large transnational businesses, has been selected as the focus for several reasons. First, it is one of the main drivers of past, present and future change. Second, it has become the main productive interface between society and the environment, forming the foundation for all modern societies. Third, it is an institution of great power based on its capacity to transform resources into useful artefacts. Fourth, it is the immediate cause of many environmental risks. Finally, its pollution is symbolic of broader flaws embedded in the main institutions of society.

Why look at national governments in the USA, UK and Australia?

It would be impossible to explore every environmental risk or response in a single volume so instead this book reviews a cross-section of representative examples and uses them to draw some general conclusions. The main case studies have been drawn from the industrialised world, with particular focus on the responses of national governments in the USA, the UK and Australia. The reason for this selective approach is threefold. First, these countries have made major contributions to environmental risks through their high resource use and pollution levels (although many problems have also been exported to developing states). The USA is the single largest user of resources and producer of waste, the UK has been criticised by other European states for its pollution, while Australia is one of the highest per capita emitter of greenhouse gasses. If the world is to become ecologically sustainable it is necessary for developed countries such as these to change the way they operate.

Second, these countries are where many of the government responses to environmental risks were originally developed. The USA has the largest environment agency in the world (see Chapter 3), led the development of environmental impact assessments and was the first to create an online pollution inventory (see Chapter 5). The UK has one of the oldest pollution inspectorates in the world (dating back to the nineteenth century) and is the cradle of the industrial revolution that generated many of the risks we face. As part of Europe, the UK has also been influenced by some interesting ideas such as ecological modernisation, risk society theory and 'Third Way' politics (see Chapter 2). Australia had the honour of creating the world's first environmental political party and was one of the first states to develop a national strategy for ecologically sustainable development through a series of public consultation forums involving all levels of government, business, unions and environmentalists (see Chapter 6).

Finally, these three countries offer enough similarities and differences to make for a useful comparison. On the one hand, all have similar institutional contexts: national political systems based on liberal-democratic principles, legal systems built on individual rights, mixed-market economies, advanced industrial production, high standards of living, public welfare support (at varying levels) and highly urbanised populations. On the other hand, the UK has traditionally had a more collective or corporatist approach to issues that encourage a larger public sector, while the USA supports a more individualistic political and legal culture. Australia provides an interesting intersection of these two approaches, sometimes exhibiting a corporatist approach and sometimes taking a more decentralised or individualistic tack. Its political system is a combination of those of the USA and UK that is sometimes referred to as the 'Washminster mutation' because of the combination of institutions derived from Washington and Westminster (Jaensch 1997; Thompson 1980). While the similarities make the cases comparable, the differences will give a useful indication of the importance of the local institutional context in influencing the effectiveness of responses.

It should be noted, however, that each chapter does not spend exactly the same amount of time on each country. While an even-handed overview is offered, more time will be spent on individual case studies from specific states that are amenable to detailed analysis. Cases are more often drawn from the USA, for example, because its industrial sector is several times larger than both the UK and Australia combined, it has faced a proportionately larger share of risk as a consequence and it pioneered many of the types of environmental governance being analysed.

Three key political players

Before embarking on a study of this kind it is important to note the political context within which national environmental governance emerged. To understand this, we need to be aware of three key political players: the state, business and the community.

The term 'the state' refers to the entire set of institutions of governance that constitute the public sector. This includes the executive government (the Cabinet and Prime Minister or President), the legislature (i.e. Parliament or Congress), the bureaucracy (all agencies, departments and authorities), the legal system, enforcement agencies (i.e. police, prisons and the military) and publicly owned enterprises. The state is internationally recognised as having sovereignty over a particular country (its territory) and group of people (its citizens) who may be grouped into several nations. By convention it has the power to make and enforce laws within its jurisdiction, defend its territory, enter into treaties and represent the collective will of its citizens. While the bulk of this book is about the state and its response to environmental risks, it is important to note the role of the other two players from the outset.

Most of the actions taken by the state have been directed at business and in particular that section of business called industry that is a major contributor to environmental risks. The response of industry to state actions is, important because it is an indicator of the effectiveness of such interventions (i.e. whether the policies, regulations or programs have resulted in an improvement in environmental performance). This will be covered in some detail in Chapters 8 and 9. Negative responses by industry can also be a major impediment to the implementation of policy decisions and examples of this are spread throughout the book.

The third key player is the community. Of specific importance are those sections of the community that have organised themselves into the environment movement, pressure groups, other non-government organisations and political parties. These have exerted a significant influence over the formulation of government policies, the creation and enforcement of regulations and changes to the behaviour of industry. The relationships between the state, the environment movement and industry are an integral component of environmental governance and merit further discussion.

The environment movement and the state

In the nineteenth century concerns about the environment had already led governments to pass several pollution laws, create a few public health inspectorates and establish some national parks. Outside the state, there was a growing social movement towards a kind of 'green romanticism' (Dryzek 1997) that established new non-government organisations and community groups like naturalist or conservation societies (Garner 2000; Bates 1992; Petulla 1987). By the middle of the twentieth century the type, distribution and magnitude of environmental risks had evolved into major hazards of global proportions and the movement began to change (Beck 1992). The 1960s–70s saw a diverse mobilisation of the community around various causes, such as the environment, peace, social justice, feminism and civil rights. Some of the older conservation societies shifted from naturalist groups to active political lobbyists or campaigners, while new groups sprang up at the local, national and international level.

By the 1980s these rapidly multiplying organisations had formed into a mass movement that began to engage its own professionals to generate knowledge that would help the cause. They eventually shifted from the status of political fringe-dwelling outsider groups to attending major policy-making forums on sustainable development both nationally (e.g. the President's Council on Sustainable Development or the Australian ESD Working Groups) and internationally (e.g. the Rio Earth Summit). Some had even formed their own political parties and successfully ran for office (such as the European, German, New Zealand and Tasmanian Greens) (Dryzek et al. 2003; Hutton & Connors 1999; Doyle & McEachern 2001; Jacobs 1997; Merchant 1992; Hulsberg 1988). By the late 1990s several movements had coalesced into a loose coalition to stage mass so-called 'anti-globalisation' protests against economic and political leaders at various forums around the world. These movements are not really anti-globalisation because they are actually demanding a more sustainable, fair and just interlinking of societies (Howes 2001a).

The environment movement remains highly heterogeneous in terms of institutional structures, goals and strategies, which makes generalisations difficult. It ranges from conservative, moderate reformers within established political parties (such as the West Australian Liberals for Forests) to radical activists (such as Earth First!). There are small, temporary alliances fighting local issues (as in the Love Canal campaign in Niagara Falls) and there are large permanent international organisations that act across a range of issues around the world (such as Greenpeace). Some work with existing institutions (such as the IUCN or WWF), while others seek to establish alternatives (e.g. green communes) (Eckersley 2004; Dryzek et al. 2003; Hutton & Connors 1999; Doyle 2000; Papadakis 1984, 1996; Doyle & Kellow 1995; Merchant 1992; Pybus & Flanagan 1990; Hulsberg 1988; Hutton 1987; Nicholson 1987). Over the last decade it would be fair to say that the general aim of the movement has crystallised into making society sustainable, although there are many different interpretations of what this requires. It has attempted to green business and government in the same way that the labour movement improved conditions of employment and helped to create the welfare state (Dryzek et al. 2003).

This diversity of structure, size and purpose is reflected in the variety of strategies adopted by the movement. These range from behind the scenes lobbying and letter writing campaigns to consumer boycotts, protests or direct actions, taking legal action and even running candidates for office. More recently, groups have sometimes adopted a partnership approach that enables them to work with individual firms or governments to improve en-vironmental outcomes. Protests and direct action campaigns are one of the most highly visible features of the environment movement.

Protests and direct actions

One of the earliest wins for US environmentalists was in 1956 with the prevention of a dam being constructed in Echo Park, Colorado (Petulla 1987). Key environmental actions in Australia were also centred on dam construction. Opposition to the construction of a dam at Lake Pedder, Tasmania, led to the creation of the world's first green political party—the United Tasmania Group—that contested the 1972 state election. Although unsuccessful, some members went on to form the Wilderness Society that successfully opposed the building of the Franklin Dam in 1983. This campaign triggered a national movement that led to the election of Green candidates in several parliaments around Australia (Hutton & Connors 1999; Pybus & Flanagan 1990; Green 1981). In the UK, one of the more recent successful actions has been the occupation of the Brent Spar oil rig in the North Sea by Greenpeace. This forced Shell to abandon its plans to sink the rig and tow it to shore for salvaging (Yearley & Forrester 2000). While many protest actions fail to achieve their objectives, the successful ones tend to make clever use of the media to generate broader public support that puts pressure on both political and/or business leaders.

Over the last decade or so protest actions have moved away from single issues, such as a particular development decision, and brought together coalitions of groups to fight for broader changes. At the 1992 Rio Earth Summit, environmental groups that were dissatisfied with the restricted formal agenda moved across town, established a parallel summit and began to discuss omitted issues. These included calls for greater wealth distribution to alleviate poverty, an end to the over-consumption of resources by rich states and the need for industry to pay for the environmental and social damage it had done (Doyle & McEachern 2000; Chatterjee & Finger 1994). A similar story of tight agenda control was evident in domestic sustainable development policy-making forums in countries like the USA, UK and Australia (UK Sustainable Development Commission 2003; Garner 2000; Howes 2000; Doyle 1998; Cushman 1996; PCSD 1996; McEachern 1993).

The most recent change to protest action has been the ability to mobilise on a global level and in a far more coordinated fashion. In 1999, for example, the World Trade Organisation (WTO) meeting in Seattle was disrupted by 30 000–40 000 protestors who were campaigning on a range of social and environmental issues. They held a general criticism of the undemocratic nature of international organisations and concerns about the social impacts of trade, as well as demands for fair trade to replace free trade, Third World debt relief and more action on environmental issues such as climate change (Howes 2001a). These mass protests were repeated in 2000 at World Bank and International Monetary Fund (IMF) meetings in Washington DC and Prague and the World Economic Forum (WEF) in Melbourne. During 2001 there were major protests at the G8 meeting in Genoa and the WEF in Davos and many stock exchanges around the world were blockaded on the first day of May. Smaller demonstrations were held at the Commonwealth Heads of Government Meeting in Brisbane in 2002, and protests again appeared at the WTO meeting in Cancun in 2003.

While some protests and direct actions have been successful in confronting decision makers with the consequences of their actions and putting difficult issues on the mainstream agenda, many don't achieve their aims. Other strategies, some involving confrontation and others involving cooperation, have been developed to engage the existing institutions of power on their own terms.

Legal manoeuvres

The USA leads the way, in terms of using the legal system to achieve environmental objectives, for several reasons. First, the US Constitution guarantees access to the courts. Second, in the 1970s the US courts relaxed the requirements for legal standing to sue, making it easier for individuals and groups to commence proceedings. Third, the USA has a much more litigious culture than most other countries so that resorting to court action is seen as both an acceptable and viable option (Murchison 1994). The Natural Resources Defence Council, for example, took action to force the US EPA to list 65 toxic substances as 'priority pollutants' for regulation because it felt the agency was moving too slowly (Petulla 1987). Together with the American Public Health Association, the council was also able to force the regulation of formaldehyde as a toxic substance through legal action (Shapiro 1990). Some environmental groups have targeted US industry directly and a few have used the Toxics Release Inventory data in their cases (Selcraig 1997).

Use of the legal system by groups in Australia and the UK is more attenuated because there is no constitutional guarantee of access to the courts, it is more difficult to get the legal standing to sue and the political culture is far less litigious. There have been some notable exceptions, however, and one of the watershed cases for Australia was actually a fight between different levels of government. In this case the Tasmanian state government sought to challenge the right of the national Commonwealth government to stop the Franklin Dam, since the Constitution did not grant it an explicit environmental power. The ban was upheld as the Commonwealth was able to argue it was using other powers granted to it, such as the external affairs power to enforce treaties such as the World Heritage Treaty (Toyne 1994; Bates 1992). More recently, Queensland activists forced the Commonwealth to review state approval of the electrocution of bats on lychee plantations under the terms of the *Environment Protection and Biodiversity Act 1998*.

Engaging the market

While the tactics discussed above try to engage the legal system, environmentalists have also attempted to engage the economic system to achieve sustainable outcomes. This involves two strategies: demand-side pressure designed to direct environmental concerns into green consumerism and supply-side pressure through the growing market for ethical investments. In terms of the demand side, green consumerism can work as both a sanction and a positive incentive. Consumer boycotts organised against products that used ozone-depleting CFCs in the 1970s in many countries preceded the government-negotiated international ban by decades (Elliott 1998; Benedick 1998; Shapiro 1990). On the positive side, the willingness of consumers to pay a premium for environment-friendly products, such as those from the Body Shop, has encouraged other firms to change their products and processes (Roddick 2000).

On the supply side, investors are increasingly concerned that firms with poor environmental or social records are at risk of being sued for compensation and/or subjected to expensive regulatory crackdowns. Added to this is a pool of investors who genuinely want to support firms that will be good to the environment, treat their workforce well and act in a socially responsible manner towards the community. These two factors have led to the development of ethical investment and its impact is growing (Callus 2000). Studies in the USA have found that firms listed in the top twelve polluters of the Toxics Release Inventory (see Chapter 5) suffer a significant fall in their share value and this continues until they get themselves off the so-called 'dirty dozen' list (Khanna et al. 1998; Hamilton 1993). The response to pollutant inventories in the UK and Australia is more muted, but there is a rapidly growing ethical investment industry in both countries.

Strategic partnerships

Another strategy for the environment movement is to engage business and government in constructive partnerships for improvement. Friends of the Earth in the UK, for example, took the UK pollution inventory (see Chapter 5), added more information to it and established a more comprehensive website for public information. Environmental groups in the USA have worked with the US EPA and business on several projects, including the 1990 Amoco Yorktown refinery eco-audit (see Chapter 4). In Australia, the National Farmers Federation, the Australian Conservation Foundation and the Commonwealth government developed the Landcare program to enable community groups that want to rehabilitate areas of degraded land to apply for government grants. The program was so successful that it was expanded into a Coastcare strategy for rehabilitating coastal regions and eventually a Natural Heritage Trust was established to fund a broad range of such programs.

These strategies of engagement with institutions such as the law, the market, business and the state have been met with mixed success. Like protests and direct actions, there have been some major wins but there are also many failures. What is clear, however, is that all these strategies have collectively put pressure on both governments and industry to change. Some parts of the environment movement have moved beyond simply trying to influence decisions and now seek to participate in government itself.

Electoral politics

Running for office can be motivated by several strategies. First, it may be an attempt to put pressure on the major parties' candidates to change their policies by threatening to siphon off some of their support, giving an advantage to their opponent. Second, it might simply be to demonstrate to the major parties that there is enough concern about environmental risks to lead a significant proportion of the electorate to vote for a Green candidate. Third, it may be an attempt to win a few seats in a legislature to be able to ask difficult questions, raise issues and propose new laws, in order to draw more attention to the issues. Finally, it might actually be an attempt to win enough seats to enable a Green party to have some say in government. The efficacy of all these strategies will ultimately depend on the electoral system that is operating and how much support is generated.

It is difficult to develop a successful national electoral strategy in countries that use the 'first-past-the-post' electoral system,[1] such as the US Congress or the UK House of Commons. In these situations the Greens would need to attract more votes than any other candidate and are up against the better-funded and well-established major parties. Electoral systems based on proportional representation, however, such as the Australian Senate[2] or the Tasmanian House of Assembly,[3] enable candidates to win seats with as little as 7.7 per cent or 16.7 per cent of the vote respectively. This means that Green candidates can, and often do, win seats and sometimes even hold the balance of power between the two major parties. In the Australian state of Tasmania, for example, five elected Green independents agreed to support a minority Labor government in 1989–92 in return for changes to environmental policies (Fullerton 2004; Haward & Larmour 1993; Eckersley & Hay 1993).[4] Nationally, both Australian Labor and Liberal parties have adopted environmental policies to attract Green voters and these have been crucial in deciding who governs[5] in several elections since 1987 (Williams 1997; Doyle & Kellow 1995; Toyne 1994; Richardson 1994; McEachern 1991). In the 2004 national election, for example, more than 7 per cent of the vote went to the Greens despite an overall rise in support for the conservative government.

Many of the changes to environmental governance examined in the chapters that follow are either a direct product of, or have been significantly influenced by, the prompting of the environment movement. Persistent protests, legal actions, market strategies, partnerships and electoral forays have had a cumulative effect over several decades. The changes that have been achieved have often been strongly resisted by some parts of the industrial sector (Beder 2002), which is why it is necessary to review its relationship to the state before proceeding.

Business, industry and the state

The rise of the political importance of industry is intimately connected with the modernisation process that began with the Enlightenment. This process created new knowledge and institutions that transformed society. A rapidly growing body of science and technology fed the industrial revolution that revolutionised what is produced, the way it is produced, the kinds of work available and where people live (Cardwell 1994; Postman 1993; Goldstein 1988; Cooley 1987). Politically, the rise of a new middle class led to demands for an expansion of the right to vote, while a growing working class used their electoral power to force the development of the welfare state (Dryzek et al. 2003). Emerging market economies spread industrialisation around the world, at first through the old colonial system and later via increased international trading regimes, transnational firms and various other forms of globalisation.

The importance of industry

Today industry is the main productive interface between society and the environment and an essential basis for all sectors of the global economy (i.e. providing the equipment and energy needed for agriculture, fishing, mining, forestry, energy production and distribution, manufacturing, transport, construction, communication, retailing, entertainment, finance, etc.). The vast majority of this industry is controlled by privately owned businesses that operate in an increasingly globalised market (CIA 2003). Firms can vary in size from the self-employed tradesperson to the transnational manufacturer which employs tens of thousands of people and has an annual turnover that dwarfs many national economies.

By its nature, industry utilises resources (raw materials, money, labour and knowledge) to create goods and services that raise the standard of living (Doyle & McEachern 2000; McEachern 1991). These benefits, however, have come at the cost of substantial ecological degradation and considerable social suffering. At its worst this can lead to disastrous incidents like Bhopal (see Figure 1.2), with thousands of casualties, or world-threatening hazards such as climate change (see Chapter 1). This makes industry the main cause of environmental risks, but paradoxically a potential catalyst for transformation (Howes 2001a; WCED 1990). The response of government, under pressure from the environment movement, has been to try to change the way industry behaves using new agencies, regulations, economic prompts, knowledge and policy goals such as sustainable development.

The responsiveness of liberal democracy

In theory, both the political and economic systems in countries like the USA, UK and Australia are supposed to be responsive to the demands and concerns of the public. As mentioned in the previous section, citizens can voice their concerns in protest actions, form interest groups to lobby government, run political campaigns, vote against politicians whose policies they do not agree with and even run for office themselves. Consumers can boycott products or firms they disapprove of and have recourse to the courts or state agencies for protection against unscrupulous practices. More recently, investors can move their money into ethical investment funds to reduce the pool of capital available to businesses that are poor environmental performers. These means of public empowerment are available through the institutions of a representative liberal democratic political system working in conjunction with a regulated market-based economy, an accessible legal system and a welfare state. While businesses are concerned about their public relations and profitability, governments that have to face periodic elections will be encouraged to establish consultative forums when formulating major policies so as to gain support and avoid an electoral backlash. This constructs an opportunity for organised interest groups to influence policy making by persuading the government to grant at least some of their demands (Beetham 1992; Rustow 1990; May 1978; Moore 1967; Macpherson 1966).

Who governs?

Under the pluralist model of liberal democracy (developed in the 1950s) business and industry are pressure groups which seek to influence policies like any other. No government can afford to favour one group, according to this theory, because it will lose the votes of competing groups (Dahl 1967). This model has been widely criticised, even by some of its early proponents, such as Lindblom (1977), because it does not adequately take into account the deployment of hidden powers that prevent public contests from forming in the first place. Being able to keep an issue off the political agenda is just as much an exercise of power as winning a contest (Crenson 1971). Further, there may be ways of influencing the way people think so that favouring some pressure groups over others is viewed as acceptable or 'natural' (see Chapter 2) (Dryzek et al. 2003; Pusey 1991; Ginsberg & Shefter 1990; Lukes 1974).

One of the main assumptions of pluralism is that the economic power of business, even large transnational industrial firms, does not translate into political power. This assumption appears to be highly unlikely given that the collective investment choices by business are a strong influence on the level of employment, tax revenue and GDP growth. Governments have explicitly adopted policies designed to keep GDP growth and employment levels high because the benefits they bring are popular with the electorate. They also need the tax revenue generated to provide popular public welfare services. Several studies have suggested that the desire of governments to achieve these goals means that they don't just favour the overt demands of business, but also try to anticipate what it needs (Lindblom 1977; Lukes 1974; Miliband 1970). Thus business and industry are in a privileged position of power and are not just another pressure group, particularly when it comes to environmental governance (Beder 2002; Doyle & McEachern 2000; Athanasiou 1996; Chatterjee & Finger 1994; Landy et al. 1994; Hoberg 1992; McEachern 1991; Crenson 1971).

Bounded democracy

The power inherent in the privileged position of business and industry is not absolute (McEachern 1991). Major US car manufacturers, for example, could not stop stricter emission regulations being imposed on new vehicles in the 1970s (Hoberg 1992). Large transnational chemical firms were unable to prevent the global ban on CFCs in the 1980s (Benedick 1991). Similarly, a large oil company like Shell had to back down on its proposal to sink the Brent Spar oilrig in the 1990s under pressure from Greenpeace (Yearley & Forrester 2000; Doyle & McEachern 2000). This is why firms still feel the need to put a great deal of effort into creating organisations and actively lobbying government on specific issues. It also explains why visible policy contests persist, so perhaps it would be more accurate to think of our political system as a 'bounded' democracy that still provides some opportunity for movements to bring about change within limits (Beck 1992; Dryzek 1987, 1992; Lindblom 1977).

The targets for lobbying for change cannot therefore just be in government but must include anyone in a position of power, particularly those in industry. This is why many environmental campaigns have been directed at both. While this book will focus on the response of national governments to the issues highlighted by the movement, it will also consider the reaction of industry to both growing environmental activism and increased governance (particularly in Chapter 9). This is important in order to assess the overall impact of government interventions.

The structure of this book

Assessing the ability of government to respond to environmental risks (within the limits set by industry and with the prompting of the community) poses three key questions:

1   What's the problem?
2   How has government responded?
3   Has it worked?

Each of these questions is addressed in separate parts made up of several chapters.

What's the problem?

Chapter 1 deals with the question of whether the planet really needs saving and begins with a brief summary of the impacts of industrial development. Key incidents and ongoing hazards are reviewed to give an indication of the scope and seriousness of environmental risks. The debate about the state of the planet between scientists, sceptics and environmentalists is then summarised. Finally, the need to take action in the face of uncertainty is addressed. Overall it is argued that it makes sense to at least behave as if environmental problems are serious, even if there is some doubt.

The second chapter covers why environmental risks are generated in the first place. It begins with a brief summary of theoretical explanations offered by different sides of politics. While each position offers some insight into an aspect of environmental risk, it appears to be some of the key institutions created by the modernisation process that have gone astray. This chapter then considers how state institutions have been developed in order to ameliorate the risks generated by altering the resource flows of industrial development. The approach creates a framework by which the effectiveness of such institutions might be assessed.

How has government responded?

Environmental risks have caused a significant restructuring of the state at the national level over the last few decades, so Chapter 3 looks at some of the organisations that have been created as a result. The first part of the chapter gives a brief account of the historical, economic and institutional context of the USA, UK and Australia. Three key national environmental institutions are then discussed: the US Environmental Protection Agency, the UK Environment Agency and the Australian Environment Protection and Heritage Council system. Each is compared according to their origins, institutional goals, structure, resources and powers. While the ultimate logic of each is to reduce environmental damage by redirecting the flow of resources through society, each has been shaped by different political and institutional contexts.

In Chapter 4 the new restrictions and incentives created by national governments are examined. The most common response to environmental risks has been to pass new regulations banning hazardous substances, specifying technology, imposing performance standards and setting ambient standards. While this approach has been responsible for considerable improvement, the experience of the US EPA over more than three decades suggests that there are problems with inflexibility, enforcement, industry resistance and a lack of incentive to go beyond compliance. The UK, on the other hand, tried to get around some of these issues with the Integrated Pollution Prevention and Control approach to regulation. Difficulties with regulations also triggered a rise in market-based interventions in the 1980s in the form of financial penalties and incentives that included tradable pollution permit systems, taxes and charges and subsidies for improving performance. Taken together, however, both regulations and economic prompts have had some positive impact but have also faced considerable resistance to change from industry and parts of the state.

Chapter 5 considers the use of information as a tool of national environmental governance. From the 1970s most industrialised states adopted environmental impact assessment legislation that forced industry to release information about proposed developments and assess the likely effect on the environment. This gave the community the opportunity to suggest improvements in projects before they left the drawing board. More recently, large industrial facilities have been forced to reveal their annual pollution emissions on government-controlled websites that are publicly accessible. The point is to inform and empower communities that are affected by industrial development. On the whole they have had a positive impact, but a comparison of US, UK and Australian national inventories reveals that their effectiveness is very much influenced by local economic, social and political circumstances. The uniqueness of all these programs, however, rests on their attempt to utilise knowledge strategically.

National environmental governance moved into a new phase during the 1990s and this transition is covered in Chapters 6 and 7. Earlier interventions were reactive and piecemeal in that they aimed to repair parts of the damage already done. The creation of sustainable development policies, however, was a concerted attempt to create a vision for a new society that fulfilled economic, social and ecological goals. Australia, the USA and the UK developed national policies while world leaders agreed to an agenda for change at the 1992 Rio Earth Summit and the subsequent follow-up Rio+10 conference in Johannesburg in 2002. Overall the policy goals were laudable, but it has proved extremely difficult to make the transition to a sustainable society. Further, it has been difficult for policies to avoid being constrained by entrenched political and economic interests.

Has it worked? ·

The final part, assessing how all these responses have worked, begins with Chapter 8. It draws together the approach developed in Chapter 2 and the analysis offered in the subsequent chapters. The chapter starts with some international assessments of how the USA, UK and Australia have fared in terms of ecological/social wellbeing and sustainable development. It then compares several techniques for assessing the effectiveness of government environment interventions: meeting the goals set, tracking changes in ambient environmental quality, overcoming resistance to enforcement and evidence that the flow of resources through society and the environment has been altered. This analysis suggests that while government interventions have not yet led to a truly sustainable society, they have had some positive impact and at least bought more time.

Chapter 9 looks in more detail at the various responses that industry has had to the increasing level of environmental intervention by government. Some firms rejected the seriousness of environmental problems, others sought to accommodate environmental concerns with minor changes, but a few tried to become good corporate citizens. Over time, firms have tended to move away from the position of rejection and governments have sought to encourage this trend with voluntary programs to reduce waste. Many firms have also begun to adopt environmental management systems that push them beyond a simple compliance mentality and towards continuous improvement. One of the key drawcards for encouraging good corporate behaviour is the growing belief in 'win–win' scenarios, where making production more efficient is good for business and the environment. While many firms have started to clean up their act, there are still a considerable number of recalcitrant industries that need regulations to force baseline improvements.

The conclusion brings together the points made throughout the book in a proposal for a possible restructuring of states and industrial economies. It revisits the underlying principles of liberal democracy and considers how they might be extended to represent the interests of future generations and the planet. The conclusion includes a 'reasons to be cheerful' section that highlights recent examples of positive social transitions around the globe. It is argued that a similar kind of transformation could build on current reforms to move from 'the winter of despair' to 'the spring of hope' in government.

PART A

What's the problem?

CHAPTER ONE

The nature of risk and uncertainty

Introduction

Rapid industrial development over the last two centuries has produced many benefits, but it has also generated negative impacts, particularly in the area of environmental damage. By the end of the twentieth century such problems had become a major concern, leading some environmentalists to warn of a crisis where the very survival of the planet is at risk. Other people have suggested that this risk is no more than a challenge that can be met with more technical innovation and economic reform. But there are also those, often in business, who deny that the risk is serious. So who is right and how should society respond? Answering this question will first require an examination of the nature of environmental risk. It will then be necessary to consider the sceptic's view to see if there are grounds for doubt. Finally, it is important to look at what strategy can be used to navigate through this uncertainty to develop an appropriate response.

What's wrong?

During the 1980s it appeared that the dire predictions about the death of the Earth were starting to come true. The decade began with the well-publicised relocation of hundreds of families from the Love Canal housing development in upper New York state, after it was discovered that the land was contaminated by hazardous chemical waste. This was followed in 1984 by thousands of deaths and injuries in Bhopal, India, after the accidental release of poisonous gas from a Union Carbide factory. In 1986 the world suffered its worst nuclear accident to date when a reactor at Chernobyl in the Ukraine caught fire and spread a radioactive cloud across Europe, shortening the lives of up to 100 000 people. To end the decade, the *Exxon Valdez* oil tanker ran aground, spilling some 50 million litres of oil in Prince William Sound, Alaska, devastating wildlife for decades to come (Simons 1998; Paehlke 1995; Rowell 1994; see Figure 1.2).

To add to our woes, in the middle of the decade the scientific community publicly identified two new global environmental risks that had emerged from long-term industrial emissions. The first was the announcement of an unnatural thinning of the ozone layer (which protects humanity from ultra-violet radiation) over Antarctica and popular perceptions of a 'hole in the sky' spread rapidly through the media. The cause was attributed to the release of ozone-depleting substances, particularly chlorinated fluorocarbons (CFCs) and related compounds that had been produced by the chemical industry for decades (UNEP 2002; Benedick 1991). A second risk emerged when research suggested that emissions from the burning of fossil fuels might be altering the climate of the planet, leading to an increase in average temperatures and a rise in sea levels (Elliott 1998). The projected impacts of these industry-induced changes included increased flooding in some areas, more frequent and prolonged droughts in others and a reduction in food production (IPCC 2001a, b).

These incidents and scientific revelations gave added impetus to the already growing environment movement as groups began to multiply and expand around the world. Larger organisations, like Greenpeace, increased their protest actions, hired their own scientists to continue researching the risk to the planet and deployed a range of professional lobbyists to influence both government and industry. Smaller groups, like the Chipko movement in India, campaigned on local issues, such as the protection of specific forests from logging. The anti-nuclear, peace and feminist movements also grew rapidly and merged with the environmentalists to form Die Grünen (the Greens) in West Germany—a political party that eventually became part of a national coalition government in 1998.

This outpouring of concern and mass mobilisation forced a change in the central institutions of many countries by the end of the 1980s. Media coverage of the environment became more serious and the 'environmental crisis' emerged as a common theme. Mainstream political parties began putting more emphasis on environmental polices and started to consult with environmental groups. Industry, while generally reluctant to admit the seriousness of the risk, started to change the way it operated and a plethora of environmental management systems were developed. Many organisations, both private and public, began to hire environmental scientists, engineers, planners, managers and policy makers. All of these changes were in response to the perceived risk to the planet, but what is known of this risk?

The rise of risk

Risk is a term used in almost all walks of life (e.g. business, politics, sport) and is studied in many disciplines (e.g. economics, science, sociology), but it appears to mean something different in each (see, for example, Adam et al. 2000; Lupton 1999; Franklin 1998). Broadly speaking, a risk can be understood to be a perceived hazard. This has two components:

1   The hazard—that is, something that has the potential to have a negative impact on the normal functioning of an entity (e.g. the physical impact of a fire on a building, or the biological impact of an injury to a person's health).
2   The perception—that is, an activity undertaken by thinking beings that enables them to interpret and respond to this hazard (e.g. the fear of being caught in a burning building and the deployment of fire safety measures).

Because risk involves perception, there are often situations where people 'see' risk differently. In their study of the US Environmental Protection Agency, Landy et al. (1994) found that the risks posed by toxic waste dumps were rated quite differently by the public, scientists, economists, policy makers and industry. Further, some people don't see risks that are apparent to others. Snakes are a source of great angst for one part of the population, yet make great pets for another. It should be noted here, however, that people are not always trying to avoid risk. Skydivers, for example, enjoy jumping out of planes despite acknowledging the risk to their life.

While Lupton (1999) offers a detailed typology of risk theory, she essentially divides the theories into two main schools of thought: realism and constructionism (for ease of reference these have been arranged in the form of a table; see Figure 1.1). The realists argue that risks are real and can be known through scientific, mathematical calculations. According to this approach, the differences in perception can be attributed either to ignorance when non-experts misinterpret the probabilities, or a lack of data that prevents rigorous calculation. This approach is often adopted by scientists and is found in many early articles on risk management (see Williams 1977; Starr 1969). It is also implicit in the study by Landy et al. (1994), previously mentioned, where they argue for a public education campaign to help people adopt a more scientific/economic approach to environmental risk.

Figure 1.1 Approaches to risk

Risk theory school of thought	Impact of hazard	Perception of hazard
Realism	Real	Expert view is correct, all other views are wrong
Constructionism, Weak	Real	Constructed by social context, no right or wrong view
Strong	Constructed by social context, no right or wrong view	Constructed by social context, no right or wrong view

One of the problems with the realist approach is that it fails to account for the impact of social context on how people make sense of things and glosses over the problem of how to determine whether something is an acceptable risk. It is often the case, for example, that children growing up near factories have a higher chance of developing respiratory disorders than those living in non-industrial areas because of the increase in air pollution. On the one hand, from an expert point of view, scientists might say that such disorders are not life threatening or they might find that the differences in rate of illness between industrial and non-industrial areas are not statistically significant. Even if the rate is demonstrably higher, classical economists would argue that the benefits of operating the factory outweigh the associated health costs. The company's investors and executives, who don't live near the factory or suffer its impacts directly, value the money derived from its operation and would see the health risk as acceptable. Local residents with children, on the other hand, would disagree. They have to face the health consequences on a daily basis and see the negative impact on something they value—their children. Each group is located within a different social context that leads them to define acceptable risk differently. Further, the attitudes of the residents may be tempered by employment in the factory and the scientists, economists, managers and investors would probably change their attitude if they also lived locally. It is not simply a case of one group being right and one wrong.

The constructionists see the differences in perception arising from varying social systems that 'construct' risk differently. Lupton (1999) differentiates between the stronger and weaker versions of this school of thought. The weaker versions assume that while the hazards and their impacts are real, our perception or anticipation of them is influenced by social and cultural factors (see, for example, Douglas 1972). Some people place a high priority on a clean environment, others are more concerned with industrial expansion and still others want both. The stronger version of the constructionist school (in which Lupton places herself) assumes that perception, hazards and impacts are all constructed (see, for example, thinkers who use the ideas of Foucault, such as Meister and Japp (1998) or Stratford (1994)). While the biological effects of a pollution-related injury may be similar in two people, for example, they may respond socially in different ways: one may perceive it as a debilitating setback and become depressed, the other may treat it as a challenge to be overcome or worked around. This suggests that both the anticipation and the impact of risk can be socially constructed.

One of the problems with the constructionist school is that it may lead to a kind of decision-making paralysis. If risks are socially constructed, either totally or partially, how do people choose between competing constructions? Some scientists employed by the energy sector say that global warming is not a serious risk, but scientists with the UN Intergovernmental Panel on Climate Change argue that it is, so what can society do? Mol and Spaargaren (2000) argue that the strong social constructionist approach in particular may result in the denial of real ecological problems with devastating consequences. Beck (2000) tries to side-step the realist versus constructionist divide by arguing that the recognition and understanding of risk is socially constructed and, while the impact is real, social contexts give it meaning (this leads Lupton (1999) to argue that Beck's view oscillates between the constructionist and realist camps). This is a useful approach that sits well with the definition of risk as a perceived hazard.

The nature of environmental risk

The first thing to note about environmental risk is that it is not new (Lupton 1999). While it has become more topical in the latter half of the twentieth century, it has appeared in many different societies throughout history. Australian foresters expressed concerns about conserving resources over a century ago (Papadakis 1993), Plato lamented the loss of vegetation in ancient Greece around 400 BC (AtKisson 1999) and hunting may have caused the extinction of some species in the Asia-Pacific region tens of thousands of years ago (Flannery 1995). What changed more recently is the number, scale and type of both environmental risk and public concern.

Environmental incidents

Environmental risks can be divided into two types. First, there is a growing list of incidents where the impacts of a hazard have been immediately realised (e.g. oil spills). Second, there are a number of ongoing risks with more diffuse impacts that often require a degree of scientific expertise to identify and comprehend (e.g. ozone depletion). Figure 1.2 summarises the impacts of a cross-section of major incidents over the last half-century.

Figure 1.2 Some major environmental incidents since 1950

1952, England: For five days London was clouded in a smog that led to the death of more than 2000 people with pre-existing respiratory problems. A Clean Air Act was passed in 1956 to cut emissions.

1956, Japan: The Chiso company released large amounts of methyl mercury into Minimata Bay, contaminating local fishing catches and causing debilitating illnesses, birth defects and over 100 deaths. The situation persisted for many years because authorities were reluctant to act against the company. About 10 000 residents were affected.

1969, USA: The Cuyahoga river became so polluted that it caught fire. This was one of the incidents that spurred the US federal government into a new phase of environmental regulation that led to the creation of the Environmental Protection Agency.

1978–80, USA: About 500 households were relocated from the Love Canal housing development (Niagara Falls) after it was found that chlorinated hydrocarbons and dioxins were leaching into the backyards of homes. It had been discovered that the estate was built on an old chemical waste dump several years earlier, but the residents had a long battle to get the state and federal governments to act.

1984, India: A Union Carbide chemical plant in Bhopal accidentally released a cloud of methyl iso-cyanate that killed an estimated 3500 people and injured 15 000. It took almost a decade for the victims and their families to win compensation from the company and in 2002 protesters entered the decommissioned site to highlight the lack of clean-up operations.

1986, Ukraine: One of the four nuclear reactors at Chernobyl caught fire, releasing a plume of radioactive material that spread across Europe. Over 100 000 people had to be evacuated from the region, 18 000 needed medical treatment and 100 died shortly after the event. It has been estimated that between 50 000 and 100 000 people will die of radiation-related illnesses over 50 years.

1989, Alaska: The oil tanker *Exxon Valdez* ran aground in Prince William Sound spilling 50 million litres of oil, killing bird life and devastating local fish breeding grounds. Eight years after the spill only one species had fully recovered.

1995, Nigeria: Ken Saro Wiwa, an activist who campaigned for the rehabilitation of traditional Ogoni lands polluted by the operations of Shell Nigeria, was killed by the then military government. This brought attention to the environmental damage done to the region and the violent repression that has led to the deaths of over 1000 Ogoni people.

1997, Indonesia: The extensive burning of vegetation led to a smoke haze covering eight countries and affecting the health of 75 million people over a period of three months. The problem recurred several times in later years. Forestry companies and local farmers blamed each other.

2002, Spain: The oil tanker *Prestige* broke up and sank off the north-east coast of Spain, spilling 21 000 tonnes of crude oil and taking 56 000 tonnes to the bottom of the sea. The resulting oil slick damaged wildlife along the Spanish and French coasts, adversely affecting the fishing and tourism industries. It is feared that oil may continue to leak from the wreck for many years.

2003, China: On 23 December a gas-field in the municipality of Chongqing released a cloud of poisonous gas that killed 234 people and forced the evacuation of more than 64 000 villagers.

Source: Reuters (2003, 2004), Simons (1996), Paehlke (1995) and Rowell (1994).

This is just a sample of the kinds of impacts that environmental risks can generate. The list is far from complete and the apparent increase in the frequency of events is more to do with the accessibility of data rather than indicating an acceleration of occurrence. Figures cited are estimates that vary according to the source of information used, but there is a general agreement that these events actually occurred with significant impacts.

The first point to note is that these incidents can occur in a variety of institutional contexts in any part of the world, in developed or developing states (e.g. Japan or India), under capitalist or socialist economies (e.g. the USA or, in the case of Chernobyl, the former USSR). Second, they can transmit their impact via several media, such as air (e.g. the Indonesian smoke haze), water (e.g. effluent in Minimata Bay) or land (e.g. contaminated soil at Love Canal). Third, events often have major economic impacts associated with them, sometimes seriously damaging entire local industries (e.g. the demise of fishing in north-east Spain or Prince William Sound, Alaska). Fourth, these incidents involved the use of the environment by industry (even the Indonesian fires can be linked to industrial production methods or products being applied to forestry). Fifth, there are often major social implications from death or injury (e.g. Chernobyl, Bhopal or Chongqing). Finally, major incidents such as these usually force a response from government (e.g. the creation of new agencies) that can either be a help (e.g. new laws forcing an improvement in air quality) or a hindrance (e.g. the coercion of people who raise concerns). All of these points indicate that environmental incidents have economic, social and political implications.

Ongoing problems

The other category of environmental risk consists of ongoing problems that don't necessarily generate discrete incidents but may contribute to them in the longer term. Impacts of these ongoing risks continue over a long period of time and often go undetected because there is no dramatic incident that indicates a hazard. Identification and understanding of these risks are therefore very heavily reliant on scientific research to construct the issue as the basis of public debate and institutional response. A complete list of such ongoing risks would be lengthy, but there are some high-profile issues that merit special mention. These include climate change; ozone depletion; the loss of biological diversity; increased chemical usage, pollution and hazardous waste; land degradation; the depletion of natural resources; and overpopulation. The following discussion focuses on the first four of these issues as a way to demonstrate both the range of ways that risks are identified and the variety of responses.

Climate change

Concerns about human-induced climate change and the greenhouse effect came to prominence at a 1985 international scientific conference in Villach, Austria (Elliott 1998). In effect, the Earth's atmosphere acts as an insulating blanket for the planet. Gases such as carbon dioxide, methane and nitrous oxide (among others) absorb heat that would normally be radiated back into space. This so-called 'greenhouse effect' naturally raises ambient temperatures to a range that allows the flourishing of existing organisms, including humans. Major fluctuations in temperatures, such as ice ages, occur naturally, but since the Industrial Revolution human activities have substantially altered the composition of the atmosphere and increased the greenhouse gas concentration. The burning of fossil fuels to power our factories, workplaces, homes and vehicles, for example, has raised the carbon dioxide level 20–25 per cent (IPCC 2001a, b; Elliott 1998). The risk is that this increase in greenhouse gases will lead to a general global warming and a significant change in many local climates.

In 1988 the United Nations established the Intergovernmental Panel on Climate Change (IPCC). This was a group of several thousand climate scientists around the globe who would review all of the research on climate change and report back at regular intervals to inform the policy debate (Elliott 1998). The IPCC released three major assessment reports in 1990, 1995 and 2001. The most recent report (IPCC 2001a) concluded that global surface temperatures increased 0.6°C on average during the twentieth century, leading to approximately a 10 per cent reduction in snow/ice cover and a rise of 0.1–0.2 metres in sea level. This warming will carry on if humanity continues to release large amounts of greenhouse gases and it is expected that by 2100 average surface temperatures will rise 1.4–5.8°C, while sea levels will rise a further 0.09–0.88 metres (IPCC 2001b). The impacts of this change will be to shift rainfall patterns, causing increased droughts in some areas and more flooding in others. This will have an adverse effect on agriculture, human settlements and the survival of some species. Damage to properties from weather events such as storm surges will grow, leading to an increase in insurance costs and remedial public works (e.g. flood barriers). Human health will be directly affected, with more people drowning during the monsoon season in low-lying areas such as Bangladesh, and diseases carried by insects such as mosquitoes may spread to more populous zones.

International responses to climate change demonstrate how difficult it is for mainstream institutions to address profound environmental risks. The first IPCC report spurred on the development of the Framework Convention on Climate Change that was signed by most world leaders at the Rio Earth Summit in 1992. It committed the industrialised world to limit their greenhouse gas emissions to 1990 levels and set in motion a string of later negotiations regarding the role of developing states, emission trading and offsets (such as tree planting to increase carbon dioxide absorption). Meanwhile, the second IPCC report (1995) suggested that a 50–60 per cent reduction in emissions was needed just to stabilise the situation. In 1997 the Kyoto Protocol was signed, which created targets for the industrialised world to reduce their greenhouse gas emissions by an average of 5 per cent of their 1990 levels. While being an important first step it was clearly inadequate, given the IPCC's recommendations and the implementation of the protocol is now under threat by the USA and Australia, who have changed their minds and refused to ratify the agreement. The rest of the signatories are attempting to salvage the situation. In late 2004 Russia announced that it would ratify the protocol, which would bring it into force for the remaining participants.

The reason that the world's response has been so inadequate is fivefold. First, burning fossil fuels, the main source of greenhouse gas emissions, is the foundation for a modern economy. These fuels power industrial manufacturing, homes, businesses and government departments and are the basis of the transport of people and goods around the globe. Second, there is no easy substitute for fossil fuels. Hydrogen cars, solar power and wind energy are all technically feasible but more costly (because environmental impacts are externalised by our accounting systems) and require a substantial investment in infrastructure. Third, the fossil fuel industries are very powerful organisations which have a vested interest in maintaining the status quo

(Beder 2002). While some of the more enlightened firms have started to invest in alternative technology, most have lobbied governments very hard to avoid anything that will reduce demand for their product. Fourth, some sceptics have claimed either that the risk of climate change is not proven, or that the cost of taking action is too high. Such claims are often used by resource companies to oppose intervention. Finally, the issue is a victim of the 'North versus South' divide that permeates international relations. Wealthy industrialised states (largely located in the northern hemisphere) argue that developing states should also be willing to submit to restrictions. Poorer developing states (usually located in the southern hemisphere) don't see why they should have to shoulder the burden of a problem they haven't created and are suspicious that any agreement would be designed to keep the North's wealth advantage. All of these factors make an effective response to the risk of climate change difficult.

Ozone depletion

In contrast to this somewhat disheartening story, the risk of ozone depletion provides a more positive case study. Ozone is a short-lived and highly reactive variant of oxygen that forms in the upper atmosphere. Oxygen exists as a gas made of molecules that are pairs of oxygen atoms (O_2). At high altitudes some of these pairs split into individual oxygen atoms (called oxygen radicals) that attach themselves to other oxygen molecules to form ozone (O_3). But ozone is unstable and breaks down into oxygen again. This constant cycle of creation and destruction absorbs and scatters ultraviolet (UV) radiation from the sun. Hence it provides a layer in the upper atmosphere that effectively shields the Earth's biosphere from a great deal of UV radiation that can harm plants and animals (e.g. causing cataracts and skin cancers in humans) (UNEP 2002; Elliott 1998; Benedick 1991). While there are some seasonal variations in the concentration and distribution of ozone, some products of industry, CFCs in particular, have severely interrupted the UV shielding cycle.

CFCs were developed in the 1930s and have some very desirable properties (Benedick 1991). First, they have a very high rate of compressibility and low boiling point. This makes them ideal for refrigeration and aerating insulating foam. Further, they have a low toxicity for humans, are non-corrosive to metals, are highly chemically inert (i.e. they will not react with other substances easily), do not conduct electricity and can absorb large quantities of other substances. This makes them a great solvent for cleaning all sorts of things (such as electrical equipment or moulds for plastic goods). CFC production therefore rapidly increased during the post-war years as consumers bought ever more fridges and air conditioners. It was given a further boost by the arrival of the consumer electronics industry based on transistors and silicon chips (the basis of radios, TVs, VCRs, calculators, computers, telephones, etc. (UNEP 2002; Elliott 1998; Benedick 1991).

The problem was that while this group of substances was so useful and apparently safe at ground level, they were having an undetected impact on the ozone layer. The low boiling point and inert nature of the substances mean that they can persist in the atmosphere for many years when released. This enables them to rise slowly to the upper atmosphere, where they release chlorine that reacts with ozone and interrupts the UV absorption cycle. In the 1960s scientists first noticed an increase in chlorine and a decrease in ozone at high altitudes. At this stage, however, neither the source of the chlorine nor the seriousness of the risk were known. In 1974 laboratory tests indicated that CFCs might be the culprit. By the end of the 1970s CFC propellants in spray cans had been banned in several states and a consumer boycott of these products was forming in many other states. The United Nations Environment Program formed a committee that eventually led to the 1985 Vienna Convention where states agreed to cooperate further. In that same year, however, it was discovered that there had been a 40 per cent reduction in ozone concentrations over Antarctica since 1979 (the so-called 'ozone hole'). This was a surprise, as most scientists had expected a roughly uniform thinning rather than the patchy development of such 'holes' (UNEP 2002; Elliott 1998; Benedick 1991).

The discovery of the ozone hole led to the 1987 Montreal Protocol where industrialised states agreed to reduce the emission of ozone-depleting substances such as CFCs by 50 per cent before the end of the century. A ten-year extension was given to developing states (Elliott 1998; Benedick 1991). A series of international meetings followed when new research indicated that the risk was much higher than previously thought and other substances in common use were also contributing to the hazard (e.g. halogenated hydrocarbons such as methyl bromide and hydrochlorofluorocarbons (HCFCs)). Eventually a total ban on the major ozone-depleting substances was adopted. This has been very effective and by 2000 it was estimated that the global production of ozone-depleting substances had fallen by 85 per cent (UNEP 2002). The chemical firms that produced CFCs were initially highly sceptical of their effect on ozone and strongly resisted attempts to restrict their use (Benedick 1991). Later, they argued that there was no viable technical alternative, but by the early 1990s substitutes had been found and the firms fell into line with the ban.

In 1994 one of the senior administrators helping to implement the Montreal Protocol explained[1] how the knowledge of the ozone depletion problem was rapidly evolving in the late 1980s and early 1990s. The development of viable alternatives was a key factor in the protocol's success, he said, but industry resistance in places like the USA did hold back action. He argued that there was a kind of sea change in such attitudes because 'by 1992 we'd had the ozone depletion in the northern hemisphere and suddenly it was dead serious and we had to get out of this'. So the increased perception of risk among northern industrialised states drove the later tightening of regulations. The most recent predictions suggest that the ozone layer will fully recover by the middle of the twenty-first century (UNEP 2002).

The loss of biodiversity

The revelation of ozone depletion and climate change in the mid-1980s added to the list of ongoing environmental risks that had been steadily growing since the 1960s. One of the central concerns was the increasing rate of species extinction that was leading to a global loss of biological diversity. Biological diversity, or biodiversity, refers to the number and variety of different organisms on the planet (e.g. plants, animals, fungi). Through billions of years of evolution these organisms have established complex networks of interdependence. Plants, for example, use water, nutrients from the soil, carbon dioxide from the air, and sunlight to create food for grazing animals, and predators use the grazing animals in turn as a food source. Plants also absorb the carbon dioxide exhaled by animals and release oxygen that the animals need for respiration. The animals rely on bacteria in their digestive system to help break down and absorb their food. Plants rely on bacteria to fix nitrogen from the air, as well as create nutrients from the breakdown of both the waste from animals and their carcasses. Plants also rely on animals to spread their seeds and pollinate their flowers. This is a highly simplified example of the interdependence of different species that make up more complex networks known as ecosystems. If a species becomes extinct it can no longer fulfil its role in an ecosystem. This has consequences for all the other species in the system, including humans (UNEP 2002; Elliott 1998).

Evolutionary change and natural disasters mean that there has always been a background rate of extinction, and there have been past events where the extinction rate was elevated, but human use of the environment has dramatically increased the number of species being lost each year (Rio+10 2002a; UNEP 2002). Sometimes the loss of species has been due to hunting or fishing to the point where a breeding population is no longer viable (Flannery 1995). At other times the introduction of a foreign species into an environment has crowded out one of the native species. Large-scale land clearing and the drainage of wetlands have accelerated the rate of extinction further by destroying the habitats needed by threatened organisms to survive. Pollution and the use of chemicals can also have unforeseen consequences. Carson (2000 [1962]), for example, pointed out how the use of pesticides was leading to a decline in several bird species in the USA more than 40 years ago. These activities have raised the rate of extinction to many times its background rate (UNEP 2002; Elliott 1998). The risks posed by such a rapid loss of biodiversity are profound and irreversible. Even from a selfish perspective, humans need the products and services provided by ecosystems, from the air they breathe to the food they eat, to survive. Further, many of the as yet unidentified species may hold the key to future medicines or useful products. Quite apart from this, it is reasonable to ask whether humans have the right to wipe out so many other kinds of life.

Several international actions have been taken to try to counter the loss of biodiversity on many fronts. The 1971 Ramsar Convention committed states to preserving wetland areas as breeding sites for migrating birds. This was followed in 1972 by the Convention Concerning the Protection of the World Cultural and Natural Heritage, where signatories agreed to nominate and protect areas of high conservation value as biological reserves. The 1975 Convention on the International Trade in Endangered Species was designed to restrict the overexploitation through trade of species that were at risk of extinction. UNEP, the IUCN and the WWF produced a World Conservation Strategy in 1980 that some states absorbed into national policies. Finally, in 1992, 150 states signed the Convention on Biological Diversity that required all participants to develop appropriate national strategies to preserve biodiversity as well as monitor species and cooperate with relevant research (Elliott 1998). Despite these efforts, indicators for forest, freshwater and marine ecosystems suggest a steady decline in biological diversity over the last three decades (UNEP 2002; Rio+10 2002b).

Chemicals, pollution and hazardous waste

Increased chemical usage, pollution and hazardous waste create another type of ongoing environmental risk. Their contribution to climate change, ozone depletion and the loss of biodiversity has already been mentioned. Further, the potentially extreme health impacts of some chemicals was dramatically demonstrated by the incidents at Bhopal and Minimata Bay, and the disposal of hazardous chemical waste was the key problem at Love Canal. Obviously not all chemicals are hazardous; the whole planet and all the life forms on it are in fact made of all sorts of chemicals. The chemical industry, however, creates substances that are either not found in nature (such as PVC) or develops processes to synthesise naturally occurring substances (such as sulphuric acid) on a large scale to reduce costs. Strictly speaking these should be labelled 'artificial' or 'synthetic' chemicals because they are human-made, but the term 'chemical' is popularly used to imply any industrially made substance.

The chemical industry developed alongside the Industrial Revolution and followed the rapidly growing science of chemistry that emerged from Europe in the eighteenth century, particularly in Germany. It produced substances with many useful applications across all sectors of society: building, machinery, transport, agriculture, food processing, health care, furniture, clothing, printing and so on. The ability to invent new substances with useful properties has been its key driving force. By the early 1990s there were more than 70 000 artificial chemicals in common industrial use and each year another 1000–1500 were being invented (Rosenbaum 1991). In the USA alone there are more than 200 000 chemical manufacturing plants (Underwood 1993).

Problems associated with the chemical industry are threefold. First, substances that at first appeared to be very useful have often turned out to have damaging side effects. CFCs were very useful in refrigerators but they attacked the ozone layer, while the pesticide DDT was promoted as a way to reduce crop losses to insects, but also killed off the bird life where it was sprayed. Attempts to test for the safety and side effects of new substances have created a new dilemma: the ethics of testing substances on animals in ways that can cause extreme suffering. The second problem for the chemical industry is that their production processes often generate a large amount of toxic waste or pollution. This can be released as an air emission, liquid effluent or a solid and can either impact on the local environment or be transported to long-term storage or dumps (UNEP 1990). Either way, the waste usually finds its way into the environment as happened at Love Canal and Minimata. The final problem for the chemical industry is that it usually relies on non-renewable resources, such as fossil fuels, for its raw materials. This means any expansion of the sector will contribute to the running down of a resource stock.

Many of the attempts to regulate the chemical industry and its side effects have occurred at national and local levels (since this is where a great deal of the impact is felt) and these interventions will be covered in more detail in later chapters. There are, however, some attempts at international action. In 1979 the Convention on Long-Range Transboundary Air Pollution committed 35 industrialised states to endeavour to limit the problem. Concerns about acid rain led to the 1985 Helsinki Protocol on the Reduction of Sulphur Emissions, which was signed by some European states. Several conventions were also formulated to reduce marine pollution with the guidance of the UN. Finally, the Basel Convention on the Control of Transboundary Movements of Hazardous Waste and their Disposal was signed in 1989 to prevent rich industrialised states dumping hazardous waste unsafely in poorer states (Kellow 1999; Elliott 1998). Despite these efforts and others, chemical use, pollution and hazardous waste remain significant problems (UNEP 2002).

These four ongoing risks (climate change, ozone depletion, loss of biodiversity and chemicals) are of course not the only ones that could be discussed. Concerns have also been raised about the depletion of non-renewable resources, land and water degradation and the impacts of increased population, to name a few. (For the sake of brevity they will not all be dealt with here, but they are very well covered in other volumes if the reader is interested, for example UNEP 1990, 2002; Elliott 1998; Ehrlich & Ehrlich 1990.) These four give a good indication, however, of the long-term problems that constitute the other half of environmental risk (as opposed to short-term incidents). The final point to make here is that all of these kinds of risk are interrelated. Chemical emissions such as CFCs, for example, can damage the ozone layer and act as greenhouse gases. Climate change can affect local habitats and increase the loss of biodiversity. Increasing population increases the demand for the products of the chemical industry, running down non-renewable resources, increasing land and water contaminated by hazardous waste and adding to climate change. A growing population also increases demand for food, leading to increased fishing, more land clearing for agriculture, a loss of forests, more soil erosion and a loss of biodiversity.

Political responses to environmental risk

By the end of the 1980s environmental risks were being acknowledged by many political leaders around the world, with some environmentalists and scientists suggesting that there was a serious threat to the habitability of the planet (e.g. WCED 1990; Ehrlich & Ehrlich 1990; Suzuki 1990). Three times during the last decade the national governments from around the world have considered these issues at major UN forums: the Rio Earth Summit (1992), the Rio+5 (1997) special session of the UN General Assembly, and the Rio+10 (2002b) conference in Johannesburg. Each time the majority have accepted that the problems exist and are getting worse. The final report from the Rio+10 summit, for example, stated that:

> The global environment continues to suffer. Loss of biodiversity continues, fish stocks continue to be depleted, desertification claims more and more fertile land, the adverse effects of climate change are already evident, natural disasters are more frequent and

more devastating and developing countries more vulnerable and air, water and marine pollution continue to rob millions of a decent life (Rio+10 2002a, p. 3).

Their concerns are backed up by investigations by non-government organisations such as the World Resources Institute and the Worldwatch Institute, which offer regular assessments of the state of the global environment. They are also supported to some extent by industry organisations such as the World Business Council on Sustainable Development, although the latter emphasises the positive improvements that have been achieved. Even individual states have acknowledged the ongoing problems.

Environmentalists suggest that these risks are indicative of a systematic failure in society that requires substantial economic restructuring and lifestyle changes. Business leaders, on the other hand, often suggest that individual incidents are isolated cases and the ongoing problems have either been overstated or provide a challenge that industry can overcome with better management and technology. Governments try to steer a course between these two sets of claims for fear of antagonising either investors who worry that regulation is bad for profitability or voters who are concerned about the environment (Richardson 1994; McEachern 1991). This illustrates the importance of social context in constructing environmental risks and their impacts and the problem of whether these risks are real.

The sceptics and their critics

There remain significant critics who are highly sceptical of environmental risk and each decade appears to produce a crop of high-profile dissenters. In the 1980s Simon and Kahn (1984), for example, argued that the planet was not in such bad shape and predicted that things would be better by the end of the century. In the 1990s North (1995) and Easterbrook (1995) also took optimistic views (a summary and critique of these kinds of views dating back to the 1960s can be found in Dryzek (1997)).

One of the most recent and well-known examples of this position is Bjørn Lomborg and his book *The Skeptical Environmentalist* (2001). His overall thesis is that the longer-term trends indicate that things are getting better for both the planet and humans, but still more needs to be done. He is therefore critical of environmental organisations such as the Worldwatch Institute, Greenpeace and the World Wide Fund for Nature for claiming that things are getting worse. His argument, however, is underpinned by a number of rather questionable premises, including that:

1   some research on specific agricultural risks (e.g. soil erosion and falls in wheat production) is based either on small-scale studies or short-term trends, therefore humanity should not be concerned;
2   shifting pollution problems between media (e.g. acidic vapours converted into a sludge for landfill disposal) should be counted as an improvement in environmental quality;
3   the loss of forests has been more than offset by increases in the area of monoculture tree plantations established for logging;
4   the costs associated with risks such as climate change are too high to justify action; and
5   some of the predictions made by individual environmentalists were wrong, therefore society should mistrust both all their claims and the studies of environmental scientists.

Many environmental scientists have written rebuttals to Lomborg's claims and a database search revealed several hundred related journal articles that have been published over the last three years. It would be a pointless exercise to summarise them all here, but the critics generally argue that Lomborg has been highly selective with his use of data and/or misinterpreted its meaning. Lovejoy (2002), for example, argues that he has misapplied measurements of species extinction rates and forest clearing, leading to an understatement of the loss of biodiversity. Holdren (2002) suggests that Lomborg missed the point on energy production because he focuses on the availability of fossil fuel reserves rather than the impact of their use. Schneider (2002) queries his selective use of cost and temperature estimates with regards to climate change. Bongaarts (2002) argues that Lomborg's calculation of the link between population growth and resource use is simplistic, missing many of the complex social issues that are entailed. Such criticisms are supported by many other scientists (see, for example, Fisher 2002; Simberloff 2002).

Baker (2002) points out that despite this concerted criticism, the financial media continue to use Lomborg as an argument against both the seriousness of environmental risk and the need for government intervention. *The Economist* (2002) even found it necessary to justify its support by attacking the scientists who disagreed with him. In January 2003 it was reported that the Danish Committee on Scientific Dishonesty found that Lomborg's book was based on 'half-truths and poor research', a verdict that the author rejected (Schang 2003). *The Economist* (2003) immediately sprang to Lomborg's defence with the surprising claim that the decision was 'incompetent and shameful' because his book was not a scientific treatise. It was later reported that the verdict had been queried by the Danish Ministry of Science and Lomborg was not guilty, which added fuel to the debate (Tribe 2003).

Such a reaction of support for Lomborg from the financial media is understandable, as acknowledgment of serious and systematic environmental risks would demand a major restructuring of modern industrial society. Those with a vested interest in keeping the status quo are therefore likely to seize any evidence, no matter how flimsy, that change is unnecessary. Further, the idea that the very foundation of our society, industrial production, is threatening our long-term survival is so profoundly disturbing that many people's initial response has been denial.

While many, including this author, do not agree with Lomborg's analysis, his book and the reaction that it has provoked is an important contribution to the debate regarding environmental risk. Scientific research and democratic decision making are both improved when there is a well-informed debate that is able to expose the weaknesses of each side and generate improvements. It is therefore important not to accept unquestioningly the claims made either by Lomborg or those he criticises. At the end of the day, however, Lomborg is only able to argue that the particular indicators that he has selected may be improving if his approach to the analysis is used. Even if this assertion is accepted and the majority of experts in the relevant fields do not accept it, by Lomborg's own admission the state of the world is still far from satisfactory.

Lomborg claims that he is not a 'demonic little free-market individualist' and is not arguing for zero environmental intervention by government. He does, however, assert that regulation and policy tools are not the main reason for improvements in environmental and social indicators. According to his view, government intervention should be rationalised to avoid resources being inefficiently used. Lomborg offers scant evidence for this claim and it is worth noting that business generally has a history of resisting changes that require an improvement in their environmental performance (Beder 2002; Doyle & McEachern 2000; Ruckelshaus 1993; McEachern 1991; UK Department of Trade & Industry 1991). It has usually been the prompt of government intervention that has forced firms to change their practices and, had government not acted, it is likely that the state of the environment would be worse. Ozone depletion, for example, is dealt with only briefly by Lomborg and he omits to mention that the chemical industry first denied the existence of a risk, then resisted attempts by governments to ban ozone-depleting substances for several years (Benedick 1991).

Lomborg's approach to environmental risk is clearly in the realist school where there is one correct answer (his) and many mistaken views. From his perspective anyone who argues that the problems considered in his book are getting worse has either been misled or is deliberately trying to mislead. He assumes that if the official data is examined using his rational, scientific, statistical approach the same conclusion is inevitable. The problem is that the majority of scientific experts who work with and create this data do not agree with his analysis or conclusions. So how does society decide between these competing views? Is one version of environmental risk correct and the other wrong, or are these simply different social constructions of risk?

Action and uncertainty

As has already been pointed out, the realist position does not take into account the ability of social context to influence how the concept of acceptable risk is constructed. In this particular case, it seems implausible that so many scientists around the world would be engaged in a deliberate conspiracy to mislead everyone. Lomborg himself points out that most scientists are working within the public sector and are conducting research funded by public money. What he fails to establish is any direct economic or political incentive to produce misleading results. They are not seeking to win political office and will not receive bigger salaries if the risks are taken seriously (their income usually being pre-set by public sector pay scales). Most are engaged in research simply because they are interested in finding out how something works, rather than pursuing a political agenda.[2] Further, the peer review process that acts as a filter for both funding and publication actively discourages scientific research with an overtly political bias.

These factors do not sit well with Lomborg's assumption that scientists have to portray their research as attempts to solve serious problems in order to obtain public funding. In fact there have been several attempts to push both opinion and scientific studies the other way. President Reagan, for example, offered extra government funding to those US scientists who were sceptical of climate change in the early 1980s. In 1997 the Australian government paid for representatives of the Australian Bureau of Resource Economics to travel to all major capital cities[3] and argue that it would cost too much to reduce greenhouse gas emissions. This was in the lead up to the Kyoto conference but little official credence was given to the IPCC findings and no effort had been made to estimate the costs of the impacts of climate change. Despite these efforts, the majority of climate scientists in both the USA and Australia continued to warn of the risk of climate change. These factors undermine the realist view held by Lomborg that society is being deliberately misled, but it still leaves a problem: are the risks real or not?

A risk management strategy

Even if humanity cannot know for sure, society should at least behave as though environmental risks and their potential impacts are real. This argument utilises two rational scientific theories: (1) a version of game theory derived from mathematics; and (2) the economic risk management principle of minimising the maximum cost.[4]

The analysis is based on two basic assumptions. First, the history of the last four decades suggests that most businesses are reluctant to address the environmental risk generated by their activities. Second, even if Lomborg's thesis is correct and some problems are improving, by his own admission the world is still far from achieving a satisfactory outcome with regards to human welfare and the environment. These very plausible premises support two logically valid arguments. First, either there really are serious environmental hazards associated with industrial development or there are not. Second, either the state intervenes by developing and implementing effective policies or it does not. The range of possible outcomes can then be drawn up (Figure 1.3).

Figure 1.3 Hazard versus response

	Real and serious environmental hazard	No real or serious environmental hazard
The state intervenes effectively	A No cost from being mistaken	B Industry is forced to invest in cleaner production in the short term, with some money recouped from efficiency gains
The state does not intervene effectively	C Industry fails to adopt cleaner production, leading to major economic, social, political and environmental costs	D No cost from being mistaken

Both outcome A (real hazard and effective intervention) and D (no real hazard and no intervention) have no cost of being mistaken since actions and perceptions match (although A would still entail some compliance costs). The cost of outcome B (state intervention but no real hazard) would be minimal. Since governments have become more active in environmental regulation and policy over the last three decades, businesses in most industrialised states have spent increasing amounts of money on cleaning up their operations. By the end of the century, industrialised states were spending an estimated 0.8–1.6 per cent of GDP on environment protection (UK Department of Environment, Food and Rural Affairs 2002; McLennan 1999; Morgenstern et al. 1998; OECD 1984, 1996a; US EPA 1993, 1994a, b; Harris 1993). It is arguable that for government intervention to be truly effective more money will need to be invested by both the state and industry to make society sustainable.

The costs of current expenditures or any increase must be discounted for two reasons. At the microeconomic level many investments in cleaner technology can actually reduce production costs and pay for themselves because they entail efficiency gains with less raw material use and wastage per unit of production (Suzuki & Dressel 2002; AtKisson 1999; Hawken et al. 1999). A chemical plant in California, for example, spent US$240 000 in 1987 on reducing and reusing their caustic soda and hydrochloric acid waste, which resulted in raw material purchase savings of US$2.4 million per annum and an annual 6000 tonne reduction in waste (Porter & van der Linde 1995). Obviously not all firms will find these kinds of changes easy or inexpensive (Athanasiou 1996; Cebon 1993), but the increasing number of positive case studies suggest that the money invested is often more than offset by cost savings. At the macroeconomic level, evidence has been emerging that government environmental intervention does not increase the level of unemployment (Goodstein 1999). Some studies have even suggested that it has a net stimulus on industrial economies working below full capacity by creating new industries, encouraging the development of new technology and shifting resources away from older, more inefficient sectors (OECD 1984, 1996a). In 1995 it was estimated that American industry could save US$1.2 trillion dollars and create 1.1 million jobs over 15 years by reducing its waste by 1.3 billion tons (NCEP 1995).

The maximum cost is therefore outcome C where the state does not intervene effectively, there is a serious hazard and industry does not perceive a benefit in changing to cleaner production methods. This outcome generates a set of severe problems that include substantial economic costs, such as increased insurance premiums against environmental damage claims, greater clean-up charges and compensation payouts after accidents and higher healthcare premiums because of illnesses caused by pollution. Some of these costs have already become apparent (UNEP 2002; IPCC 2001b). On top of these economic costs are the negative social impacts (e.g. death, injury or poverty through loss of livelihood, as in Bhopal), political costs (e.g. civil unrest, as in Nigeria) and ecological harm (e.g. damage to ecosystems or loss of resources, as in the *Exxon Valdez* oil spill in Prince William Sound). The US Department of Defence, for example, was concerned about the possibility of increased conflict due to reductions in food production, energy supplies and fresh water that may result from climate change (Schwartz & Randall 2003).

This analysis can go one step further by assigning probabilities to each of the outcomes in Figure 1.3 (readers who find such numerical analyses unhelpful can skip to the next paragraph). If there is a 50:50 (or equal) chance that the hazards are real and a 50:50 chance that government intervention will be effective, all four outcomes would have a probability of 25 per cent (i.e. 50 per cent for the reality of hazard multiplied by 50 per cent for the chosen response). Given the review of the data presented in this chapter, however, it would be reasonable to assert that there is a greater than 50 per cent probability that environmental hazards are real. Further, the review of incidents and ongoing problems suggests that there is a greater than 50 per cent chance of governments not intervening effectively. The probability of outcome C is therefore greater than 25 per cent (the odds of each factor multiplied together) while the odds for outcome B (effective intervention but no real hazard) would be less than 25 per cent. Hence the most probable outcome is that the world will incur the maximum costs of outcome C unless there is a renewed effort to take action. This supports major changes in the way environmental risks are addressed.

Based on this line of reasoning, if humanity adopts a risk management strategy to minimise the maximum costs associated with industrial development, it would be reasonable to accept the need for effective state regulation, policy making and implementation. Further, it would be reasonable to demand changes that will increase the effectiveness of these interventions. This is the case even when faced with contradictory constructions of environmental risk by a range of different experts.

Conclusions

In short, a risk is a perceived hazard that has the potential to cause damage and perceptions of acceptable risk are influenced by social context. Environmental risks are a complex set of interrelated incidents and ongoing problems that are generally associated with industry and have potentially serious consequences for both society and the environment. While there is some dispute over the reality and severity of environmental risk, the bulk of expert opinion suggests that there are serious problems and even the sceptical environmentalist admits that things are far from satisfactory. Finally, it is wiser to behave as if the planet does need saving rather than risk the major costs that could result from sceptical inaction.

CHAPTER TWO

The origins of risk and modern governance

Introduction

Even if the sceptic's dilemma (discussed in Chapter 1) is overcome and society behaves as if environmental risks are real there is the immediate challenge of how to develop an appropriate response. This requires an understanding of what creates environmental risks in the first place so that the underlying causes are treated, not just the symptoms. It also requires an understanding of the nature of governance to determine what is likely to be the most effective strategy for intervention—there is no point in prescribing cures that are beyond the capacity of the state to implement.

This chapter will address these issues in turn. First, a range of explanations for the possible causes of environmental risk is outlined. It is argued that all of these causes are institutions that are either a product of, or integral to, the process of modernisation. The link between the development of modern institutions and environmental risk is explored in more detail via the work of Ulrich Beck (1992, 1994, 2000) in Part B. Particular attention is paid to the role of the state, which is central to any study of environmental governance. An analysis of the different discourses generated by the state, industry and the environment movement, together with a more detailed consideration of state power, is developed in Part C which draws on the ideas of Michael Foucault (1977, 1990, 1991) and John Dryzek (1987, 1992, 1997). Finally, these strands are brought together into a theoretical model that can be used for assessing the effectiveness of state interventions and the politics in which they are enmeshed.

Debating the origins of environmental risk

Why have environmental risks been generated? This is a deceptively simple question, but the answer is highly contentious. There is an ever-growing sea of conflicting explanations and simply describing the many different schools of thought has filled many volumes (see, for example, Eckersley 1992, 2004; Hay 2002; Palmer 2001; Dobson 2000; Dryzek & Schlosberg 1998; Dryzek 1997). The intersection of the political left and the environment movement has created a wide range of views (Doyle 2000). Eco-socialists, Marxists and critical theorists blame the market for encouraging industry to exploit both people and the environment (Bell 1995; Gorz 1994; Broad 1994; Chatterjee & Finger 1994; Pepper 1993; Lele 1991). Eco-anarchists blame hierarchies within both the state and the market for alienating humans from nature (Bookchin 1982, 1990, 1994). Eco-feminists argue that patriarchy encourages the exploitation of both women and nature (Shiva 2000; Warren 1997; Stratford 1994; Harcourt 1994; Mies & Shiva 1993; Merchant 1992; Plumwood 1986). Deep ecologists blame the anthropocentric (human-centred) views and institutions that fail to value the non-human environment adequately (Foreman 1998; Devall & Sessions 1985; Naess 1974, 1984; Fox 1984a, b).

There is an equally broad array of ideas on the right of politics. There is a group of thinkers, for example, who blame state 'interference' in the market for creating or exacerbating environmental risks by preventing the optimal allocation of resources (Hardin 1998 [1968]; Howard 1994; DiLorenzo 1993; BCA 1991a, b). This group includes neo-liberals (in the UK and Australia), neo-conservatives (in the USA), libertarians, utilitarians, economic rationalists and some business leaders (Holland & Fleming 2003; Dryzek 1997; Pusey 1991). For simplicity they will be referred to collectively as 'neo-liberal' because their beliefs have been extrapolated from classical liberal ideas. (This should not be confused with US liberals who are generally on the centre-left of politics.)

To make matters even more confusing, various streams of institutionalism identify a broad range of social structures as key influences on development trajectories. While many of these studies only deal with environmental governance as a side issue, they do have considerable relevance to the area because they are concerned with uncovering what influences both human behaviour and society's historical, economic or political development. (See, for example, Fosnot 1996; Zysman 1994;

DiMaggio & Powell 1991; Garrett & Weingast 1991; Haas 1990; Johnson et al. 1989; Piore & Sabel 1984; Hardin 1982; Berger 1972, 1981; Tyson & Kenen 1980; Wolf 1979; Stigler 1971.)

It is not the purpose of this book to try to resolve all the disputes between these various schools of thought. The point is simply to note that the ground is contested and provide an indication for the reader of how to follow up any ideas they find interesting. One thing that all of the different theories appear to have in common, however, is that they focus on a particular set of institutions that either have been created by the process of modernisation or have become an integral part of the modern world. While environmental risks are very old (as noted in Chapter 1) it is only during the modern period that the type and scale have become so profound as to threaten the future of the entire planet. Air pollution, for example, was a local problem for many medieval European cities, but emissions on a scale that cause climate change or of a type that destroys the ozone layer are recent phenomena. Perhaps it is therefore the path taken by modernisation that is the root cause of environmental risk.

Three theorists who have made considerable contributions to the understanding of this area are Ulrich Beck (1992, 1994, 2000), Michael Foucault (1977, 1990, 1991) and John Dryzek (1987, 1992, 1997). Beck dissects the process of modernisation, the creation of global risks and the adequacy of state responses in considerable detail. Foucault offers a dynamic historical account of the way society constructs and transforms institutions, particularly those relating to the state and governance. Dryzek has used these ideas to develop some useful analytical techniques for the study of environmental governance. Before proceeding, it is important to understand something of these theories, so a brief summary is offered below. Together, they offer a plausible explanation of how the world came to be in its current predicament and a basis for assessing how the state has responded.

Modernisation and environmental risk

Modernisation refers to the historic process of transformation of traditional societies that began in Europe and North America with the Enlightenment, the rise of the liberal-democratic state, the rapid development of science and technology, the Industrial Revolution and the spread of market-based economies. This transformation entailed a series of profound changes to social institutions (Cardwell 1994; Postman 1993; Goldstein 1988; Cooley 1987). Traditional artisan production and farm labour was replaced with mass production, machine technology and the specialisation of labour.

Economies that were based on land ownership and agricultural commodities were replaced by private capital, industrial production, the investment market and manufactured goods. Socially, the population shifted from small farming communities to large industrial cities. Science usurped religion and reason challenged belief as the basis for knowledge. Politically, the American and French revolutions set in train a process that continues today of replacing authoritarian regimes with elected governments, while the role of the state expanded to deliver more social goods such as security, infrastructure, welfare and education. These changes generated great benefits, such as reduced mortality rates, longer lifespans and a higher standard of living for a large part of the human population, but they also entailed considerable social and ecological costs. This transformation has been referred to as the 'simple' phase of the modernisation process that ended the early twentieth century (Giddens 1998a).

From class society to risk society

In his now famous book *The Risk Society*, Beck (1992) argued that the process of modernisation changed at some point in the twentieth century and started to undermine itself with the negative impacts that were produced as part of its normal operation. As industrial production spread, it became the main foundation on which modern society was built. The side effect, however, was to generate environmental risks that seriously threaten the survival of humanity and the planet. This effect spilled over into politics where the struggle between classes over the distribution of goods has been overlaid by a struggle over the distribution of 'bads', such as pollution and toxic waste. Both the state and industry have been unable to address these risks adequately, leading to a rise in public disenchantment and a growing sub-politics of the environment movement.

The idea of risk society is also pursued by Giddens (1994, 1998a) and he is particularly interested in the rise of uncertainty and the loss of faith in expert knowledge. Both Beck (1998a) and Giddens (1994) offer a framework strategy for managing the uncertainty inherent in expert knowledge through a more accessible public review process that re-engages the sub-politics of environmentalism. This could include public consultation forums on major issues, community representation on major decision-making bodies within the state and industry and the possibility of community–state–business partnerships on specific projects (Giddens 1998b). While there have been some patchy moves towards implementing a limited version of these ideas the world is still nowhere near the kinds of ecological democracy that have been proposed by these thinkers and others (Eckersley 2004;

Dryzek et al. 2003; Dryzek 1987, 1990, 1992). Lash (1994), for example, suggests that the re-engagement of the sub-politics with decision makers requires access to information and communication networks to assist non-government organisations (NGOs) to take up neglected issues (a point pursued in Chapter 5).

Modernisation becomes reflexive

Beck (1994, p. 6) defines reflexive modernisation as 'self-confrontation with the effects of risk society that cannot be dealt with and assimilated in the system of industrial society'. As modernisation proceeded it generated risks that were beyond the capacity of the state and industry to address adequately. This is largely due to the fact that society was trying to address complex twentieth-century issues (such as nuclear disasters) with institutions designed in the nineteenth century (like insurance). The rise of environmental risks caused a reaction by the community that created the environment movement. Many within the movement then questioned whether modernisation was such a good idea and began proposing alternatives. The apparent failure to avoid a growing list of incidents and ongoing hazards resulted in a loss of faith in both the willingness of industry to behave responsibly and the capacity of the state to respond. Environmental groups therefore increasingly took their own actions, often turning the products of industry against itself. They used the Internet and the electronic media, for example, to confront industry publicly with the consequences of its actions in campaigns such as Brent Spar (Yearley & Forrester 2000) or mass rallies outside major international economic and political forums (Howes 2001a).

Giddens (1998a, p. 31) is careful to point out that reflexive modernisation goes beyond simple modernisation (the phase prior to the mid-twentieth century) because it 'implies coming to terms with the limits and contradictions of the modern order'. Scott (2000) argues that rather than there being an identifiable switch between simple and reflexive modernisation, these features have always been part of industrialisation. Mol & Spaargaren (2000) group both risk society theory and the stronger versions of ecological modernisation theory under the reflexive modernisation umbrella. Fundamentally, ecological modernisation argues that while the institutions of modern society (liberal democracy, the state, industry and market economics) have gone astray, they can be saved with appropriate restructuring (Mol & Spaargaren 2000; Dryzek 1997; Christoff 1996). At its core is the assertion that economic growth can be decoupled from increased resource use and waste by deploying better technology and alternative decision-making routines. (Representative thinkers of this school would include Gore

(1992), AtKisson (1999) and Hawken et al. (1999), although they do not use the term.)

Later versions of this school of thought have moved away from a narrow technological focus on efficiency and sought to encompass broader social, economic and political transformations. Hajer (1995) and Curran (2001) suggest that the spread of ecological modernisation as an idea may explain the popular rise of environmental policy goals such as sustainable development (see Chapters 6 and 7). Weale (1998) found that political culture was a significant factor in the uptake of ecological modernisation ideas among policy makers. Blowers (1997) and Cohen (1997) suggest that both environmental policy making and the rise of the environment movement can be explained by the reflexivity of risk society and ecological modernisation (see also Howes 2001a).

So far so good, but it would be useful to understand how these institutions of modernity evolved and operate in more detail. This would then help explain why there is a kind of institutional inertia within the state and business that makes it difficult to address environmental risks. It may also explain the rise of alternative views that challenge prevailing attitudes and give rise to protest movements. This is where Foucault can help.

Looking deeper: The rise of modern governance

Foucault's understanding of the modernisation process and the institutions of governance that it has created begin with two fundamental premises. First, he asserts that power and knowledge are inextricably linked, like two sides of the same coin. Second, he claims that power comes from below, not above, because any institution or power structure ultimately depends on the acquiescence of the people that it attempts to control (Hindess 1996; Rabinow 1991; Foucault 1985). He offers an ingenious explanation for how this works through a social fabric where the power of institutions is transmitted through individual relations (e.g. the police officer who fines you for a smoking vehicle exhaust pipe, or the environmental inspector who visits your workplace).

Discourses and power

When two or more people enter into an unequal association, Foucault argues, a force or power relation is formed in which one person is dominant and the other is subordinate (Foucault 1990). Associated with this force relation is a discourse that reinforces the situation. A discourse is a kind of mini-ideology that includes constructed knowledge which gives the dominant person strategic information about the subordinate that helps maintain their relative positions. It also produces a way of looking at the situation that justifies the relation, encouraging both the subordinate and dominant person to accept the legitimacy of the situation.

A doctor–patient relationship is perhaps the best example of a force relation with an associated discourse. The doctor's medical knowledge and the specific information derived from testing or examining a person constitutes part of the discourse that puts them in a position of authority because the patient usually cannot understand the highly technical information and has to rely on what the doctor tells them. Further, there is a shared view that the doctor will act in the interests of the patient, that it is legitimate for them to examine the patient's body (even if it may be embarrassing) and that the course of treatment should be followed even if it is costly, inconvenient and painful. This shared view and highly technical knowledge reinforces the patient's subordinate position to the doctor and constitutes a discourse so powerful that they literally put their lives in the hands of the doctor. While most of the time this is a good idea, it has been abused on some occasions. A recent case in the UK, for example, involved a doctor called Harold Shipman who had been killing scores of his elderly patients while pretending to treat them. He was able to get away with this crime for years because of the trust placed in doctors by patients and their relatives under this medical discourse.

Discourses manifest themselves in the ideas, values, categorisations, practices and self-discipline that cause people to participate in their own control (Hajer 1995; Foucault 1985). In the example above, people willingly submit to the control of doctors, nurses, hospital rules and regimented treatments because they have been classified as a patient (i.e. someone who needs medical attention) and believe that this will make them well. This happens even if the doctor is not acting in their interests, as in the Shipman case. With regards to environmental risk, Dryzek (1997) suggests that discourses are a way of interpreting the world which influence the way humans collectively acknowledge or understand a risk and shape what is viewed as a legitimate response.

Unlike the Marxist notion of a single dominant ideology, there is a multiplicity of ever-changing discourses that pervade the fabric of society which are constantly clashing or reinforcing each other. When discourses reinforce, an institution grows. Patients, for example, may have a great deal of faith in science that encourages them not only to accept treatment but also to participate in the trials for new cures that creates knowledge to strengthen the institution. When discourses clash, an older institution can be undermined and decline, while a new one is born. The struggle between Christianity and science, for example, has led to the establishment and growth of many scientific research institutions and falling church attendances. Finally, anyone can be affected by many different discourses at the same time. A person may be in a subordinate relationship with their doctor or their priest, but they may be in a dominant position over their children as a parent or over members of the local sports club of which they are president.

Surveillance and the possibility of observation is a key feature of the way discourses operate because individuals modify their behaviour and discipline themselves if they think they are visible (Foucault 1977). Rutherford (1994) finds evidence that current attitudes towards environmental problems are examples of an ecological discourse at work that assumes scientific surveillance and management is the solution. The kind of surveillance of industry undertaken by environment agency officials or environmental organisations is a good example. As long as a firm feels that an agency may be watching, it is more inclined to comply with regulations. It may also feel more inclined to adopt more environmentally friendly practices if it feels that community groups are watching its operations and threatening a campaign that would damage its public relations or profitability.

Discourses of the state, industry and environment movement

Dryzek (1997) identifies four key elements of discourses. First, discourses influence how nature is viewed, what is acknowledged as an issue, what is construed as a problem and what institutions are seen as legitimate players in the situation. Second, they influence which relationships are seen as 'natural' (e.g. competition between people or human dominance of the environment). Third, they influence how the actors in environmental governance are perceived and motivated (i.e. altruistic or self-interested). Finally, they affect the metaphors and rhetoric used to justify different positions (e.g. whether nature is portrayed as fragile or robust). These four elements influence both the construction of, and responses to, environmental risk. They can be used to differentiate the discourse emerging from the three main players in environmental governance: the state, industry and the environment movement.

State institutions, for example, often generate and operate under a discourse of 'administrative rationalism' (Dryzek 1987, 1990, 1997). In this discourse risks are constructed as something that can be adequately managed by the state. People and the environment are seen as subordinate to the experts within state institutions who are supposed to be better able to understand the problems and find solutions. It is assumed that agents of the state will act in the public interest, while those in business and the community may be self-interested. Finally, the state seeks to reassure the public that everything is under control. These elements will be evident in Chapters 3, 4 and 5, which deal with the creation of new agencies, the deployment of new regulations and the implementation of new Environmental Impact Assessment procedures.

Industry, on the other hand, often generates a discourse of neo-liberalism which Dryzek sometimes refers to as 'economic rationalism' (1997) or 'market liberalism' (Dryzek & Schlosberg 1998). Here risks are constructed as minor problems that can be easily managed by the market. Competition is assumed to be the natural relationship between people, institutions and species, while firms assert the right to use the environment as both a resource and a waste disposal system. It is assumed that all actors are motivated by self-interest and this naturally produces the greatest public good. In terms of rhetoric, state regulations are labelled 'command and control' to generate the sense that they are an authoritarian interference in the market. These elements are apparent in the resistance of industry to regulation and the switch to economic prompts covered in Chapters 4 and 9 and the way in which sustainable development policy was narrowed (Chapters 6 and 7). Meister and Japp (1998), for example, found that the discourses underpinning sustainable development policies internationally support the dominant position of business by constructing the environment as a resource to be used and promoting consumerist behaviour. Neo-liberalism is supported by a closely related discourse, which Dryzek (1997) refers to as the 'Promethean response', that denies the seriousness of environmental risks, is critical of the state and environmentalists and portrays nature as bountiful. This is the kind of discourse generated by sceptics such as Lomborg (discussed in Chapter 1) and used by recalcitrant firms to justify their resistance to change.

The environment movement is more difficult to associate with a single discourse because it contains such a diversity of views (Doyle 2000). There is a component of what Dryzek (1997; Dryzek & Schlosberg 1998) calls 'green romanticism' prevalent within eco-centric groups which constructs environmental risks as a serious threat, rejects the legitimacy of modern institutions, subordinates the wants of humans to the needs of nature and portrays nature as benevolent. On the other side of the spectrum is the discourse of ecological modernisation, which constructs risks as a challenge, supports the ongoing use of nature, calls for reforms to enable existing institutions to recognise a common interest in a healthy environment and uses the language of partnership and efficiency. Those at the weaker (technocentric) end of this discourse share some common ground with neo-liberalism, while those at the stronger (reflexive) end share much in common with eco-democracy and risk society theorists (Mol & Spaargaren 2000; Dryzek & Schlosberg 1998; Dryzek 1997; Christoff 1996).

There are some common themes which emerge from this range of environmental discourses. First, all believe that the risks are serious and neither the state nor industry has done enough to address them. Second, there is the assumption that sustainable relationships can and should be established between humanity and nature. Third, most view the motives of industry with suspicion and many advocate increased state intervention with more public scrutiny.[1] Finally, there is often a call for increased community information, consultation and empowerment because it is assumed that green NGOs will act in the public interest. The discourses of environmentalism will become apparent in the discussion of Environmental Impact Assessment (EIA) procedures, online pollution inventories and the making of sustainable development policies (Chapters 5–7).

In short, the three main groups of actors involved in environmental governance (industry, the state and the environment movement) operate under different discourses. This has important implications for environmental governance. It explains why debates about the seriousness of environmental risks persist. It is also one of the key reasons why it has been so difficult to generate consensus on environmental policies (see Chapter 1) and why the implementation of regulations or programs can be cumbersome.

The mentality of government

Foucault (1991) applied the notion of discourse to the state in a very specific way. He used the term 'governmentality' and gave it three definitions: a description of the discourses associated with governance by the modern state, an historical trend towards this kind of governance and the switch to this kind of governance by sixteenth-century European states. Most theorists have picked up on the first definition and for the purposes of this analysis governmentality can be understood as the mentality of both the governed and those who govern which rationalises and legitimates the sovereignty of the state. It is a set of discourses that influences subjects to accept the legitimacy of the existence and actions of state institutions and guides these institutions in their calculations and strategies of intervention. Many of the early interventions on the environment, for example, treated risks as minor problems that required individual management. Hence there was separate legislation for air pollution, water pollution and solid waste. One of the problems, however, is that pollutants can move between these media: solid waste might release chemicals that leach into a waterway, or airborne radioactive particles may settle to contaminate land. The move towards more integrated pollution prevention and control has only come more recently as the mentality of government has changed towards more holistic approaches and the priority assigned to such risks by the public has increased.

Miller and Rose (1993) argue that governmentality is apparent in the normal operation of state institutions: the assumption that government reports and collected data can adequately transmit information to decision makers; the attempts to deploy programs and promulgate norms in response to issues; and the use of experts to interpret and guide decision making. Miller and Rose also suggest that the underlying assumption about these activities is 'an eternal optimism that a domain or a society could be administered better or more effectively, that reality is, in some way or other, programmable' (Miller & Rose 1993, p. 78). One example would be the preparation of Environmental Impact Statements (EISs) as part of the government approval process for major developments (see Chapter 5). In this case the EIS is assumed to represent the reality of the impacts of the proposal to decision makers and good management practices can therefore be programmed into the project as part of the conditions of the permit to proceed.

Foucault (1977) offers an explanation as to why the state operates in this way which relates to his second and third definition of governmentality. He argues that from the sixteenth century onwards, European states grew to a size and population that made it impossible for traditional means of medieval governance to continue. In order to survive, the rulers developed two innovations. First, they propagated the discourse that the state was for the benefit of the citizens, rather than the monarch. Over time citizens began to see their submission to the authority of the state as being in their own interests. Second, it became important to understand the population better, in order to detect the early signs of sedition, anticipate any resistance to the exercise of state power and develop more effective strategies for exerting authority. The citizenry therefore became the subject of study by the state. This generated so much data that the state had to adopt statistical methods to identify averages and trends in order to create usable knowledge.

In their attempts to impose order, state technocrats assumed that the populace would be easier to rule if all citizens exhibited behaviour that was close to a scientifically defined 'norm' or average. This led to a discourse that deviant behaviour needed to be normalised. Three techniques of power were devised. First, dividing practices were established that isolated deviants in institutions such as prisons or mental hospitals. Second, classification of 'the natural order' was defined and promulgated in state institutions such as schools and the military. Third, normalisation technologies were deployed so that citizens accepted the legitimacy of state assessment and correction. Foucault (1977, 1980, 1985) mentions several specific powers of state institutions: the power to judge, the power to restrain, the power to punish, the power to determine good and bad and the power to enforce laws. These powers are founded on the 'bio-power' of subjectification in which individuals come to understand themselves, perceive their society and define 'truth' through the discourses of state authorities. This discourse is socialised into citizens through the 'mode of subjection' in state institutions such as schools, hospitals and the military. This analysis can be extended to the disciplining of society by environmental authorities.

Putting the pieces together: Governmentality and risk

Lupton (1999) points out that the key to governmentality is to try to normalise risks through surveillance, regulation and discipline. First, risk avoidance is constructed as a moral norm by the discourses of governmentality. Then 'risky' people or organisations, those that deviate from the norm, are identified and put under surveillance. Finally, disciplining regulations are imposed as mechanisms of power to try to normalise these 'deviants'. The discourses of risk therefore influence decision making and service delivery by the state. A prime example would be pollution inventories that identify high emitters as risky and deviators from the norm (see Chapter 5). The inventories put firms under surveillance and discipline 'deviant' high polluters with public pressure to normalise their behaviour by reducing their emissions.

Foucault's model of a dynamic web of force relations/discourses provides a possible explanation of how social institutions, including those related to environmental governance, might arise, grow or decline. His theory of the state says something about the purpose of such institutions: to discipline and normalise the use of nature. While this is an elegant way of considering environmental governance, there are some difficulties and he has many critics from both left and right (see, for example, Newton 1998; Diamond & Quinby 1988; Poster 1984). Foucault's theory does not, for example, indicate why industry generated so many serious environmental risks in the first place, although it does explain why there are so many varying explanations and schools of thought. His approach also does little to generate a strategy for change. Despite these limitations, he still offers some useful insights.

Hajer (1995) has demonstrated how Foucault's analytical techniques can be used in conjunction with other theories, such as Beck's concept of reflexive modernisation, to explain why the mainstream institutions of power have such difficulty addressing serious environmental risks. Consider, for example, if the state is hemmed in by neo-liberal and Promethean discourses that undermine government intervention and deny the reality of a hazard.

Effective action would therefore need to transform both existing institutional structures and prevailing discourses. This book will use a similar theoretical and methodological approach, synthesising the key insights offered by Beck, Foucault, Dryzek and ecological modernisation. The overlaps between these schools of thought are represented in Figure 2.1.

Figure 2.1 The theoretical framework

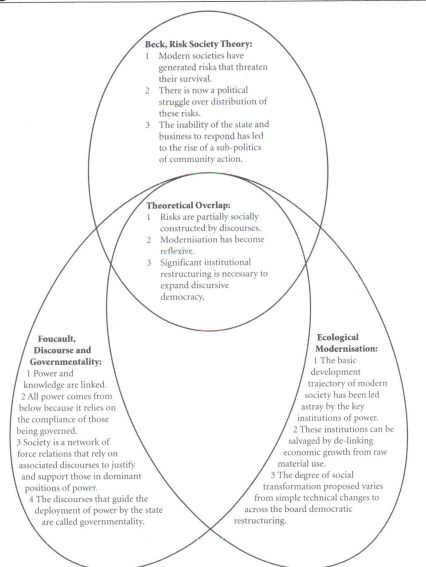

Beck, Risk Society Theory:
1 Modern societies have generated risks that threaten their survival.
2 There is now a political struggle over distribution of these risks.
3 The inability of the state and business to respond has led to the rise of a sub-politics of community action.

Theoretical Overlap:
1 Risks are partially socially constructed by discourses.
2 Modernisation has become reflexive.
3 Significant institutional restructuring is necessary to expand discursive democracy.

Foucault, Discourse and Governmentality:
1 Power and knowledge are linked.
2 All power comes from below because it relies on the compliance of those being governed.
3 Society is a network of force relations that rely on associated discourses to justify and support those in dominant positions of power.
4 The discourses that guide the deployment of power by the state are called governmentality.

Ecological Modernisation:
1 The basic development trajectory of modern society has been led astray by the key institutions of power.
2 These institutions can be salvaged by de-linking economic growth from raw material use.
3 The degree of social transformation proposed varies from simple technical changes to across the board democratic restructuring.

A framework for assessing environmental governance

Beck's idea that modernisation is being undermined by its own success is perplexing, but it could be the underlying cause of the institutions of modern society being targeted by the various schools of thought that were reviewed in the first part of this chapter. Adding Foucault's insights, the application of various discourses of rationality to the creation of knowledge, production processes and the organisation of society has led to the rapid spread of institutions such as industry, capitalism and the state. The nineteenth-century reaction to the social risks of capitalism led to the creation of the labour movement, the creation of the welfare state (Dryzek et al. 2003) and arguably the experiment with state socialism during the twentieth century. Similarly, the reaction to the growing ecological risks in the late twentieth century led to the rise of the environment movement within the community and the generation of alternative development discourses.

The crucial institution of modernisation is industry: a result of the modernisation process and the primary source of many benefits, costs and risks. It is where the knowledge generated by science and technology is blended with new methods of institutional organisation. It is also the cause of much of the damage to people and the environment (in capitalist and socialist states, as well as developed and developing states). Further, it is para-doxically where many of the innovations and solutions to environmental damage are to be found (WCED 1990). In short, industry is the main produc-tive interface between society and the environment: the rationale for its existence is to take resources (knowledge, capital, labour and raw materials) from both and return products, services, income and waste (McEachern 1991). This flow of resources is filtered, directed and distributed by the network of force relations and discourses that make up the social fabric and create or undermine existing institutions.

The underlying rationale (or governmentality) of any state intervention is therefore to redirect this flow in a way that will reduce social and environ-mental risks. This gives some indication of what to look for when assessing the effectiveness of both state intervention and the progress of industry towards sustainability. That is, we would expect a redirection of knowledge, labour, capital and raw materials into more environmentally friendly activi-ties and a subsequent reduction in environmental risk. In terms of knowledge, there should be some indication of an increase in better infor-mation regarding the impacts of industrial development available to the state, industry and the community. On the labour side, it would be reasonable to expect that a growing proportion of the labour force would be employed in industries related to environmental protection and a growing number of environmental professionals would be employed in both the private and public sectors. In terms of capital, a rise in expenditure on pollution abatement and cleaner production technology would be expected. Finally, raw material flows should have been altered so that less damage is done during their extraction and less pollution is produced during the manufacturing stage. This point will be developed further in Chapter 8, after the various kinds of response have been explored.

Conclusions

This chapter began with a brief tour of different explanations of the potential causes of environmental risks. Three kinds of discourse emerged that will be referred to throughout this book. The first is neo-liberalism, which is generally opposed to increased state intervention and has emerged from both industry and the right of the political spectrum. The second is administrative rationalism, which supports the governmentality of increased state regulation and is often supported by agents of the state and parts of the political left. The third is environmentalism which, although diverse, is generally critical of mainstream institutions like industry or the state and usually supports some form of increased community empowerment. Clashes between these three discourses form the underlying dynamic of environmental policy making and regulation (as summarised in the introduction to this volume).

Many of the discourses on the causes of, and cures for, environmental risk have provided a useful but limited insight. Market failures, poorly designed state intervention and various social hierarchies do appear to be significant factors, but these are themselves products of the modernisation process and longer-term trends in governance. Looking at these underlying causes is therefore more productive. If modernisation is being undermined by its own success, or if state intervention is having an impact, it should be apparent in changes to the flow of resources through society. A key place to look for such changes will be in the behaviour of industry, which is at the centre of most environmental risks. The next chapter reviews the historical development of national environment protection institutions in the USA, UK and Australia. It demonstrates how the goals, structure, resources and powers of each institution are the tangible consequences of reflexive modernisation, clashing discourses and governmentality.

PART B

How has government responded?

CHAPTER THREE

National environment protection institutions

Introduction

The previous chapters explored the nature and causes of environmental risks; now it is time to consider the responses of governments. This chapter considers how the state has created very different environment protection organisations in the USA, UK and Australia. The first section offers a very brief overview of key institutional contexts of the three states as a background for developing the analysis. The next section then looks at the way environment protection organisations were created and altered over the course of several decades. The following sections go on to compare the goals, structure, resources and powers of each as they stand today. The chapter finishes with a summary of the key legislation being administered; this is discussed in more detail in Chapter 4. Overall it is argued that the very existence of such institutions are evidence of reflexive modernisation at work and their particular form is heavily influenced by prevailing social discourses and the governmentality of each state.

Setting the historical scene

Having spent much of the previous chapters discussing the importance of social context, it is appropriate to start this analysis with a short overall comparison of the three states being used as the source of case studies. The idea is to set the scene before the entrance of the main actors in the play of environmental politics. Obviously there are a great many similarities between the three, based on a common historical root, a shared language and related social institutions. There are, however, differences that have shaped the ability of each state to recognise, construct and respond to environmental risks.

Uniting a kingdom

The UK system of government is one that has evolved in fits and starts over centuries, which gives it several interesting features. The foundation of the current monarchical system was established after the Norman conquest of 1066, although the line of succession has been interrupted by various wars and rebellions. The first parliaments were restricted to councils of advisers drawn from the most important nobles, but participation was gradually extended to the rest of the population (although women had to wait until the twentieth century to vote). Over time power shifted away from the monarch and today they play a largely ceremonial role. The parliament at Westminster consists of two chambers: the House of Commons with 659 members elected to represent particular constituencies for a maximum period of four years and an unelected House of Lords (currently being reviewed). While the monarch remains the official head of state, whoever leads the party with the most seats in the Commons becomes the head of government (Prime Minister) and selects a cabinet of ministers from both houses to manage particular policy areas (e.g. the environment) (CIA 2003; Dunleavy et al. 2002; UK Office of Statistics 1998).

There is no single written document which functions as a Constitution, nor is there a constitutional bill of rights for citizens (although a legislative bill of rights was recently adopted that was based on a European Union agreement). The lack of a written Constitution gives enormous power and flexibility to the central Westminster government. During the Thatcher years, for example, the government was able to restrict the right to protest by various environmental groups and abolish elected local governments that it did not like, such as the Greater London Council (Dryzek et al. 2003; Garner 2000). At present there remain some 235 local governments of various kinds spread throughout the UK (CIA 2003). They have the prime responsibility for delivering services to the community and although they can raise their own local taxes they are heavily dependent on Westminster for funding.

The UK was formed in 1801 from four countries: England, Scotland, Wales and Ireland. Ireland was partitioned in 1921 when the Republic of

Ireland won its independence, so that today Northern Ireland is the only part of that country which remains in the union (Tomancy 2000). Originally there were only two levels of elected government: national and local. In 1998, however, the Blair government created regional assemblies as a middle tier for Scotland, Wales and Northern Ireland. These have limited powers to raise taxes and control expenditure in some public policy areas. The majority of revenue is still raised by Westminster and it remains the major policy-making body (Bradbury & Mitchell 2001; Garner 2000; Brown 1998).

Of the three states being studied, the UK provides a number of unique features. First, it has the longest continuous development of governing institutions, which has thrown up many anachronisms. In large part this is due to two competing discourses: conservatism, which supports the continuation of the monarchy and House of Lords, and liberalism, which promotes representative democratic government and individual rights. Second, it does not have a single constitutional document, which leaves the Westminster government with enormous scope and flexibility in the powers it can exercise. Third, despite the move towards devolution, it remains the most politically centralised. Finally, the UK has an added feature—its membership of the European Union (EU). Since joining the EU in the early 1970s several initiatives on environmental regulation have come from European Environmental Directives and the European parliament. The UK, in turn, has been able to prompt changes to some EU policies, such as the move towards integrated pollution prevention and control (Dunleavy et al. 2002; Garner 2000). Neither Australia nor the USA has an equivalent regional institution with such influence.

Uniting the states of America

The first thirteen states[1] that formed the USA were created from British colonies that rebelled against the Crown in 1776. After winning their war of independence the colonies attempted to stay in a loose confederation, but eventually drafted a new Constitution in 1787 which created a stronger federation with a broad sweep of powers for the new national government (Anastapolo 1989; Brogan 1985). When this document came into force in 1789, it embodied many of the political institutions that had emerged from British liberalism: elected governments, the separation of powers and the rule of law. The new republic, however, took it further with a bill of citizens' rights (the first ten amendments to the Constitution), an independently elected head of state (the President) replacing the monarch and a bicameral Congress with an elected upper house (the Senate). Over time the republic grew and absorbed French and Spanish colonies until the number of states had reached

50 by the middle of the twentieth century (Brogan 1985). The USA is therefore left with three levels of government (federal, state and local) operating under a federal Constitution. Each state elects its own governor and assembly, has its own Constitution, legal system and set of agencies or departments (Wagman 1995).

The federal government, located in Washington DC, has a Congress made up of the House of Representatives with 435 members (elected every two years to represent specific constituencies) and a Senate with 100 members (two for each state) elected for six years (one-third go to the polls every two years with the House). The President and Vice-President are elected separately from Congress for four-year terms and can be re-elected only once. The President selects their own Cabinet (e.g. Secretary of State), which does not include members of the legislature and appoints the most senior positions within the public sector. On the one hand, the President needs Congress to pass laws or budgets and confirm senior appointments. On the other hand, the President can veto an act of Congress, but this veto can be overturned by a two-thirds congressional majority vote. The Supreme Court is the last court of appeal and has the power to strike down laws or actions that it deems to be unconstitutional (CIA 2003; Wagman 1995).

Despite the bill of rights, the USA continued to use slaves until the end of the Civil War in 1865. Further, many African Americans who were descended from these slaves were still fighting for their full civil rights in the 1960s. Indigenous groups also suffered displacement from their traditional lands during the frontier wars and expansion of European settlement across the continent (Brogan 1985). These historical events have left their mark on many policy areas. The environmental justice movement, for example, was formed during the 1980s when it was found that African, indigenous and Latin American communities were more likely to live in polluted environments or near hazardous waste sites than richer, largely white citizens (Everett & Neu 2000). By the mid-1990s the US government had acknowledged this inequality (US EPA 1994b) although it remains a major point of contention (Dryzek & Schlosberg 1998).

There are several important differences between the US and UK systems. First, the USA has more political checks and balances on government, with a separately elected legislature and executive that have to negotiate public sector funding and new laws. Second, state governments have more powers and responsibilities for delivering services than the recently created UK regional assemblies. Third, the power of the federal government is constrained by a written Constitution and the ability of citizens to appeal to the Supreme Court. Fourth, historical differences mean that an environmental justice movement is prominent in America but not the UK. Added to this, the USA has a more litigious political culture and fewer barriers to the legal system than both the UK and Australia. History has shown that individuals and groups are willing to use the courts to achieve political ends, including changing environmental policies or regulations (Dryzek et al. 2003; Murchison 1994).

Constituting Australia

Like the USA, Australia developed from the British colonisation of a country with a much older indigenous culture. The first colony, New South Wales, was established in 1788 and by the middle of the nineteenth century there were six separate colonies. In 1897 a Constitution was drafted by a convention of representatives from each colony. This was then endorsed by a national public referendum and passed as an Act of the Westminster Parliament in 1900 (coming into effect on 1 January 1901) which created the Commonwealth of Australia. Women had the vote at the federal level from the beginning, but indigenous people could only vote in some state jurisdictions until universal suffrage was extended to them in 1962. The national capital was located in a specially created city called Canberra and the Commonwealth Parliament moved there in 1927 (Jaensch 1997; Clark 1980).

The Australian Constitution is a mixture of the US and UK systems. In line with the US federal brand of liberalism there are three tiers of government: Commonwealth, state and local. Nationally, there is an elected Senate with equal representation for each state and the High Court acts as the last court of appeal and defender of the Constitution. Each state has its own Constitution (not always written), elected Parliament and governor, although the governor is appointed and ceremonial. As in the UK system, with its residual conservatism, the British monarch remains the head of state (represented by the Governor-General and state governors) and there is no constitutional bill of rights. Government is formed by a Prime Minister and Cabinet drawn from the party that has the majority in the lower house. This hybrid of the two systems is sometimes referred to as the 'Washminster mutation' (Jaensch 1997; Thompson 1980). In all there are now six states and two territories that make up the federation. At the Commonwealth level, there is a bicameral Parliament consisting of the House of Representatives (with 150 members elected to represent specific constituencies for three years) and a Senate of 76 members (twelve from each state and two from each territory, elected for six years) (Jaensch 1997).

There are some unique features to the Australian system that differentiates it from the other two. First, the Constitution was deliberately written by colonies jealously guarding their autonomy, so it provides only a limited range of policy areas in which the national government can operate. All powers of the Commonwealth are specified and anything not listed is assumed to be a residual power that automatically falls to the states (Bates 1992). Second, later changes to the system introduced proportional representation to elect the Senate and one of the two chambers in several states. This has allowed minority parties, such as the Greens, to win seats at both levels—something that is not possible in the first-past-the-post systems used in Westminster and the US Congress. Third, the other chambers use a preferential voting system which encourages the major parties to take on policies proposed by the Greens in order to win their preferences (these electoral systems are explained in more detail in the endnotes to the introduction of this book). In short, the Australian system makes it easier for environmentalists to get elected to the legislature.

Figure 3.1 Country comparison in brief

	USA	**UK**	**Australia**
Area (000s sq. km)	9 159	242	7 618
Irrigated land (000s sq. km)	214	1	24
% arable land	19	26	7
Climate	Mostly temperate, tropical south, artic north-west	Mostly temperate	Arid centre and west, temperate south and east, tropical north
Population (millions)	280	60	20
GDP (billions)*	10 082	1 470	465
GDP per capita*	36 300	24 700	24 000
Exports (billions)*	723	287	69
Imports (billions)*	1 148	337	70
% GDP per sector:			
• agriculture	2	2	3
• industry	18	25	25
• services	80	73	72
% electricity production:			
• fossil fuel	71	73	90
• hydro	7	1	8
• nuclear	20	23	0**
• other	2	2	2
National government budget (billions):*			
revenues (% GDP)	1 828 (18%)	565 (38%)	87 (19%)
expenditures	1 703	540	84

cont'd.

Figure 3.1 Country comparison in brief *(cont'd)*

	USA	UK	Australia
Political system	Federal: national government in Washington DC, 50 states, one district and 14 dependent territories	Mainly centralised in Westminster, regional assemblies with limited powers in Scotland, Wales and Northern Ireland	Federal: national Commonwealth government in Canberra, six states and two territories
Constitution	Written, came into force in 1789	No single document, accumulated set of laws, agreements and conventions	Written, came into force in 1901
Head of State	President	Monarch	Monarch of Britain represented by the Governor-General
Executive	President, elected separately from Congress for four years, appoints their own Cabinet	Prime Minister and Cabinet drawn from Parliament, government formed by the party with the majority in the House of Commons after an election	Prime Minister and Cabinet drawn from Parliament, government formed by the party with the majority in the House of Representatives after an election
National legislature	Bicameral elected Congress: House of Representatives (435 seats) and Senate (100 seats)	Bicameral Parliament: elected House of Commons (659 seats) and non-elected House of Lords (about 618)	Bicameral elected Parliament: House of Representatives (150 seats) and Senate (76 seats)
Highest national court	Supreme Court	House of Lords	High Court

Source of all figures cited in Figure 3.1: CIA (2003).

* Measured in US$ purchasing power parity.

** Australia has one research reactor but its output is negligible compared to the total energy market.

Comparable but different

Figure 3.1 summarises some of the other similarities and differences in key geographical, political and economic areas of all three countries (CIA 2003). There are some important points to note. The UK has a population of 60 million in a relatively small temperate country. In comparison Australia has a much smaller population (20 million) and a very large landmass that ranges from a tropical north, through a large arid centre and west, to a temperate south and east (where most of the population live). The USA has both the largest population (280 million) and landmass, stretching across temperate, tropical and arctic climates. In economic terms, while the proportion of GDP generated by agriculture, industry and service sectors is similar in all three states, the USA clearly dominates in terms of sheer size and wealth. Australia, as the smallest economy with the highest per cent GDP exported, is the most vulnerable to global economic change, while the UK's economy is linked to the highly regulated EU market which is of a comparable size to the USA. In terms of the energy industry, while the USA and UK have a sizeable nuclear power sector, Australia has only one small research reactor but it does produce significant quantities of uranium for export. Finally, the UK supports a proportionally larger public sector than the other two countries with the majority of revenue raised and distributed by Westminster. Both Australia and the USA raise considerable funds through state taxes (not included in this table) and the states are a major provider of community services.

The final point to consider is that there is a significantly different political culture in each country. This culture is the combination of community values and beliefs that influence its collective behaviour and response to the state (for a more detailed explanation see Hague et al. 1998). It is very much influenced by the combination of social relations, discourses and governmentality of each state. The USA, for example, has a highly individualistic and litigious political culture that is supported by the neo-liberalism that pervades the mentality of both the governed and those governing. The UK political culture, on the other hand, tends to be more conservative and collective (although a strong dose of neo-liberalism was injected during the Thatcher years) and continues to support a class system and large public sector. This may explain why the workings of government tend to be less open, more centralised and incremental in their approach to reform. Australia is an unusual mixture of the two. It has more of a collective ethos than the USA and supports a proportionally larger public sector, but has a less closed approach to governing than the UK. American liberalism has certainly influenced the design of many institutions (e.g. the federal system and the Senate), yet Australia still retains a conservative streak (e.g. in 1998 a national referendum proposing the removal of the British monarch as the head of state was defeated).

In short, although each society shares a common historical root and has developed comparable institutions, there are some significant differences that make for interesting contrasts. Technically, all have highly industrialised production processes and a well-developed scientific knowledge base, although the USA has a larger cutting-edge research and development sector. Economically, the USA is clearly in a league of its own, although the UK membership of the EU makes it part of a comparable regional market. Socially, Australia and the USA have issues arising from colonial pasts, the treatment of indigenous people in particular and in America there is the added complication of dealing with the legacy of slavery. Politically, all three have constructed governing institutions under the influence of liberalism, but these have been moderated to a large extent by conservatism in the UK and to a lesser extent in Australia. Finally, each state faces significantly different challenges with regards to their diverse domestic environments. These different contexts significantly affect the way each state constructs and responds to environmental risks. In particular, they shape the kind of environmental organisations that were created in the latter half of the twentieth century.

Institutional construction and reconstruction

Up until 1970 there were no national environment protection agencies as such in these three states, yet as discussed in Chapter 1 the risk from environmental incidents and ongoing problems had become apparent many years before. Further, there was already a growing patchwork of environmental regulation being administered by various departments and agencies operating in the areas of public health, land management and industry. So why did these governments feel the need for change? The answer lies in the process of reflexive modernisation discussed in Chapter 2, in particular the consequences of the rapid increase in industrialisation and consumption that occurred in the long post-WWII economic boom. The negative side effects of these developments, coupled with the growing counter-culture movements across the developed world during the late 1960s, sowed the seeds for change.

Politics and the rise of the US EPA

Nowhere was this transformation more evident than in the USA. By the end of the 1960s, the USA had experienced a number of serious environmental incidents caused by industry including a major oil spill off the tourist beaches of Santa Barbara, the declaration that Lake Eerie was biologically dead and the Cuyahoga River becoming so polluted that it caught fire (see Chapter 1, Figure 1.2). Added to this, at the start of the 1960s (Carson 2000 [1962]) had pointed out the dangers of overusing pesticides and by the end of the decade Ehrlich (1969) was warning of the risk of overpopulation. These fed into environmentalist critiques that questioned the desirability of industrial development and modernisation. The initial response of Congress was to pass laws dealing with specific problems on an individual basis, which was indicative of the highly compartmentalised, legalistic and incremental governmentality of the time.

Although environmental intervention can be traced back at least as far as the 1880s, it had built up slowly as legislation passed by state governments. The federal government began to take on more responsibility after the failure of a joint waste water treatment construction program with the states (Petulla 1987; Lazarus 1991). Senator Edmund Muskie was one of the key instigators of the reform and expansion of many federal environment laws (Hoberg 1992). The *Air Pollution Control Act 1955*, for example, was substantially upgraded by both the *Clean Air Act 1963* and the *Air Quality Act 1967*. In 1965 a new federal *Motor Vehicles Pollution Control Act* was the first law to set national emission standards. The federal *Insecticide, Fungicide and Rodenticide Act 1947* was amended and strengthened in 1964. In 1965 the *Solid Waste Disposal Act* was passed, as were Muskie's amendments to the *Water Pollution Control Act* which introduced tradable pollution permits and the mentality of the market mechanism approach (Portney 1990).

In 1969 Congress passed the *National Environmental Policy Act* (NEPA). This Act established the Council on Environmental Quality, a small group of technical experts who were supposed to advise the President on environmental issues (US Government 1991). The Act also contained what at first appeared to be a relatively minor clause that required federal agencies to take into account the impact of new government projects on the environment. This clause led to the creation of Environmental Impact Assessment (EIA) procedures that rapidly spread from federal government to the states and the private sector (Hoberg 1992). EIA was also quickly picked up in other industrialised countries that were reforming their own laws. President Nixon at first opposed the NEPA but relented when he realised the extent of public concern and the possibility that it could support the presidential aspirations of Senator Muskie (Dreyfus & Ingram 1985). The Act became law in 1970.

Seeing the need to take some initiative on the environment, Nixon created the Environmental Protection Agency (EPA) in 1970 to administer both the NEPA and the growing body of federal environmental legislation. The idea for a new agency originated from a presidential commission reviewing options for restructuring the federal bureaucracy headed by Roy Ash. The Ash Council (as it became known) initially wanted to reorganise the whole federal bureaucracy into four functional units, one of which would include a Cabinet-level Department of Environment. This was overturned by Cabinet because many members feared losing some of their powers, so a more narrowly defined agency was recommended instead. Nixon carefully crafted the responsibilities of the new agency to appease the conflicting demands of his favoured Cabinet members, and several environmental functions that the US EPA logically ought to have taken over were kept by other departments (Marcus 1991; Petulla 1987).

In short, Nixon sought to consolidate administrative control of the new environmental laws, reassure favoured Cabinet members that they would not lose authority, head off Muskie's use of the environment as a campaign issue and shore up his own public support (Hoberg 1992; Williams 1993; Ruckelshaus 1993). The institution was therefore a product of political deals made in response to growing environmental criticisms. Neither Nixon nor the Congress fully trusted the US EPA. Half the Congress did not trust the Nixon administration and were concerned that the agency might be 'captured' by the large business interests that it was supposed to regulate. Nixon and the other half of Congress raised concerns about the possible negative economic impacts of imposing the extra costs believed to be carried by environmental regulation (Lazarus 1991). The main result has been that Nixon and subsequent presidents have made sure that several other agencies, committees and offices kept the power of the US EPA in check. The Office of Management and Budget in particular has played an active role in challenging US EPA actions (Ruckelshaus 1993; Percival 1991). It should also be noted that because of the federal nature of the USA, the state governments have created their own environment protection institutions and their relationship with the US EPA varies from cooperation to competition.

An emerging environment agency in the UK

As in the USA, the UK had passed laws to deal with specific problems generated by industry back in the nineteenth century. An Alkali Inspectorate, for example, was established in 1863 to monitor waste from industry and its role was gradually broadened as more types of pollution became acknowledged as risks (Garner 2000). The UK had its share of environmental incidents and responded with specific laws; the London smog of 1952, for example, led to the *Clean Air Act 1956* (see Chapter 1, Figure 1.2), which was expanded in 1968 (UK Government 1990). Added to this, the counter-culture movement was also emerging along with environmentalism to challenge industry.

In response to these developments the Westminster government established the Royal Commission on Environmental Pollution (RCEP) in 1969. Its ongoing role has been to investigate environmental risks and make recommendations on possible responses. The first RCEP report in 1970 outlined the broad scope of environmental risks as they were understood at the time, but also noted a decline in some types of air pollution, such as sulphur dioxide, since the implementation of the *Clean Air Act 1956*. Some elements of the RCEP report do appear to have been influenced by neo-liberalism: with regards to pollution abatement, for example, it suggested that actions should only be taken on the grounds of sound science if the benefits outweighed the costs. It did, however, support the creation of a Department of Environment as a positive step (RCEP 1971). The RCEP continues to investigate and issue reports every year or so and advises Westminster on various topics, such as environmental best practice, waste management, integrated pollution control, public access to information and so on. In this respect it fulfils a similar function to the US Council on Environmental Quality and has been one of the key sources of innovations in UK environmental regulation.

The creation of the Department of Environment in 1970 was a means of consolidating the administration of the growing body of environmental laws. It was initially part of a ministerial portfolio that included related departments such as Housing, Local Government, Public Buildings and Works and Transport. As with the US EPA, however, not all the relevant responsibilities were handed over to the new department. Some powers stayed with departments such as Agriculture, Trade or Industry, but it did provide an umbrella for the burgeoning number of specialised inspectorates (Jordan 2002; RCEP 1971). After the UK joined the EU in 1973, the department became a conduit for implementing national versions of European environmental directives and plans. It also liased with the European Environment Agency after its creation in 1990 (Hawke 2002; Garner 2000). Some analysts suggest that up to 80 per cent of the policies now being implemented by the department have their origin in the EU (Jordan 2002). The department has undergone a series of major reorganisations over the last 35 years.

In 1987 Her Majesty's Inspectorate of Pollution was created from the merger of several specialised inspectorates. The catalyst was a repeated recommendation from the RCEP pointing to the need for a more coordinated regulatory approach, a point first made in the 1970s, backed up by pressure from the EU (Garner 2000). The new inspectorate took over responsibility for much of the pollution-related legislation, particularly the *Control of Pollution Act 1974*. Another idea that emerged from the RCEP was Integrated Pollution and Control (IPC) that was enshrined in the

Environmental Protection Act 1990 and *Environment Act 1995*. The idea was expanded by a European Directive on Integrated Pollution Prevention and Control (IPPC) and reabsorbed in the UK by the *Pollution Prevention Act 1999* (Hawke 2002; Duxbury & Morton 2000).

The UK Environment Agency (UK EA) was created within the department by the *Environment Act 1995* from the merger of Her Majesty's Inspectorate of Pollution, the National Rivers Authority and Waste Disposal Authorities (Garner 2000). This reorganisation had been proposed but deferred in Westminster's 1990 White Paper on the environment, *Our Common Inheritance* (Garner 2000; UK Government 1990). While the term UK Environment Agency has been used to differentiate it from the US and Australian institutions, it should be noted that the jurisdiction is restricted to England and Wales. Scotland has its own agency and Northern Ireland has a separate Environment and Heritage Service. Further, local authorities retain responsibility for smaller facilities and less hazardous substances through their own local Air Pollution Control System that runs in parallel to UK EA (UK Office of Statistics 1998). Conservation responsibilities are held by a variety of institutions—the two main ones are English Nature and the Countryside Agency (Garner 2000). To simplify the analysis the focus is mainly on the UK EA because it covers the majority of UK territory and citizens. The agency is currently part of the Department of Environment, Food and Rural Affairs and a committee of the House of Commons reviews its operation. In order to improve interdepartmental cooperation, the Blair government has appointed junior environmental ministers to all other departments to provide relevant input into their decision making.

Establishing a national environment protection system in Australia

Australia has taken a very different path from the USA and UK to creating national environment protection institutions. Like the other two states, environmental laws can be traced back to the nineteenth century; there was a steady expansion of such laws after WWII and a counter-culture movement generated alternative environmental discourses in the late 1960s (Doyle 1998; Rutherford 1994; Bates 1992; Vogel & Kun 1987). The early response of passing new laws is again indicative of the piecemeal, incremental and legalistic governmentality that prevailed among all three governments and shaped their response to the rising public concerns about environmental risk. There are, however, two significant differences that affect the trajectory of institutional change in Australia.

First, because of the small population, large landmass and historical reliance on primary industry, Australia did not face the same intensity of urban environmental risks (Doyle & McEachern 2000). There were no equivalent events to the London Smog of 1952, nor the US Cuyahoga River catching fire in 1969 (see Chapter 1, Figure 1.2). This is not to say that there are no urban risks; air pollution is certainly a hazard in the larger Australian cities for example, but historically the major issues have tended to be about conservation, water resources, the marine environment and land management (Doyle 2000; Walker & Crowley 1999; Hutton & Connors 1999; Doyle & Kellow 1995). These have usually developed from the application of industrial products and processes to the primary sector. Second, the lack of a specific environmental power for the national government in the Australian Constitution and the absence of a suitable general power (such as the one available to Washington) made Canberra reluctant to intervene (Toyne 1994; Murchison 1994; Rutherford & Fowler 1992). Hence the majority of responsibilities have stayed with state governments and they established their own environmental departments, agencies and commissions in parallel (Gilpin 1980).

During the 1970s Canberra began to take a serious interest in environmental risks and developed three strategies for intervention. First, purely Commonwealth initiatives were taken to manage those areas within its accepted jurisdiction. The Commonwealth Department of Environment, Aborigines and the Arts was created in 1971, but was initially restricted to an advisory role. The department was later given oversight of a number of pieces of legislation, including the *Environment Protection (Impact of Proposals) Act 1974* which allowed the Commonwealth to demand an EIA for any project in which it was involved or that required its approval (Crommelin 1987). The *States Grants (Nature Conservation) Act 1974* and *Environment (Financial Assistance) Act 1977* gave the Commonwealth some influence over the states through the control of funding for environmental programs. Like its UK counterpart, the department has gone through several phases of expansion, contraction and reorganisation and is currently constituted as the Department of Environment and Heritage. There was a short experiment with a small Commonwealth Environment Agency 1991–96, but this was disbanded after the Howard government was elected in 1996 and Environment Australia was created as the umbrella organisation for environmental responsibilities within the department (although this label had fallen into some disuse by 2004).

The second strategy of the Commonwealth was to use creatively some of its constitutional powers to intrude into what was traditionally considered to be state jurisdictions. When the Queensland state government refused to stop oil exploration on the Great Barrier Reef, the Commonwealth declared it a national park. Similarly, the refusal of Queensland to stop sand mining on Fraser Island led Canberra to shut down the operation by refusing to grant export licences for the minerals extracted (Toyne 1994; Formby 1986). In 1983, the Hawke government moved to prevent the construction of the Gordon-below-Franklin Dam in a World Heritage listed area of Tasmania. This action relied on the use of the external affairs powers granted to the Commonwealth under section 51 of the Constitution. It was argued that because Australia was a signatory to the World Heritage Treaty, the Commonwealth could intervene to protect listed areas (Bates 1992). This interpretation was upheld by the High Court in 1984 and the Commonwealth went on to use the same tactic to protect areas of the Daintree rainforest in 1987 and Kakadu National Park in 1992 (Toyne 1994).

The third strategy saw cooperative Commonwealth–state institutions developed to deal with interjurisdictional issues. Several joint ministerial councils were established; the most enduring was the Australian and New Zealand Environment and Conservation Council (ANZECC) that until 2002 was charged with gathering information and generating ideas for change (a similar role to the US Council on Environmental Quality and the UK Royal Commission). In 1992 the Commonwealth, states and territories signed the Inter-Governmental Agreement on the Environment that led to the creation of the National Environment Protection Council. This was a council of the environment ministers from all jurisdictions chaired by the Commonwealth. Majority decisions by the council became national measures that had to be enforced by each jurisdiction's environment protection institution. In the Commonwealth's case this fell to the Department of Environment. During its existence the council created several measures dealing with pollution, air quality, hazardous waste, packaging materials, contaminated sites and vehicle emissions. In 2002 both ANZECC and the council were absorbed into a larger joint ministerial body—the Environment Protection and Heritage Council (EPHC) (NEPC 2002). Together the EPHC and the Commonwealth Department of Environment constitute the main national environment protection institutions created in response to the negative side effects of the modernisation process and rising counter-culture discourses on environmental risk.

Chalk and cheese by comparison?

This brief history demonstrates the effects of similar stimulis (growing environmental risks and discourses) on different institutional contexts in the USA, UK and Australia. In terms of similarities, all three governments were initially reluctant to create environment protection institutions. As a result, the new organisations had to work within a network of other, often hostile, state organisations and inherited a set of pre-existing piecemeal environmental laws (indicating some similarities in the initial governmentality of each state). This means that these selected institutions are not the sole agents operating in the field of environmental regulation. While other departments, local and regional authorities are also at work, these subjects have been selected for further analysis simply as an indicator of how states have responded as the process of modernisation has become more reflexive and constructed more risk.

It should also be noted that there are some significant differences between the three responses. The US EPA has a fairly consistent basic structure, while the UK EA, Commonwealth Department of Environment and the EPHC have emerged quite recently from an apparently ongoing process of institutional reform. The UK has the added dimension of having to work with EU directives, while Australia has a far more decentralised system. These differences have affected the goals, structure and powers delegated to each institution.

Institutional goals

The goals set for any new institution of governance reveal several interesting features about the society that created them. First, they reveal the way the executive government has constructed the risks they intend to address, that is, they implicitly contain assumptions about the seriousness of the hazard, its cause and the most appropriate remedy. Second, the goals tell a great deal about the governmentality of the day, including the way policy area is to be divided up within and between different state institutions, the tools of intervention that are considered to be legitimate and the new governing routines that are to be established. Finally, these goals give an indication of power relations and justifying discourses that pervade society at the time. This manifests itself in the way some things are left off the agenda or the way some major perpetrators of serious environmental damage are treated with some deference because they are in a dominant position of power.

US EPA goals

When President Nixon established the US EPA he sent a message to Congress outlining the goals he had set for the new agency.

The principal roles and functions of the EPA would include:

- The establishment and enforcement of environmental protection standards consistent with national environmental goals.
- The conduct of research on the adverse effects of pollution and on methods and equipment for controlling it, the gathering of information on pollution and the use of this information in strengthening environmental protection programs and recommending policy changes.
- Assisting others, through grants, technical assistance and other means in arresting pollution of the environment.
- Assisting the Council on Environmental Quality in developing and recommending to the President new policies for the protection of the environment.

Essentially the Council [on Environmental Quality] is a top-level advisory group (which might be compared with the Council of Economic Advisers), while the EPA would be an operating 'line' organisation.

The EPA would be charged with protecting the environment by abating pollution. In short, the Council focuses on what our broad policies in the environmental field should be; the EPA would focus on setting and enforcing pollution control standards (Nixon 1971, pp. 582–3).

Nixon's reluctance to take federal action made him emphasise that the US EPA should take joint action with the states where possible and that many responsibilities could be handed back to the states in future, with the US EPA becoming more of a support mechanism for other authorities (Nixon 1971). In an interview published by the agency in 1993, William Ruckelshaus, the first administrator of the US EPA, believed that Nixon was forced to act by the electoral weight of public opinion. Ruckelshaus had worked with the Indiana State Board of Health and the Deputy Attorney General's Office on reducing local pollution emissions during the early 1960s. Most of his work focused on gross violations of existing state emission and effluent laws. He became convinced of the need for federal action because he believed that many southern states were deliberately neglecting environment protection in order to encourage industrial development. He also pointed out that he and many other people underestimated the size and complexity of the risks (Ruckelshaus 1993).

These goals and supporting statements show how difficult it has been for the state to come to terms with the seriousness of environmental risk. Note that the cause was seen as lax state-level regulation, rather than the process of industrial development itself, and it was assumed that federal intervention would only be needed temporarily. The goals compartmentalise the issue of pollution for special treatment and ignore related issues such as conservation, land management or increasing population. They assume the appropriate response was to set standards, conduct more research and assist with the deployment of better technology. Finally, they neglect to identify private industry as the prime locus of pollution and focus instead is on assisting some anonymous 'others' to develop better technology. This, combined with the reluctance to intervene in the market, suggests that American business was in a powerful position with respect to government policy.

Having been in operation for more than three decades, the goals of the US EPA have obviously adapted to the rapidly changing political environment. The concepts of sustainable development and ecological modernisation, for example, did not become major features of global debates until after the late 1980s (see Chapters 6 and 7 for more detail). In late 1990, US EPA administrator William Reilly suggested that the agency needed to move beyond its traditional functions to encourage pollution prevention and sustainable development, but tempered these statements with a recognition of the need for sustainable economic growth (Reilly 1990). In 1993, after the Rio Earth Summit, Congress asked the US EPA to outline its role in sustainable development. The response was a report from the Office of Policy, Planning and Evaluation which approached the idea with a note of caution and pointed out the lack of a clearly agreed definition while stressing the need for economic growth to pay for environmental protection. It proposed three tenets for institutionalising sustainability: a long-term planning perspective; recognition that the economy and ecology are interdependent; and 'new, integrative approaches to achieve economic, social and environmental objectives' (US EPA 1993, p. 2). It was argued that all of these would need a concerted effort by the entire state, not just the US EPA alone.

In the US EPA's 2001 Financial Year Annual Report, the current goals are stated quite simply: 'to protect human health and to safeguard the natural environment—air, water and land—upon which life depends' (US EPA 2002, p. I–1). There is a commitment to work with all levels of government and the 'regulated community' to achieve these goals. These goals clearly hark back to the original aims set by President Nixon.

UK Environment Agency goals

Some 27 years after the formation of the US EPA, the UK EA was created in significantly different circumstances. The agency listed its goals in its first corporate strategy paper.

Our aims are to:

- achieve significant and continuous improvement in the quality of air, land and water, actively encouraging the conservation of natural resources, flora and fauna;
- maximise the benefits of integrated pollution control and integrated river basin management;
- provide effective defence and timely warning systems for people and property against flooding from rivers and the sea;
- achieve significant reductions in waste through minimisation, reuse and recycling and improved standards of disposal;
- manage water resources to achieve the proper balance between the needs of the environment and those of abstracters and other water users;
- secure, with others, the remediation of contaminated land;
- improve and develop salmon and freshwater fisheries;
- Conserve and enhance inland and coastal waters and their use for recreation;
- maintain and improve non-marine navigation;
- develop a better informed public through open debate, the provision of soundly based information and rigorous research;
- set priorities and propose solutions that do not impose excessive costs on society (UK EA 1997, p. 2).

Some of these goals are similar to the US EPA, particularly those relating to pollution and technology. It is apparent, however, that there has been some broadening of the understanding of environmental risk to include conservation (although these responsibilities fall mainly to other agencies, such as English Nature and the Countryside Agency). The references to fisheries, coastal and inland waters, however, are largely due to the origins of the agency, which took over from the National Rivers Authority. Proposals to integrate efforts in several areas, such as pollution, waste, water and public engagement, do suggest that a more holistic governmentality has prevailed. Residual concerns about imposing excessive costs and the absence of industry as a target suggest that UK business, like its US counterpart, is in a position of power.[2]

In its 2001–02 annual report the concept of sustainable development is very prominent (UK EA 2002). The report lists five future goals for the agency: to be more 'efficient operators'; to match efforts to risks; to be 'influential advisers to Government'; to be an effective communicator; and to 'champion the environment within the context of sustainable development'. The contrast between these goals and the initial US EPA goals demonstrates how constructions of environmental risk have moved on over the last three decades.

Australian goals

In contrast to the US and UK situations, Australia has two key national environment protection institutions (as noted in the earlier sections of this chapter). The main coordinating body is the Environment Protection and Heritage Council (EPHC), which has environment, conservation and heritage ministers from the Commonwealth, all states and territories. It has the power to formulate national measures, which are implemented by relevant agencies in each jurisdiction. The Commonwealth also has the Department of Environment, which is the main agency of enforcement for the national government within the Department of Environment and Heritage. The EPHC is charged with the goal of creating national measures to ensure that:

- the people of Australia enjoy the benefit of equivalent protection from air, water and soil pollution and from noise, wherever they live;
- decisions by businesses are not distorted and markets are not fragmented by variations between jurisdictions in relation to the adoption or implementation of major Environment Protection Measures (NEPC 2002, p. 1).

These goals were derived from the earlier National Environment Protection Council (NEPC), established under the 1992 Inter-Governmental Agreement on the Environment, which was absorbed into the EPHC in 2002.[3]

The new EPHC publicly identifies several priority areas for action:

- air quality;
- waste management;
- eco-efficiency;
- financial sector initiatives;
- management of chemicals;
- participation by Aboriginal and Torres Strait Islander people;
- integrated national heritage policy;
- innovative policy tools and information (NEPC 2002, p. 3).

As with the US and UK agencies, reducing pollution and human health are a central focus in the construction of environmental risk. There is also the absence of targeting private industry as a culprit and a desire to avoid negative economic consequences for business. These priority areas for action, however, have been broadened to encompass broader issues of heritage and indigenous inclusion. Further, the uptake of ecological modernisation and sustainable development is apparent in the references to 'eco-efficiency', 'financial sector initiatives' and 'innovative policy tools and information'. So after more than three decades of explicit environmental regulation by the state, there are some attempts to integrate related policy areas and link goals to tools for intervention.

The Commonwealth Department of Environment plays something of a support role to the EPHC but also fulfils some specific functions for the Commonwealth government. These are stated as three outcomes that are to be achieved in the latest annual report (DEH 2002):

1 To ensure that 'the environment, especially those aspects that are matters of national environmental significance, is protected and conserved'.
2 To ensure that 'Australia benefits from meteorological and related science and services'.
3 To ensure that 'Australia's interests in Antarctica are advanced'.

These goals are more specific and reflect the narrower focus that Canberra takes to environmental issues compared to Westminster or Washington. This leaves the bulk of environmental regulation to the state and territory agencies.[4]

Goals in comparison

What, then, do these different sets of goals tell us about the response of each state to the environmental risks generated by reflexive modernisation? The first point is that the construction of environmental risk has changed over time. While the overall approach is still very much anthropocentric, with a focus on human health, the interconnectedness of issues has become more apparent in the way the expression of goals has become more general. Second, all three states have demonstrated a similar governmentality in terms of focusing on particular kinds of environmental degradation, such as pollution. Institutional differences between the three, however, have altered the scope of goals. Finally, it is apparent that private industry and business has remained in a position of considerable power throughout the last 35 years (Beder 2002). This is why they are not singled out for blame and why reservations about the possible negative economic impacts of regulation are added as qualifiers.

Institutional structure

As with the goals set, the structure of each institution embodies the prevailing perceptions, social context and habits of governance of the day. Individual sub-units were created to deal with specific goals and operating routines were established in accord with the existing landscape of political and economic institutions. One of the factors that made constructing environment protection organisations difficult was that they did not conform to the pre-existing division of policy areas. Established departments were designed to both promote and/or regulate particular economic sectors, such as agriculture, forestry, fisheries, mining, energy, manufacturing, transport, housing, communications, retailing, health care, finance and tourism. The new institutions, however, were not created to promote any particular sector. They were expected to intervene across all areas where there was an environmental risk. This is one of the reasons why they were viewed with suspicion by industry and many parts of the public sector.

In 1970 the US EPA began as an agglomeration of responsibilities and 5000 staff transferred from several existing branches of the federal bureaucracy (Williams 1993). The Federal Water Quality Administration was transferred from the Department of the Interior (DOI), although responsibility for fish, wildlife and forestry remained with the DOI. Pesticide research and standard setting was taken from the Food and Drug Administration, although it retained the power to set and police residual pesticide levels in food. Pesticide registration was transferred directly from the Department of Agriculture, but the department kept the ability to research into the effectiveness of pesticides. From the Department of Health, Education and Welfare came the National Air Pollution Administration, Bureau of Water Hygiene, Bureau of Solid Waste Management, Bureau of Radiological Health and Pesticide Tolerances and Research. Federal Radiation Control, the Environmental Radiation Standards section of the Atomic Energy Commission and the Environmental Systems Studies section of the Council of Environmental Quality all came from the Executive Office of the President. The council retained its ability to conduct research into environmental quality and the Atomic Energy Commission kept the power to set standards and issue licences for the nuclear industry (Williams 1993; Nixon 1971).

There was considerable debate about how to integrate the variety of responsibilities and personnel into one coherent agency and three proposals were put forward:

1   A functional structure with offices built around five main roles: '(1) planning and management; (2) standards and compliance; (3) regional programs; (4) national programs; and (5) research and monitoring' (Marcus 1991, p. 26).
2   A media focus with offices dealing with air, water and solid waste, to fit in with existing legislation (Williams 1993; Marcus 1991).
3   A regional approach with a decentralised network of regional offices that would work closely with state and local authorities.

The final structure was a compromise between these three proposals and it remained largely unchanged until the addition of three new functional offices in 1997 (see Figure 3.2).

In comparison to the US EPA, the creation of the UK EA involved the bringing together of far fewer disparate elements. The agency emerged from what was the latest in a series of mergers between several authorities. The three main areas of responsibility came from Her Majesty's Inspectorate of Pollution, the National Rivers Authority and Waste Disposal Authorities. As with the US EPA, the structure includes a number of functional, media and regional offices (see Figure 3.2).

In a similar fashion to the UK, Australian agencies are responsible ultimately to a minister at the state or Commonwealth level (Figure 3.2). A council made up of ministers with responsibility for the environment, conservation and heritage in all jurisdictions, the EPHC, provides the main link between these agencies, as well as acting as an overall coordinator for agreed national measures. The Department of Environment implements the Commonwealth's part in this system and the functional, media and regional factors are also apparent within the subdivisions of the organisation.

Figure 3.2 Institutional structures

US EPA	UK EA	Environment Australia and EPHC
The Office of Administrator Administrator, deputy and three associate administrators	**Ministerial portfolio** Department of Environment, Food and Rural Affairs (DEFRA)	**Environment Protection and Heritage Council** Main policy coordinating body empowered to make binding national environment protection measures. Made up of 13 ministers responsible for environment, conservation and heritage from each jurisdiction
Head office Nine assistant administrators who head up the offices of: • Administration and Resource Management • Enforcement and Compliance Assurance • Policy, Planning and Evaluation • International Activities • Research and Development • Air and Radiation • Prevention, Pesticides	**UK Environment Agency Board** Consisting of 13 members drawn from all business, the community and the public sector *Directors* Eight regional directors that head up the regional offices plus seven functional directors dealing with: • Legal services • Personnel • Environment protection • Finance	**Commonwealth portfolio** Department of Environment and Heritage (DEH) **Environment Australia** *Divisions* • Australian Antarctic • Australian World Heritage • Marine and Water

Figure 3.2 Institutional structures *(cont'd)*

US EPA	UK EA	Environment Australia and EPHC
and Toxic Substances • Water • Solid Waste and Emergency Response There are also the offices of: • General Counsel • Inspector General In February of 1997, the creation of three new offices were announced: • Children's Health Protection • Reinvention • Centre for Environmental Information and Statistics **The regional offices** There is a broad network of EPA branches that stretch across the country, including: • Ten regional offices whose structure mirrors that of the head office and which are led by regional administrators • A number of laboratories and field offices concerned with specific investigations and administration issues	• Operations • Water management • Corporate affairs *Head office* Located in London and Bristol, responsible for setting national policy *Other offices* • Eight national centres for scientific and technical support • Twenty-two functional service offices (e.g. laboratories, library and information services) • Eight regional offices • Twenty-six area offices coordinated by their local regional office **Related DEFRA agencies:** • English Nature • Countryside Agency	• Natural Heritage • Parks Australia • Strategic Development • Policy Coordination • Environment Quality • Approvals and Legislation **Related DEH offices:** • Supervising Scientist • Bureau of Meteorology • Great Barrier Reef Marine Park Authority • Australian Greenhouse Office • Office of Renewable Energy Regulator • National Parks • Australian Heritage Commission • National Oceans Office • Sydney Harbour Federation Trust

Source: NAPA (1995), McGarity (1991), US EPA (1997, 2002), UK EA (2002), UK Government (1990), DEH (2003) and NEPC (2002).

Resources and powers

While the goals and structures of each institution are good indications of the governmentality and prevailing discourses at the time, the best indicators of the construction of the seriousness of the risk are the level of resources allocated by government. Obviously the higher the priority given, the more money, staff and powers that will be given to the institution. Figure 3.3 summarises the current level of resources for each. Since the EPHC consists mainly of a ministerial council with a small secretariat, it has not been included in the column for Australia (the budget for the NEPC in 2000–01, just prior to its restructuring and the creation of the EPHC, was only US$480 000).

Figure 3.3 Institutional resources

	US EPA	UK EA	Environment Australia
Staff	17 850	8 950	1 400
Budget US$ (millions)*	7 600	721	170
Key legislation	• National Environmental Policy Act 1969 • Clean Air Act • Clean Water Act • Safe Drinking Water Act • Comprehensive Environmental Response, Compensation, and Liability Act • Resource Conservation and Recovery Act • Federal Insecticide, Fungicide and Rodenticide Act • Toxic Substances Control Act • Pollution Prevention Act • Marine Protection, Research and Sanctuaries Act • Uranium Mill Tailings Radiation Control Act	• Pollution Prevention Act 1999 • Environment Act 1995 • Environment Protection Act 1990 • Control of Pollution Act • Radioactive Substances Act • Water Act • Water Resources Act • Water Industry Act • Land Drainage Act • Salmon and Freshwater Fisheries Act • Diseases of Fish Act • Salmon Act • Wildlife and Countryside Act	• Renewable Energy (Electricity) Act 2000 • National Environment Protection Council Act 1995 • Environment Protection and Biodiversity Conservation Act 1999 • Natural Heritage Trust Act 1997 • Ozone Protection Act 1989 • Hazardous Waste (Regulation of Exports and Imports) 1989 • Environment Protection (Sea Dumping) Act 1981

Source: US EPA (2004), NAPA (1995), UK EA (1997, 2002), Environment Australia (2001a) and DEH (2003).

* US$ calculated using the most recent figures available for each agency prior to publication with currency exchange rates of A$1 = US$0.67; £1 = US$1.52

Three things are apparent from the resources and powers allocated to each institution. First, clearly the US EPA is the largest and most well financed of the three, although this is commensurate with a much larger economy, population and landmass. Second, the key areas of legislation overseen by the US EPA and UK EA are largely pollution and media focused. Third, while the Commonwealth Department of Environment is the smallest institution of the three, with the majority of regulation occurring at the state level, it has a broader portfolio to administer in terms of legislation.

Conclusions

Overall it is clear that significant differences have arisen in the three states' responses to the environmental risks produced by reflexive modernisation. Historical factors have helped to set significantly different institutional contexts and there are varying political cultures at work. As a result, responses to similar stimuli (increased concerns about environmental risk and a growing counter-culture in the 1960s) set them on comparable but significantly different trajectories of governance. In terms of similarities, all governments appear to have been initially reluctant to act, all underestimated the risks, all compartmentalised their response in ways that limited the powers of the new institutions and all have been wary of blaming or unsettling industry. In terms of difference, the US EPA has the longest continuous history and is the largest of the three. The UK has undergone a series of reformations with entry into the EU and the creation of separate parliaments in Scotland, Wales and Northern Ireland having an impact on its agency's form and function. Australia has also undergone a history of continuous administrative change but has settled on a centralised consultative forum coordinating a decentralised enforcement regime.

CHAPTER 4

Restrictions, regulations and economic incentives

Introduction

The previous chapter reviewed how different institutions had been created as a response to environmental risk. This chapter will consider the kinds of interventions undertaken by these institutions. The first four sections deal with banning or restricting activities, specifying the technology to be used, setting emission standards and creating ambient environmental standards respectively. Such regulations,[1] based on the discourses of administrative rationalism and, more recently, ecological modernisation (see Chapter 2 and Dryzek 1997), form the bedrock of most regimes of environmental governance. Most of the cases cited in this part of the story are drawn from the USA because it has the oldest agency, pioneered many of the regulatory interventions and has the most experience with them. Where possible the cases have been related back to British and Australian situations, and there is a separate section on integrated pollution prevention and control in the UK. Current neo-liberal discourses have encouraged a shift towards economic prompts to generate rewards or penalties and these will be dealt with in the fifth section, which includes examples drawn from the Australian experience. This brief history illustrates how different discourses, governmentality and reflexive modernisation are at work in the design and implementation of interventions and there are lessons for all industrialised states.

Environmental regulation

One of the first responses of governments to environmental risk has been to create laws that enable state institutions to enforce regulations that address specific risks in individual media (air, water, or soil). Regulations can take a number of different forms, including:

1   the complete prohibition of an activity or product where the level of risk is deemed to be too high (e.g. the ban on CFC production and use, or the removal of asbestos from building materials);
2   specifying the technology to be used in either the production process or product to reduce risks (e.g. fitting scrubbers to chimney stacks or catalytic converters to motor vehicles);
3   setting emission standards or licensing conditions for individual plants to minimise risk (e.g. specifying an upper threshold for smoke emissions from a specific chimney or facility); or
4   creating an ambient environmental standard for a region that is deemed to be an acceptable level of risk (e.g. setting a maximum limit on the average concentration of airborne sulphur dioxide in a given air-shed).

In practice all the different kinds of regulation operate simultaneously and work in conjunction with other state programs or interventions, so the barriers between the categories are very porous (Clayton et al. 1999; Gunningham et al. 1998). Regulations formed the vanguard of responses to environmental risk up to the end of the 1970s and persist as the foundation of most environmental governance. The next four sections will review each kind of regulation in turn. Some of the problems associated with these interventions will be considered and Chapter 8 demonstrates how many of the improvements in environmental quality can still be attributed to their deployment.

Banning or restricting processes and products

Chapter 1 considered the nature of environmental risk and one of the ongoing hazards mentioned was ozone depletion, which has been caused by chemicals such as CFCs. The response of the international community was to eventually ban the production and use of such ozone-depleting substances. This provides a classic example of the most stringent version of regulations and illustrates four interesting points. First, it shows that sometimes a risk can be constructed in a way that makes it unacceptably high in the minds of decision makers. Second, as a result of this construction, the response of the state is a total ban on the activity or product that creates the risk because it can see no other alternative. Third, this perception of unacceptable risk forms part of the governmentality that justifies to both the public and the state the legitimacy of the action, even if it potentially has a negative economic impact (as was argued forcefully by the CFC industry). Finally and particularly in the ozone case, the discourse of weak ecological modernisation that now underpins a great deal of environmental regulation assumes that improvements in technology will play a major role in resolving risks by finding alternatives (see Chapter 2 and Eckersley 2004; Dryzek 1997; Christoff 1996; Rutherford 1994). The optimism prevailed in this case even in the face of early chemical industry denials that there were alternatives to CFCs (Benedick 1991).

The fortunate coincidence of social forces in the ozone case created a positive institutional context for regulation, but this is not always the case and agencies often have to battle against competing constructions of risk, clashing discourses and an institutional setting that doesn't leave much room for change. When this occurs, resistance to regulatory intervention can come not just from industry but from other parts of the state, political leaders and even from inside an environment agency itself. The origin and structure of state institutions can exacerbate these tensions, as can the prevailing discourses of the executive government of the day. These difficulties are part of the reason why the mainstream institutions of governance have difficulty responding to environmental risk and are another indication of modernisation becoming reflexive (Eckersley 2004). As Beck (1992) pointed out, society is trying to use nineteenth-century institutions to address twentieth-century problems and, as Foucault (1977) highlighted, many governing institutions and ideas have even earlier origins. The US case studies in this section indicate the difficulties regulators face when they attempt to determine if a substance is an unacceptable risk and ban its production or use.

Banning pesticides

One of the first hurdles that an agency may face is infighting and tensions with other parts of the state. Take, for example, attempts by the US EPA to ban the pesticide DDT, which had been criticised at the start of the 1960s (Carson 2000 [1962]). The office responsible for pesticide regulation had been transferred intact from the Department of Agriculture to the US EPA and was staffed with technical agricultural experts who had primarily been concerned with the most effective use of pesticides to increase farm production (Hoberg 1992). The US EPA's Office of General Council, however, was staffed by young lawyers who did perceive a problem with the widespread use of pesticides (Lazarus 1991). Infighting between these two offices hampered the US EPA's overall efforts to regulate and delayed the ban on DDT until 1972 (Williams 1993; Hoberg 1992). Further, when the US EPA banned the use of another pesticide, EDB, as a soil fumigant in 1983, the US Agency for International Development continued to encourage its use in other countries and the US Department of Agriculture continued to demand that it be sprayed on imported produce (Rosenbaum 1991).

Regulation can also be hampered by a lack of knowledge about the impacts of products. This strategic use of knowledge is part of the neo-liberal discourse that maintains industry in a position of power over the state. The 1972 amendments to the federal *Insecticide, Fungicide and Rodenticide Act 1972* required the US EPA to assess all the pesticides on the market to decide which should be banned (Howard 1994). However, these amendments did not require suspending any pesticide that might be suspect while it was being tested. Such legislative weaknesses were due to the influence of major companies within the pesticide industry, which had a virtual monopoly on knowledge about the safety of their products. The inability of the US EPA to challenge industry on technical grounds allowed major chemical firms to set much of the early political agenda in opposing legislation (Hoberg 1992). In 1975 the US EPA issued new regulations regarding the information requirements that industry should meet for a product evaluation but there were still difficulties with implementation (Hoberg 1992).

Even when the US EPA began to test pesticides and other substances, it faced a further set of difficulties. First, there was (and still is) a heated debate about how to test substances adequately for their environmental and health effects (Rosenbaum 1991). Regardless of how thorough the scientific studies are, there will always be an element of choice about how to interpret results and construct regulations. Even defining what is meant by 'safe', 'toxic' or 'acceptable risk' can be problematic (see Chapter 1). These choices will be affected by the prevailing technical information, economic imperatives and political discourses (Landy et al. 1994; Petulla 1987). A further complication to this scientific uncertainty is that much of the testing work is subcontracted to private firms and in 1976 it was revealed that one of these firms had falsified results (Hoberg 1992).

The context created by political and legal institutions can also influence the capacity to respond to environmental risks. By the mid-1970s, those politicians who identified their interests with the industry under neo-liberal discourses accused the US EPA of over-reaching its responsibilities in these regulations. Those who were influenced by environmentalism or administrative rationalism criticised the US EPA for its lack of action. The result was a proliferation of conflicting demands for the agency to explain itself before numerous congressional committees and investigations, side-tracking many of the resources that could have gone into pesticide regulation (Lazarus 1991).

During the 1970s American judges relaxed the requirements for proof of legal standing, allowing industry, community groups and environmental organisations to challenge a regulatory decision in court without having to show a strict economic interest. Some of the time this institutional expansion worked to slow down the US EPA's activities (Lazarus 1991). US EPA rule-making routines became more complex as they attempted to anticipate and head off possible legal challenges with pre-emptive comprehensive legal analysis and the generation of sufficient technical knowledge to support any decision in court (Landy et al. 1994).

So what was the overall impact of these reflexive barriers to change? Howard (1994) complained that after 22 years the 'EPA has only gotten around to judging the safety of about thirty pesticides' (p. 58) and sees the US EPA as bureaucrats indulging in pointless 'perpetual analysis' (p. 84). In 1991, Rosenbaum (p. 220) claimed that 'useful information about toxicity is absent for 64 percent of all pesticides and inert ingredients of pesticide formulations'. Lazarus (1991) pointed out that by 1984 less than half the 600 active and 900 inert ingredients of pesticides had even been registered. The situation was not much better in 1987 with only 10 per cent of pesticides being tested each year (Petulla 1987). Despite these hurdles the situation appears to be improving and by the mid-1990s the US EPA had banned some 230 pesticides (US EPA 1995a). Problems with pesticide regulation have persisted throughout both the later Clinton and Bush (Jnr) administrations (*Consumer Reports* 2001), at both the federal and state level (Powell 2001), and there remain broader concerns about the general lack of resources that inhibit the ability of the agency to enforce regulations across all areas of its responsibility (*Chemical Week* 2003).

Restricting toxic chemicals

The US EPA's record on regulating toxic substances also demonstrates some of the barriers to responding to environmental risks, but there are some interesting contrasts to the pesticide case. The *Toxic Substances Control Act 1976* gave the US EPA the power to identify, test, evaluate and regulate the full life cycle of substances, from manufacture to use and final disposal. In 1977, the agency completed a register of about 60 000 chemicals used by industry, but by 1985 less than 100 of these had been assessed for health risks (Shapiro 1990; Lazarus 1991). Meanwhile, the number of chemicals in common commercial use had increased to about 70 000 in 1990 and 80 000 by the end of the century.

In some instances the US EPA appears to have been reluctant to restrict the use of some chemicals. Legal actions brought by the Natural Resources Defence Council in 1973 and 1974 forced it to nominate 65 toxic 'priority pollutants' for regulation (Petulla 1987). Formaldehyde, for example (a solvent used in the textile industry for fixing dyes), was determined to be a carcinogen by the Office of Toxic Substances in 1979. The agency decided in 1982, however, that it did not need to be regulated as a toxic substance. The Natural Resources Defence Council and the American Public Health Association began a legal challenge so the agency announced a reopening of its investigation. In 1984 the US EPA reversed its decision but it was not until 1986 that a standard for the safe exposure of textile workers was established (Shapiro 1990). These examples demonstrate how a context of more open legal institutions can be used by the sub-politics of environmental groups to re-engage with the state and force change.

In fairness to the US EPA, the Congress had asked for the impossible on toxic substances because of three factors. First, the number of existing industrial chemicals is simply overwhelming. It would be impossible for the US EPA even to test each existing chemical without a dramatic injection of funds, facilities and personnel. Estimates for costs of a full assessment of each chemical vary between US$1 million and US$7 million and the time taken for each assessment would be four to five years (Shapiro 1990; Petulla 1987). Based on these figures, the total cost of testing all 80 000 chemicals would therefore be between US$80 billion and US$560 billion (which is 12 to 80 times the total US EPA budget or 1–8 per cent of total US GDP). There is no likelihood of such resources being committed to this program by Congress.

The second point is that the number of chemicals is growing rapidly. As 1000 new chemicals are added each year, US$1–7 billion would be required just to keep up with the new substances being introduced. At present this is well beyond the resources of the US EPA. To deal with these problems the agency adopted a graduated approach to risk analysis that screens substances according to their perceived likely impact. This process relies on current knowledge about similar substances or functional groups to give an indication of probable risks. Of the 7595 risk analyses carried out by the US EPA in 1993, the majority (6166) were quick screenings that took less than two days and only 249 were major assessments (NAPA 1995).

The third point is that the US EPA was starting from a very low baseline of knowledge about the effects of these chemicals on humans and the environment. Laboratory tests may highlight the most lethal substances and information about known compounds with similar functional groups may be a rough guide, but there is little extensive data on long-term toxicological or epidemiological effects because these substances are so new. Further, there is little information on how they will be dispersed or accumulated in the environment and there is no indication of which species will be most vulnerable to their effects.

While the size of the problem explains why the US EPA cannot meet the unrealistic goals set by Congress, it does not explain why so few have actually been regulated. According to Russell Train (a former US EPA administrator), the chemical industry was not united in its resistance to the *Toxic Substances Act* (Train 1993). The industry was singularly unsuccessful in propagating its view of acceptable risks with a public that remains wary of synthetic chemicals. It therefore appears that the problems have had more to do with the internal disunity of the agency and the general lack of a knowledge base from which to work, exacerbated by the tendency to contract work out to private companies (Landy et al. 1994).

Banning asbestos

Asbestos used to be one of the boom products of the building industry because of its ease of fabrication, fire resistance and insulating properties. By the late 1970s, there was a general consensus that asbestos dust causes a fatal type of lung cancer. Yet when the US EPA decided to ban 95 per cent of asbestos use in 1979, the Office of Management and Budget (OMB), under the influence of neo-liberal discourses, waged an arduous campaign against the ban that lasted until 1983 (Percival 1991). First, it delayed regulations by demanding that the US EPA provide a comprehensive cost–benefit analysis. When this analysis came out in favour of the ban, the OMB queried the figures and pushed for a less comprehensive restriction (Fraas 1991). When this tactic failed, it tried to have responsibility for regulating asbestos shifted from the US EPA to the Office of Health and Safety Administration (which could only regulate asbestos use in the workplace, not in the home) (Percival 1991). The OMB even went as far as seeking help from the Canadian government, which wanted to support its asbestos industry (Percival 1991). This demonstrates the extraordinary power of neo-liberalism, which led a US state institution to form an alliance with a foreign government and the asbestos industry against other parts of its own state. In the end, however, the institutional power of the OMB was not sufficient to prevent the US EPA imposing a ban on 95 per cent of asbestos use. The remaining 5 per cent of use was permitted (under tight control) because there was no technically feasible substitute. Of course there remain a large number of buildings contaminated by asbestos (Rosenbaum 1991).

Bans and restrictions in the UK and Australia

Governments in the UK and Australia have also been prepared to ban or restrict certain products and processes such as CFCs, pesticides like DDT and toxic substances like asbestos. They faced similar hurdles to action, including a lack of knowledge, the problem of constructing a safe or acceptable level of risk, a lack of resources for comprehensive testing and a shortage of funds for remedial action. The US cases, however, suggest that even these barriers and a hostile institutional context can still not prevent opportunities for the state to take authoritative action in response to an environmental risk. Where there is a coincidence of discourses supporting action, on the other hand, regulation can be far quicker and more effective. This is why the idea of aligning the whole of the state, industry and the community behind sustainable development could be an important aid in regulation (see Chapters 6 and 7).

Specifying technology

Next to banning or restricting a product, specifying the technology to be used is one of the most 'hands-on' approaches the state can take to environmental governance. It engages with the optimism of ecological modernisation which assumes that there are technical solutions to environmental risks and the governmentality of administrative rationalism which assumes state bureaucracies have the expertise and capacity to micro-manage individual production choices for the benefit of society (Eckersley 2004; Dryzek 1997; Paehlke & Torgerson 1990). As in the previous cases, the counter discourse of neo-liberalism utterly opposes this latter assertion and argues that such regulation constitutes an unnecessary interference in the workings of the market and leads to the inefficient allocation of resources (DiLorenzo 1993).

The state in many countries has used technology-specifying regulations to curb pollution with some degree of success. The USA, UK and Australia, for example, now require the engines of new vehicles to run on unleaded fuel and have catalytic converters in their exhaust systems. In the UK, the *Clean Air Act 1956* required building heating systems to stop burning high-sulphur coal by switching to 'smokeless' fuels like natural gas to reduce urban smog. The Australian government requires energy producers to source a percentage of their power from renewable sources to reduce their greenhouse gas emissions. Some of the most interesting experiences of trying to respond to environmental risks with technology-specifying regulations have been in the USA, as the following cases demonstrate.

Case study: Refining the refinery

The case of the Amoco Yorktown Refinery in Virginia demonstrates some of the difficulties associated with specifying technology. A chance meeting between a US EPA official and an Amoco manager led to a joint environmental audit of the plant to look for better ways to reduce emissions (Howard 1994). Howard Klee (1990), the Amoco director of the project, presented the study to an oil industry conference as a positive model. The project involved more than 200 people from 35 organisations, cost US$2.3 million and was able to uncover many cost-effective alternatives to meeting emission standards. Using the techniques specified by the *Clean Air Act 1970* the refinery spent US$2400 per ton to reduce its emission of hydrocarbons by 7300 tons per year. The audit found that alternative techniques could reduce the emission of 7500 tons of hazardous chemicals (including 7100 tons of hydrocarbons) for US$500 per ton, or less than 25 per cent of the original cost (NAPA 1995).

One example of how this would work was with regards to benzene emissions. Under the *Clean Air Act* regulations, Amoco was required to install filters in its refinery smokestacks to prevent benzene escaping into the atmosphere at a cost of US$31 million, but the audit found that the majority of benzene emissions came from the loading dock. Further, these emissions could be captured and recycled for a fraction of the cost of the benzene filters (Howard 1994). Initially the US EPA did not have the discretion to allow alternatives to technology specified by legislation, so even if this had been known before the money was spent on the filters, the US EPA could not have granted Amoco an exemption (NAPA 1995). The agency acquired this flexibility in 1995 through the *Pollution Prevention Act*, the Common Sense Initiative and Project XL (US EPA 1995a). Interestingly these changes were more in line with ecological modernisation and a move away from administrative rationalism.

This project is a special case. Clearly neither the US EPA nor industry could afford to go through the same process for every plant but many of the findings could be adapted to other refineries and similar manufacturing processes. Two lessons about the adequacy of environmental regulation have been taken from this experience. First, regulations that specify technology appear to reduce the incentive to innovate and find better solutions. Second, a more flexible statutory mandate can sometimes allow state agencies to adopt more effective strategies for environmental protection (NAPA 1995; Howard 1994). At the end of the day improvements will happen only if there is a predominant discourse among industrial leaders which encourages them to pursue cleaner production methods. The story of this refinery, for example, does not have a happy ending and a decade after the audit the refinery was fined for exceeding the CAA emission limits (Doggett 2000).

Sulphur dioxide scrubbers and the Clean Air Act

Another example that highlights some of the issues associated with technology-specifying regulations arises from the attempts of the US EPA to reduce the power industry's sulphur dioxide (SO_2) emissions that lead to acid rain. These emissions produced in the heavily industrialised US mid-west region are carried to the north-east coast and across the Canadian border by the prevailing winds. Acid precipitation in these regions reduces crop yield, erodes buildings, contaminates surface waters, kills aquatic species and damages native forests. The SO_2 regulations were an attempt to address the acid precipitation problem, particularly in the north-eastern area of the USA, the Great Lakes and Canada (Rosenbaum 1991).

In 1971 the US EPA set New Point Source Performance Standards for coal-burning power stations that limited emissions to 1.2 pounds of SO_2 for every million British thermal units (Btu) of electricity produced. This was opposed by industry and unsuccessfully challenged in court on the grounds that it would require the installation of smokestack scrubbers that produced hazardous sludge (Hoberg 1992). The 1977 *Clean Air Act* amendments tightened the regulations further by specifying that emission reductions had to be achieved by the implementation of technology and could not be met by burning cleaner fuels, but this was not the most effective means to reduce emissions. A switch to low-sulphur western coal would have reduced emissions more and may have avoided as much as US$4 billion in scrubber installation costs (Howard 1994).

Guruswamy (1991) claims that the total economic impact of pollution control equipment (such as scrubbers, precipitators and cooling towers) may increase the capital costs of a coal-fired plant by as much as 45 per cent and running costs by up to 30 per cent. He suggests that these costs could be halved if the emission reductions were achieved by more integrated pollution controls. These estimates seem extremely high and could be questioned, but the point that there are better and cheaper ways to achieve the same result is generally accepted. It has been estimated that for each ton of SO_2 removed by a scrubber, 3–6 tons of sulphurous sludge is produced that has to be disposed of by landfill. This in turn often leaches into groundwater and may lead to other costs.

The decision to require smokestack scrubbers seems to be a concession to the Appalachian coal producers. Coal from the Appalachia region has a high sulphur content and producers would have suffered if it had been replaced by the cleaner western coal. Once it was realised that some form of regulation was inevitable, these coal producers formed an alliance with clean air activists to push for the adoption of mandatory smokestack scrubbers

(Hoberg 1992). Although SO_2 emissions were reduced, the level is still high enough to cause persistent acid rain problems in the north-east. This has led to calls for more regulatory measures (both within the USA and from the Canadian government). The Reagan administration delayed further action on acid rain by claiming that more research was needed to uncover causes, even though there was a clear link to coal burning (Rosenbaum 1991; Landy et al. 1994; Gibson 1990). This tactic was also used in the UK by the Thatcher government during the 1980s to counter criticisms about the impacts of its SO_2 emissions on other European states (Dryzek et al. 2003). The current US administration is also sceptical of the risk and has moved to change the CAA.

To specify or not to specify technology?

In some cases technology-specifying regulations have provided a direct and appropriate response to particular environmental risks. Requiring vehicles to run on unleaded fuel and be fitted with catalytic converters, for example, has helped to improve urban air quality by reducing the concentration of some airborne pollutants, and the fuel switching necessitated by the UK *Clean Air Act 1956* certainly contributed to a reduction in smog. In other cases, however, these kinds of regulations may lead to reductions in emissions but not encourage the most effective solution, as in the SO_2 case. There is also the real possibility that these regulations will misdirect efforts and target the wrong source, as in the case of benzene emissions at Yorktown. Ultimately, any shift towards a more flexible system of regulation requires an ongoing commitment from both business and government leaders to avoid back-sliding and this in turn requires a change of discourse among leaders in both institutions.

Concerns about the costs of specifying technology have led to a moderation in the demands made by such regulations. US rules on industrial effluent, for example, were initially tightened during the early 1970s then moderated as difficulties in achieving compliance became apparent. In 1977 the *Water Pollution Act* was amended to require industry to use best practicable technology for reducing effluent and made allowances for the economic costs of effluent-reduction technology. This was a deviation from the stricter requirement for best available technology (regardless of economic cost) that had been adopted in earlier Acts (Freeman 1990). The change in technological specification was a response to the National Commission on Water Quality report in 1976 that found 'some of the technologies suggested by the US EPA to meet best available technology requirements actually did not meet water quality standards for some pollutants' (Petulla 1987, p. 75). The current Bush administration, operating under a very strong neo-liberal discourse, has moved to reduce technology-specifying regulations in a number of areas.

A similar shift has occurred in the UK. Here the regulatory focus shifted from requiring firms to adopt 'best available technology' to 'best practicable environmental option' or 'best available technology not entailing excessive costs' under the *Environment Protection Act 1990* and EU Directive 84/360 (Hawke 2002; Clayton et al. 1999). This again indicates the influence of the prevailing neo-liberal discourses during the Thatcher years.

Setting emission standards

A more flexible approach to regulating environmental risk is to set performance standards for industrial facilities to meet. This can be done in several ways; for example:

- setting upper limits for the total level of emissions for a single type of pollutant emanating from a specific part of a site (e.g. the amount of benzene released by a particular chimney stack);
- setting upper limits for a particular pollutant from the whole site (e.g. total benzene emissions from an entire factory complex); or
- setting emission standards for a set of pollutants for a whole site (e.g. the total amount of hazardous hydrocarbons released by a factory complex).

These standards are usually set according to the level of risk associated with each pollutant—the more toxic or mobile the substance, the smaller the amount allowed to be released. In regions where there is considered to be a significant problem with overall pollution, restrictions may be tightened for existing plants and/or tougher standards set for new plants. Standards can be set for air emissions, liquid effluent and solid waste. There may also be some differentiation between different forms of the same substance (e.g. airborne lead is more hazardous to human health than solid lead waste because it is more mobile and more quickly absorbed by the body).

Standards are more flexible than technology-specifying regulations because they give each firm the ability to choose how to meet the performance goals set. For this reason, a whole-of-site approach is preferred by industry because it maximises their range of options. In the Yorktown refinery case, for example, it was cleaner, easier and cheaper for the company to stop benzene emissions at the loading dock rather than install chimney traps. Another advantage of standards is that they do not require the regulator to have a detailed knowledge of the latest production technology.

They only have to set the goals, based on the current knowledge of a specific environmental risk, while industry decides how best to comply.

US steel and emission bubbles

The US EPA had a long and difficult battle with the US steel industry over meeting the goals of the *Clean Air Act*. Pollution problems from the steel industry had been recognised long before the existence of the US EPA (Crenson 1971). Integrated steel mills (those that produce steel from iron rather than recycle scrap) require large quantities of water and energy and produce airborne hydrocarbons, SO_2 and particulate matter, especially from coking ovens. In 1977 the US *Clean Air Act* was amended to require firms to adopt reasonably available control technology. The complexity of specifying technology for each type of plant was eventually replaced in 1981 with the adoption of emission 'bubbles', that is, an aggregate level of emissions would be set for a whole production site as if a bubble had been placed over it. The firm could then make internal trade-offs between wastes produced by different parts of the site. Reductions in emissions from one part might offset the need for reductions in another, as long as the total emissions stayed below the aggregate permissible level. In theory, this gave the firm the opportunity to meet pollution standards in the most cost-efficient way by allowing it to select the cheapest and easiest emission control options for the site (Landy et al. 1994). Initially bubbles were set for particular pollutants (such as SO_2) and were allowed only in regions which attained the national air quality standards. Eventually generic bubbles for a collection of pollutants were accepted and were used in non-attainment areas if a company could provide trade-off reductions in other pollutants. The bubbles in these areas were set at a level that would approximate the total site emissions if the reasonably available control technology had been applied to each part of the site.

The bubble proposal had originally come from industry during a series of tripartite negotiations with unions and the agency from 1978 to 1980. These negotiations were designed to resolve some of the problems of implementing the 1977 amendments. The unions sided with industry and environmentalists were initially excluded from the bargaining, but were later given the chance to comment on the outcome of the negotiations. Individual firms could apply for a 'stretch-out' of the deadline for compliance if they could demonstrate a capacity to comply. This created an incentive to industry to moderate their claims of the costs of compliance so actual spending fell to US\$49.4 million from original industry estimates of over US\$500 million (Landy et al. 1994). This is a graphic demonstration of how neo-liberalism tends to encourage an overstatement in negative economic impacts of regulation.

The early outcome of this process was not encouraging. Some emission bubbles allowed companies to reduce dust by sealing roads and watering stock piles instead of limiting plant emissions. This did not take into account different health and environmental impacts from the dust's varying chemical composition or size. It was also difficult to police, which was a problem for the US EPA's Office of Enforcement (Landy et al. 1994; McGarity 1991). Of the ten 'stretch-outs' applied for, nine were violated by industry (Landy et al. 1994; US Department of Commerce 1985). Despite these difficulties, bubbles are still believed to be more economically efficient than technology-specifying regulations (NCE 1993) and are supported by the prevailing neo-liberalism as a fallback position (i.e. better than specifying technology but not as good as no regulation at all).

Eventually the industry underwent a massive restructuring in response to changes in the world market and continued to displace employment. As many older integrated mills were shutting down, there was a high growth in the construction of 'mini-mills' that were cleaner and recycled scrap metal. These facilities found it easier to achieve compliance but were largely ignored by the tripartite agreements (Landy et al. 1994). The older integrated mills, however, have continued to win regulatory concessions and the 1990 *Clean Air Act* amendments granted a thirty-year extension in the deadline for coke oven compliance with new tighter emission rules (OECD 1996b). The current Bush administration has continued the tradition of granting concessions by trying to protect the industry from foreign competition with new tariffs, although it was forced to back away from this decision in late 2003 under pressure from the World Trade Organisation and major trading partners.

Although the US steel industry has put up a major fight and won many concessions, it is not so powerful as to prevent the imposition and progressive tightening of emissions standards. Further, the demands of the international market place and the deployment of new, more efficient production technology has undermined the dominant position of the industry. To some extent modest ecological modernisation has come to many parts of the industry despite its resistance.

Integrated pollution prevention and control (IPPC)

The UK has developed its own approach to pollution control that addresses some of the issues raised by the previous cases and is similar to the bubble concept. Being the cradle of the Industrial Revolution, the UK suffered some of its worst environmental hazards early on and established pollution inspectorates back in the nineteenth century on the basis of public health concerns (see Chapter 3). Regulators tended to negotiate with firms for pollution reductions rather than set and enforce strict standards, but after the UK's entry into the European Community in 1973 things started to change (Hawke 2002). European administrative rationalism was far more support-ive of the strict enforcement of standards and promoted them in successive environmental directives (Weale 1998). Blending of these two approaches produced integrated pollution prevention and control.

In England and Wales, enforcement of the IPPC falls to the Environment Agency[2] for the larger, more complex, or more hazardous facilities, otherwise it falls to the local authorities, and there is a lot of liaison and cooperation between the two. A team of inspectors is employed by the agency and assigned specific industrial sites. Each site has a licence to operate that speci-fies standards for the total emissions from the site that are derived from the relevant legislation. These cover all media (air, water and land), allow for the different toxicity or mobility of each substance and can require abatement actions using the best available technology not entailing excessive costs. The inspectors audit the operations of each site to check for compliance with the licence and laws. Over time they develop a hands-on knowledge of the processes they inspect and an ability to spot when things are amiss with the reporting of emissions.

The integrated approach was proposed by the Royal Commission on Environmental Pollution and enshrined in the *Environment Protection Act 1990*. EU Directive 96/61 added pollution prevention, which was reincor-porated into UK regulation through the *Pollution Prevention Act 1999*. In parallel to these legislative changes, an institutional consolidation was occurring. This led first to the merger of several bodies into Her Majesty's Inspectorate of Pollution in 1987, followed by its integration with the National Rivers Authority and Waste Disposal Authorities into a new Environ-ment Agency in 1995. The new agency was therefore able to work across all three media—air, water and land (Hawke 2002; Duxbury & Morton 2000; Garner 2000; House of Commons Select Committee on the Environment 2000; Bell 1997; UK Government 1990).

There was some early resistance from industry, particularly to the disclosure of their emissions, but over time this has abated. Further, the system appears to be having some positive impact as the emission of regulated pollutants has declined (see Chapter 8). Things are not all plain sailing, however, and Richards et al. (2000) suggest that knowledge of the process and practicable alternatives is the key to integrated pollution control. The superior technical knowledge of the firms, a lack of agency resources and a negotiated approach often puts polluters in a position of advantage.

Emission standards versus specifying technology

These cases suggest that emission standards, particularly when applied on a factory complex scale, do have some advantages over specifying technology, but they can require considerable resources to police. The more combative environment of the USA has seen strong industry resistance, especially from powerful sectors such as the steel industry, and this has undermined attempts to reduce environmental risk. The negotiated approach of the UK has caused less visible industry resistance, but both appear to be achieving some positive results despite the limitations.

Setting ambient standards

The fourth approach to regulation is that of setting ambient environmental standards. This is a goal-setting approach that adds another level of flexibility to regulatory regimes. Instead of restricting a particular product, specifying the technology to be used or limiting the emissions coming from a particular site, ambient standards require that a particular region should not fall below a certain level of environmental quality. It might be specified, for example, that all surface waters within a particular catchment should not contain more than a certain concentration of dissolved salt, or that soil in the area should not contain more than a certain amount of pesticide residue. Alternatively, it may be deemed that the total level of atmospheric lead within an air-shed should not exceed some maximum limit. The advantage of this approach is that it allows local authorities to trade off between different pollution sources over an entire region.

The USA, UK and Australia have all constructed national ambient air quality standards for a handful of the most common pollutants that are deemed to have unacceptable negative health risks. These include particulate matter, carbon monoxide, atmospheric lead, oxides of nitrogen, ground-level ozone (or the volatile organic compounds that cause photochemical smog and ozone formation) and sulphur dioxide. Ambient standards for these substances are established under the US *Clean Air Act 1970*, the UK *Clean Air Act 1956/69* and EU directives and the Australian National Environment Protection Measure 1997. While ambient standards are another useful string for the state regulators' bow, there are several difficulties, not the least of which is that it is a very selective approach to environmental quality that risks ignoring significant hazards that don't make it on to the list of standards. There are two further problems. First, there is the challenge of establishing an acceptable concentration of these pollutants. Second, there is the difficulty of taking the hard enforcement actions to ensure such standards are met.

Setting ambient ozone standards

One of the reasons that volatile organic emissions are important is that some of them cause the formation of ozone in the lower atmosphere, particularly in urban areas. While ozone is an important shield against UV radiation in the upper atmosphere, in urban airspace it is a respiratory irritant and has some corrosive effects. The case of ozone emission regulations demonstrates the difficulty of setting and maintaining environmental standards in the face of scientific uncertainty. The US EPA set ambient standards for ozone at 0.08 ppm in 1971 on the basis of an epidemiological study, but by 1976 this standard proved unattainable because the natural background level of ozone sometimes exceeded this concentration (Landy et al. 1994). By 1978 a series of other studies had produced conflicting results. Two clinical trials suggested temporary health effects at levels of 0.15 and 0.25 ppm. A new epidemiological study then suggested effects on school children at levels below 0.10 ppm. Finally, animal trials suggested effects as low as 0.01 ppm.

The US EPA came under pressure to loosen the standard from President Carter's Regulatory Analysis Review Group which was concerned that economic development in urban areas would have to be stopped in order to meet the standard. Industry wanted the standard no lower than 0.25 ppm and used the scientific uncertainty generated by the conflicting results to support its case. In the end, US EPA administrator Costle was forced to make a political choice between 0.08 ppm and 0.15 ppm based on the range of scientific results. In 1979 the new standard was set at 0.12 ppm; both industry and environmentalists attempted to challenge the new standard in court but failed to have it overturned (Landy et al. 1994; Percival 1991). Ground-level ozone levels have generally fallen but despite the standard's revision many urban and industrial areas still did not comply (Landy et al. 1994; Rosenbaum 1991).

Enforcing ambient standards

Under the *Clean Air Act*, the US EPA could negotiate individual State Implementation Plans (SIPs) that specified how each state government was going to attain the national ambient air quality standards (Landy et al. 1994; Rosenbaum 1991; Portney 1990). By 1977, it was apparent that the SIP process was not working. States were either producing lax regulations or not enforcing agreed standards and there was widespread non-compliance across the steel industry. Congress tightened the law and required all states to attain the national ambient air quality standards by 1982. The amendments specified that reasonably available control technology was to be used to meet these standards so most SIPs had to be redrafted. The split between state and federal powers made regulation more difficult. At first the agency concentrated on hydrocarbon emissions and left particulate matter to the states. Three of the four key mid-western states then relaxed the standards for particulate emissions (Landy et al. 1994). By 1995 many states had failed to meet their commitments, even after threats of funding cuts had been made (Anderson & Howitt 1995).

The US EPA had even tried creating separate arrangements for steel producers that offered lower standards in return for compliance. The steel industry consistently claimed that regulations would increase costs dramatically, force plant closures and lead to mass layoffs. Given the size and importance of the steel industry to the US economy, this job threat kept state and local governments at bay and put the US EPA in a difficult position. Even President Ford (1977) publicly criticised the US EPA on this point. There is now considerable evidence that this perception is inaccurate and the job losses would have occurred even if there had been no environmental regulations (Goodstein 1999; Landy et al. 1994; US Department of Commerce 1985). Further, several studies have even suggested that they may provide a slight positive stimulus to GDP growth in some circumstances (OECD 1996a; NCEP 1995).

Russell Train, the second US EPA Administrator, admits that the agency did shut down the coke ovens of one firm in Birmingham as a last resort (Train 1993). This was unusual, however, and a study by the US Department of Commerce (1985) of the US steel industry found that the majority of redundancies and closures were due to changes in the market, downturns in the business cycle, the reformulation of products with less steel and foreign competition. Heavy debt servicing, the rising cost of labour, stagnant productivity, conservative management, inefficient use of materials and the two energy price shocks were also cited as major factors in the industry's demise, not environmental regulations. Despite these studies, the neo-liberal claims that environmental regulations and air pollution controls in particular cost jobs remains a persistent limitation on the power of the US EPA to protect the environment (Goodstein 1999; Landy et al. 1994).

Standard setting and implementation

The US *Clean Air Act* offers several useful lessons for both the UK and Australia because the SIP arrangements indicate how difficult it is to address environmental risks in multiple jurisdictions effectively. In the UK, the *En-*

vironment Act 1995 and the *Air Quality Strategy 2000* require local councils to implement air quality action plans to meet national ambient standards (Beattie et al. 2002). At the supra-national level, the EU sets standards by issuing directives and it is left to member states like the UK to decide how to meet or enforce those standards. In Australia national standards are set by the Environment Protection and Heritage Council but enforcement falls to the state or territory governments and their agencies. Historically, levels of environmental enforcement have varied dramatically between states (Kellow & Niemeyer 1999; Briody & Prenzler 1998). These situations are comparable to the SIP system in the USA and the level of enforcement will depend on the political will of the relevant authority.

Creating economic prompts

The rise of neo-liberalism during the 1980s had a major impact on environmental regulation and governmentality in general (Eckersley 2004; Dryzek et al. 2003; Weale 1998; Fraas 1991; Pusey 1991; Johnson 1991; Dallek 1984). Regulations were perceived to be out of step with this shift, so attempts were made to engage market forces by creating economic prompts (also known as 'market-based' or 'new policy' instruments). These prompts can be divided into two main types: those that are designed to generate a financial disincentive (like tradable permits and charges), to discourage damaging activities such as polluting and those that are designed to create an incentive to make positive improvements (Eckersley 1995, 2004). It is artificial to separate economic prompts from other forms of regulation. Regulations often carry financial penalties in the form of fines for non-compliance, so it should be borne in mind that these interventions operate together. The idea of a financial disincentive, however, is to go beyond a simple penalty to generate a constant motive for improvement, as well as force the firm to pay for some of the damage it does.

Consider a factory that releases pollutants like SO_2 into the atmosphere. As pointed out in previous chapters, this can have several health and economic costs for the local community. It can lead to an increase in respiratory disorders for the local population that will then require medical treatment, as well as contributing to acid rain that can corrode metal roofs, gutters, water tanks and vehicles, or damage local crops. As a result, the costs of the emissions are borne by the local community, nearby farmers and health funds (public or private), not the firm causing the problem. This is what is known as a negative externality, where some of the costs associated with an activity are borne by people or organisations outside the firm that creates the problem. In an ideal economic model, these costs could be internalised by making the polluter pay for the health care and property damage. This would also provide an incentive for the polluter to reduce their payments by cutting their emissions. The problem, of course, is being able to calculate accurately the true level of costs and ensuring that all those affected are given adequate compensation. In practice, governments often set pollution charges fairly low because they do not want industry to leave the area in search of lower production costs (Hahn 1995).

Tradable emission permits

In the USA, a scheme to reduce SO_2 emissions, using tradable permits, was introduced in the *Clean Air Act 1990* amendments as a way to make the polluter pay. This scheme involves the issue of tradable permits to industry, which were progressively reduced by the government in order to cut SO_2 emissions (US EPA 1995a; Rosenbaum 1991). The program is similar to the scheme used to phase out lead in petrol and it is supposed to give firms the flexibility to choose how to reduce their emissions, or whether to buy more permits from other firms. The theory is that the most efficient means to reduce emissions will be adopted by the best firms, which will then sell their excess rights to pollute to firms that cannot afford to clean up their operation easily. This will assist better firms to modernise ecologically and leave high polluters paying more.

One estimate of the cost savings of this system was US$8.9 billion–12.9 billion over 18 years (NCE 1993). The US EPA estimated an annual saving of US$400 million–600 million (Passell 1994). Rosenbaum (1991) suggests that the bubbles, in conjunction with tradable permits, have produced more modest savings in the costs of compliance. He cites a total figure of about US$435 million spread over 132 sites by the mid-1980s. This is considerably less than predicted and overall the US EPA's performance on SO_2 emissions is uneven. Arrangements are currently being made to establish an international CO_2 trading system under the Kyoto protocol. Only a minority of countries will be involved as both the USA and Australia have refused to ratify this agreement and many other states were not signatories. It will include, however, the majority of OECD countries, and the UK has established its own internal carbon trading system.

Environmental charges

Another method of internalising the costs of environmental risk is to impose a charge or tax on a polluting industry that can be used to pay for remedial action. In the USA, Superfund legislation of 1980 was designed to deal with contaminated waste sites that posed a threat to public health or the environment. Its main purpose was to provide the US EPA with the resources to locate contaminated sites and force firms responsible for the waste to clean them up. For sites where polluters could not be identified, a special fund was created for remedial action to be undertaken by the US EPA financed by a levy on certain chemical products (Landy et al. 1994).

The chemical industry fought the Superfund legislation and was able to get some politicians whose electorates relied heavily on the industry for employment on side. By using their influence over key congressional committees these politicians, together with the OMB, were able to weaken the legislation and gain significant exemptions. One of the key sticking points was the assignment of liability. The proposed legislation invoked strict, joint and several liability in assigning costs for site redemption. Strict liability meant that a firm would have to pay even if it had not been negligent. Joint and several liability meant that where only a few of the responsible firms could be identified, they would have to pay the whole cost of a site clean up, even though other firms had contributed to the problem. This concept was invoked to side step the difficulty of identifying all firms and apportioning blame in difficult cases. Industry argued that if the waste disposal had been carried out legally, firms should not be held liable and claimed that it was unfair for minor contributors to pay for the consequences of other firms' actions (Landy et al. 1994). The law was significantly expanded by the *Superfund Amendment and Reauthorization Act 1986* (*SARA*) that increased the funds to US$8.6 billion for remedial actions (US EPA 1995a; Wise 1992; Dower 1990).

Charges have also been used in the UK. Under the *Environment Protection Act 1990*, firms that dispose of waste are liable for releases of pollutants from contaminated land (Duxbury & Morton 2000). The *Environment Act 1995* enabled local authorities to impose environmental charges. In 2003 the Lord Mayor of London used a similar power under the *Transport Act 2000* to impose a congestion charge on vehicles entering the centre of the city. The result was an almost immediate 18 per cent drop in traffic. A landfill tax was introduced in 1996 to encourage recycling and reductions in solid waste (Garner 2000; Helm 1998).

In Australia, the chemical industry has strongly resisted paying for the clean up of contaminated sites (ESD Working Groups—Manufacturing 1991).

Positive incentives

The other side to economic instruments is to reward good behaviour in various ways. The USA, UK and Australia offer some type of tax deduction or subsidy for investment in cleaner production technology or pollution abatement work. In Australia, there have been several projects designed to extend environmental subsidies to both business and the broader community. In 1993 the Commonwealth Department of Environment and the Australian Taxation Office launched a booklet detailing the available tax deductions for capital investment in cleaner technology. In particular, it targeted expenditure on avoiding, treating or cleaning up waste. It also included deductions for the costs of environmental audits, monitoring and the implementation of environmental management plans (*Greenweek* 1993a).

The tax incentive approach has been tried before in Australia, but with disappointing results. From 1984 the Commonwealth offered a 150 per cent tax deduction for research and development (R&D) by industry. Despite this, private investment in R&D remained relatively low. From 1986 to 1988, the percentage of production reinvested in R&D by the manufacturing sector was only 0.6 per cent in Australia, compared to 3.4 per cent in the USA. The rate of investment in high technology (electronics, pharmaceuticals, motor vehicles, non-metallic minerals and petroleum refining) was 11.8 per cent for the USA but only 2.4 per cent for Australia (OECD 1993). This suggests that the response by the manufacturing industry to incentives for investment in cleaner technology may be somewhat lukewarm and the deduction rate was reduced to 125 per cent in the 1996 budget when the Howard government came to power.

The question of the effectiveness of state intervention was addressed by the Australian Manufacturing Council (AMC 1994) when it compared firms in New Zealand and Australia to determine what made them adopt best practice across all areas of management. Despite having substantially different tax regimes the proportion of firms achieving best practice was about the same. This led to misguided suggestions that government policies have very limited impact on the behaviour of business but the report findings do not support this argument (Megalogenis 1994). While the study did find that many firms change in response to an external crisis, it also pointed out that these crises may be induced by lowering tariffs, changing infrastructure costs, economic downturns and exchange rate fluctuations. Clearly the state can influence these factors, particularly tariffs and infrastructure costs. Further, many of the examples cited in the report have used government programs to achieve best practice. The reliance on government support is also acknowledged in the report's conclusion. The AMC report stresses the importance of the internal management culture of a firm with a consultative approach considered to be a sign of preparedness to improve and innovate. All of these are heavily influenced by neo-liberalism.

In terms of specific projects, the Department of Environment in Australia announced in 1993 that it would spend A$760 000 over three years to fund several EcoReDesign projects at RMIT's Centre for Design. The idea was to undertake a partnership with four to six firms to work with the centre in redesigning products to be more environmentally friendly. The project began with a whole life cycle analysis of raw material extraction and use, production, consumption and disposal (*Greenweek* 1993b). By June 1994, a joint project with Kambrook was under way to design a plastic kettle that was easier to recycle (RMIT Centre for Design 1994). This sort of project was not meant to provide a solution to all current technical and environmental problems. It was more of an attempt to seed green technical knowledge into the manufacturing sector at the design stage in the hopes of encouraging imitation by other companies.

Australia has also established a Natural Heritage Trust to help fund the rehabilitation of local environments. It was initially created with A$1 billion from the partial sale of the publicly owned telecommunications corporation Telstra and was later boosted to A$2.5 billion to extend its life. The scheme requires groups to apply for funding from Environment Australia and has been accessed mainly by local community groups, farmers, local councils and state government agencies (although it is possible for businesses to get involved). Schemes funded can be anything that may improve the environment, such as revegetating a tract of land, stabilising the banks of a river or cleaning up the water quality in an estuary. The scheme is an expansion of the Landcare program started by farmers and conservationists in the late 1980s.

In Australia both state and Commonwealth governments also offer free technical support to firms that want to adopt cleaner production processes. Participating firms then get free advertising on the government's online database of positive case studies. A similar scheme operates in the UK to support voluntary waste minimisation clubs for industry (Pratt & Phillips 2000) and the US EPA has run various programs of a similar kind (Gunningham et al. 1998; US EPA 1995b). While all of these economic prompts sit more comfortably with neo-liberalism, industry is still not keen to take on new charges or taxes. Although it is quite happy to accept subsidies or tax deductions the overall effect can still be reduced by reflexive resistance and scepticism.

Conclusions

While regulations form the bedrock of most governance, there has been a shift towards using economic prompts. One of the overriding features of all these cases is that the reaction of industry can have a significant impact on the ability of the state to make and enforce policies. These cases also demonstrate that resistance to change from business and within the state is not insurmountable. It is simply another manifestation of how modernisation has become reflexive and highlights a key role for the sub-politics of environmental groups. While all of these regulations and economic prompts have their limitations, some improvements have clearly been made (see Chapter 8). A second major conclusion is that knowledge and the control of information is important. It is difficult to develop effective regulation without an understanding of the level of pollution, the impacts of substances, the technical options for production processes or the economic impacts of implementing change. The next chapter considers the role of knowledge in environmental governance in more detail.

CHAPTER 5

Knowledge, environmental assessment and pollution inventories

Introduction

The previous chapter reviewed a range of regulations and economic prompts that have been deployed to try to alter the way industry relates to the environment. These interventions relied on either the force of law or the power of money to achieve change. This chapter will consider the way that knowledge can be used in highly innovative ways to improve environmental governance and ecologically modernise industry. The first section briefly reviews the importance of information and revisits the problem of uncertainty. The second section then considers the way knowledge has been utilised in Environmental Impact Assessment procedures. Most of the rest of the chapter offers an analysis of the way online information is used via a study of pollution inventories. The chapter concludes with a review of the broader implications of the Internet on governance and democracy in general. Overall it is argued that these developments offer some exciting opportunities for change, despite considerable resistance from industry.

The importance of information and knowledge

Information and knowledge are related but distinct concepts. Human minds receive sensory data from the outside world in five forms: sight, sound, taste, touch and smell. The combination of this sensory data creates information. This information is then interpreted and given meaning by discourses that construct the knowledge that affects behaviour. Imagine, for example, that you were looking at a river downstream from a factory. Your senses pass on data that the water has a cloudy appearance, a strong smell, an acidic taste, causes some skin irritation when you dip your hand in the river and you can see no fish. This sensory data is then combined to create the information that the river contains substances other than water. An environmental discourse may predispose you to assume that factories cause water pollution that has undesirable impacts on human health and the environment. Together the information and discourse construct the knowledge that the river is polluted, that this is a bad thing and that the nearby factory is probably the source. This knowledge may then influence your behaviour by encouraging you to campaign for the factory to reduce its pollution.

It is important to note that most useful knowledge carries an inherent risk of being mistaken. The only certainties we have are usually rather bland (e.g. the assertion that 'a factory is a factory' is always right, but not very illuminating in telling what a factory is, what it does or whether it is a good or bad thing). In the example above, for instance, the actual source of the pollution may be a sulphurous mineral outcrop further upstream that you didn't know about. Further, discourses influence what people choose to observe, what they overlook and what they decide is important. No one thought to test for the effects of CFCs on atmospheric ozone, for example, until decades after they were in common use. This means that human knowledge is piecemeal and prone to error. Chapter 1 outlined one approach using game theory to dealing with the uncertainty that results from imperfect information and the idea that humans should choose actions that would minimise the maximum cost (both possible and probable). Underpinning this strategy is the method of triangulation where information is taken from a variety of sources with different economic/political interests (e.g. business, government and NGOs) and compared to compensate for the bias in each. Such strategies are the best humans can do in dealing with the problem of uncertainty in knowledge and have been used in the creation of this book.

Prevailing models of market economics and liberal democracy suggest that in theory better information should make for better decisions (Hawken et al. 1999; Gunningham & Grabosky 1998; Eckersley 1995). If, for example, consumers know all about the social and ecological impacts of different products or processes they should be able to make informed purchases. Producers could also use this knowledge to guide their decision making regarding the efficiency of their resource use. In short, the market is supposed to work better with better information and in an ideal situation there should be perfect information to guide supply and demand decisions. Similarly, democratic politics is supposed to work better when there is an electorate that is well informed about all areas of policy, competing political parties are honest about what they plan to do in government and state institutions are open about their activities and effects. In practice, of course, we never have perfect information, but anything that improves knowledge should make the systems work better.

On the other hand, knowledge is power so the strategic release or withholding of information is widely practised by economic, social and political institutions. Firms invest heavily in the research and development of new technology, processes and products. This is jealously guarded by legal institutions such as patents and confidentiality agreements to prevent competitors utilising the same knowledge. Firms are also keen to promote a good corporate image and information about the benefits of their products, but rarely advertise their negative impacts (Beder 2002). Political parties generally keep unpopular policies quiet until after elections and often promise things they know they are unable to deliver. Similarly, government agencies or departments are never very keen on revealing their mistakes to the public (Colebatch et al. 1997).

So knowledge and information have a strategic value that translates into power with tangible consequences (see Chapter 4). Negative information about the impact of a product can combine with health or environmental discourses to reduce sales and create real economic losses for a firm (e.g. asbestos). Ultimately it may even lead to the banning of the product (as in the case of CFCs). Alternatively, information about damaging policies may combine with environmental discourses, leading to the alienation of some voters or the undermining of an agency's authority, as happened to the US EPA during the Reagan administration (Dryzek et al. 2003; Johnson 1991; Burford & Greenya 1986; Dallek 1984).

Knowledge-based environmental interventions are interesting because they attempt to utilise the strategic value of information and prevailing discourses to create knowledge that could make the economic and political systems theoretically work better. They also, however, are a challenge to entrenched institutions that perceive an interest in restricting the flow of information. Two of the main interventions of this kind have been the introduction of Environmental Impact Assessment procedures and the creation of online pollution inventories. Both were generally supported by the environment movement but resisted by industry.

Environmental Impact Assessment (EIA)

The idea of Environmental Impact Assessment (EIA) is to create knowledge that anticipates and minimises environmental risks before a development goes ahead. It is a prime example of the governmentality of administrative rationalism because it assumes that the essence of complicated issues can be reduced to reports and effective changes programmed in by the state (Rutherford 1994). While there are many different ways this can be done, EIA often requires the developer to produce an Environmental Impact Statement (EIS) that details the likely effects of a project on a local area and the measures to be taken to minimise the risks. There is also usually some public consultation before a decision about whether to proceed is taken.

Legislation

In 1969 the US Congress passed the *National Environmental Policy Act* which contained what at first appeared to be a relatively minor clause that required federal agencies to take into account the impact of new government projects on the environment. This clause led the US EPA to create EIA procedures for new developments which rapidly spread from federal government to the states and the private sector around the world (Hoberg 1992). President Nixon at first opposed the Act but relented when he realised the extent of public concern (Dreyfus & Ingram 1985).

In Australia, Commonwealth EIA procedures were created under the *Environment Protection (Impact of Proposals) Act 1974*. These procedures covered any project in which the national government was directly involved or which required its approval. Australian state governments developed similar procedures around the same time. As with the USA, the procedures were progressively expanded to cover most large-scale private sector developments. By the early 1980s the Commonwealth and most states had signed bilateral agreements to coordinate EIA procedures and avoid duplication for approvals (Crommelin 1987). The 1992 Inter-Governmental Agreement on the Environment included a more detailed agreement and the Commonwealth *Environment Protection and Biodiversity Conservation Act 1998* provided for states to have prime responsibility for EIA, although there have been some delays with the administrative arrangements.

The UK government was more reluctant to adopt formal EIA procedures and instead preferred to rely on existing town planning regulations. In 1985 Westminster's hand was forced by European Directive 85/337 which required all member states to adopt formal EIA procedures (Bulleid 1997). After three years of deliberation the *Town and Country Planning (Assessment of Environmental Effects) Regulations 1988* were passed (Smith, R. 2001; Weston 1997). Local government authorities have the prime role in administering EIA procedures, but the Secretary of State for the Environment and the Department of Environment may also be involved in England and Wales. Separate arrangements exist for Scotland and Northern Ireland. The British government was also reluctant to use the term 'impact' so EIA in the UK is usually referred to as environment assessment and EIS is known as an environment statement (Weston 1997).

General procedures

While specific procedures vary, EIA involves a number of common steps (Smith, R. 2001; Bulleid 1997; Thomas 1996; Paehlke & Torgerson 1990). First some state institution (e.g. the US EPA, an Australian state EPA or a Local Government Authority in the UK) must determine if a proposed project requires an assessment. There are then several options for how to proceed. For very large projects a public inquiry may be convened (in the UK and Australia this could be in the form of a Royal Commission; in the USA there may be congressional hearings). Minor projects, on the other hand, may just require a simple administrative report. For all other projects, the developer may be required to prepare an EIS which is released for public consultation. This document is supposed to assess the local environment that is to be affected, detail the productive activity to be undertaken, outline the likely impact of the development and list the steps to be taken to mitigate this impact.

The EIS is prepared either by the proponent or a consultant engaged by the proponent. A draft EIS is released for public comment and review. The proponent may then be required to produce a revised or supplementary EIS based on this input. The final EIS is assessed by the relevant state institution and a report sent to the relevant minister or administrator for a final decision. In theory, a project should only proceed if: (1) the final EIS is satisfactory; (2) the environmental impacts are acceptable; (3) the strategy for mitigating environmental impacts outlined is adequate; and (4) the mitigation strategy will be put into practice by both the developer and operator.

Proportion of projects covered

EIA procedures appear to be somewhat cumbersome and have attracted a considerable degree of criticism. One of the first disputes is the adequacy of the number of projects affected. Industry, acting under a neo-liberal discourse, often claims that too many developments are being held up, while environmental groups argue that not enough projects are being subjected to full EIA procedures. In Australia, from 1974 to 1993, 2600 proposals had been considered under the Commonwealth legislation but only 132 EISs had been prepared (Commonwealth EPA 1994). In the USA 80–90 per cent of development proposals do not undergo EIA (Thomas 1996). In the UK there were 2000–2500 EIAs conducted from 1988 to 1995 (Smith, R. 2001; Bulleid 1997). These relatively small proportions do not appear to support the industry view.

Time for approval

Another dispute arises over the time taken to undertake the EIA process. Industry has claimed that EIA procedures unnecessarily delay project approvals. Environmentalists complain that they often don't have enough time to review an EIS properly. It is difficult to give a definite figure on how long an approval takes, since this will be largely determined by how long it takes to prepare the particular EIS. In Australia, after receipt of the EIS there is a 28-day period of public comment, then the final decision is made within 42 days. This makes the total time of state involvement about three months for the minority of projects which are required to prepare an EIS; other projects are approved more quickly (Commonwealth EPA 1994). In the UK the public consultation time is limited to 20 days and the whole process usually takes six months total (Lee-Wright 1997; Weston 1997). Most major development projects take several years of planning, costing and financing before construction work actually begins. The preparation of an EIS can often be incorporated as part of this internal process and the few months of state involvement usually run concurrently with these other preparations. Governments are often willing to speed up the process. In the UK developers can apply for EIA waivers and a Project Facilitation Unit was created within the Australian Department of Prime Minister and Cabinet in 1992 to fast-track approvals (Bulleid 1997; Toyne 1994).

Costs

One of the other complaints that industry has about the EIA process is the fact that it has to pay for the preparation of the EIS document. It is often claimed that this adds substantially to the cost of the project since expert consultants often have to be employed. One US study found that the average cost of preparing an EIS was less than 0.2 per cent of the total construction cost (Thomas 1996). It also found that the changes that were brought about in the project because of suggestions at the public review stage reduced the costs of the project in more than half of the cases surveyed. These cost reductions more than offset the cost of preparing the EIS and in one instance the costs of a project were reduced by more than 50 per cent. In the UK the estimated cost of an EIA ranges from £25 000–50 000 (US$40 000–80 000) (Bulleid 1997; Lee-Wright 1997). These figures suggest that in general the preparation of an EIS is an insignificant cost to development projects as a whole, so again the neo-liberal view is not supported. Further, it may often be the case that the process can substantially reduce the costs of a project.

Accuracy

Another point of criticism is whether an EIS can construct an adequate model of the environment in which a development is to take place or accurately predict what impacts will arise from the development. Clearly the neo-liberal discourse, which favours a speedy approval, clashes with the scientific discourse, which values thorough investigation. This means that the understanding of the existing environment within an EIS will almost always be partial. Studies in the UK suggest that at least 25 per cent of EISs are unsatisfactory (Smith R. 2001; Weston 1997). In Australia, the contrast between discourses was highlighted when a long-term scientific study by the CSIRO assessed the area proposed for the Kakadu Stage III National Park extension as a high-value conservation zone. An EIS for a proposed mine in the area, on the other hand, played down this value and highlighted the problem of introduced species (Toyne 1994). In another case involving the proposed Tasmanian Wesley Vale Pulp Mill, the EIS completely neglected to raise the issue of dioxins and was criticised in a confidential report by the Department of Deep Sea Fisheries for ignoring the effects of tidal flows on the dispersal of effluent (Economou 1992; McEachern 1991). These examples suggest that the accuracy of EISs is problematic.

EIA revisited

This analysis suggests three main points. First, EIA is an attempt by state institutions to pre-empt potential risks and conflicts which is guided by the governmentality of administrative rationalism. Its limitations are an indication of the limits of state power and imperfect knowledge. Second, while EIA doesn't appear to fulfil expectations generated by administrative rationalism (i.e. that the world can be programmed by the state (Miller & Rose 1993)), it is not as cumbersome as business and neo-liberalism suggest. Third, EIA offers some benefits for business because it anticipates and sometimes helps to avoid conflict, it can improve the environmental credibility of business and it may even save business money by revealing development options that are more ecologically modern. While there are problems, it appears to be better to have an imperfect process than nothing.

One of the main innovations that EIA procedures have introduced is to utilise knowledge, rather than the force of the law or money, as a tool of governance. The partial success of this change has encouraged the state to experiment with other knowledge-based interventions. Relatively recent changes to communications and information technologies have spurred on the development of these programs. The rapid rise of the Internet in particular has led to a vast improvement in the accessibility not only of EIAs but also of other environmental reports and data. The next section considers how this capacity has been utilised in the public disclosure of emissions via online pollution inventories.

Online pollution inventories

The US Toxics Release Inventory (TRI) was the forerunner for many similar programs around the world, including the Australian National Pollutant Inventory (NPI) and the UK Pollution Inventory. Under pressure from community-based NGOs and in the wake of Love Canal (see Chapter 1), Congress passed the *Emergency Planning & Community Right to Know Act* in 1986 that created the TRI. The inventory was based on the principle of community 'right to know' that asserts the entitlement of residents to be informed about hazards that may affect them (US EPA 1995b). Under the TRI, the US EPA identified a list of hazardous substances (initially 329, later expanded to 647), set threshold levels for the emission, production or use of these substances and issued guidelines for calculating and reporting their release. Any firm that uses, produces or releases more than the threshold amount of one of these substances in a year must calculate and report their level of emission to the US EPA. The agency checks and collates the information then releases it on a publicly accessible database. Data was first collected for 1987 and published in a paper format that was supplied to public libraries. It made the transition to computer disk and web versions as the technology became available. The public can now use the TRI website to search for specific substances or investigate emissions from individual plants, companies or geographical locations. Aggregate data and historical trends are also available (US EPA 2000).

The UK Pollution Inventory works in a similar fashion to the TRI and is administered by the UK Environment Agency. It started as the Chemical Release Inventory in 1990, was restructured into its current form in 1997 and has 150 substances on its reporting list (UK EA 2000). The Australian NPI was first proposed in 1992 in the wake of the Rio Earth Summit in Brazil (Keating 1992). After lengthy consultations and trials it began to collect data for 1998–99 and the website was formally launched in 2000. The joint Commonwealth–state ministerial body, the National Environment Protection Council, was initially given the role of overseeing the inventory; this responsibility then passed to the restructured Environment Protection and Heritage Council (see Chapter 3). State and territory agencies collect the emission data, while the Commonwealth Department of Environment runs the website. The NPI is the most modest of the three inventories, having only 36 substances or groups of substances initially, but was later expanded to 90.

Cause and effect

International research into the effect of online pollution inventories has been patchy. Early work by Habitch (1990) for the US EPA suggested that the TRI did put pressure on firms to reduce their emissions. Over ten years the TRI itself indicates a fall of 40 per cent in emissions of the original listed substances (US EPA 2001). The normalising mechanisms that put pressure on industry to clean up its act appear to be threefold. First, industry executives were actually surprised at the amount of raw material being wasted when the TRI started and ordered improvements in production efficiency (Gottlieb et al. 1995). Second, NGOs have been willing to take legal action against polluting firms which has effectively scared some firms into action (Shapiro 1990; English 1997). Third, firms that appear high on the TRI's list of polluters tend to lose share value as investors are wary of potential losses through court actions and clean-up costs (Khanna et al. 1998; Hamilton 1993). Of course the aggregate results may overstate the impact of the inventory. Some of the reduction in total emissions may be due to older industries shutting down or more polluting processes being moved offshore. But the size of the drop during a period of strong economic growth suggests that industries have gone at least some way towards reducing their emissions per unit of output (i.e. they may at least be starting to ecologically modernise).

As would be expected the clash of discourses continues and industry has tended to be critical of the imposition and expansion of the inventory (Fairley 1996) while NGOs have been supportive and pushed for a more comprehensive system of accountability, fewer exemptions and more accurate reporting (English 1997; Hearne 1996). Similar reactions have occurred in response to the UK inventory (Finer 2000; Maslin 2000; Society of Chemical Industry UK 1994) and the Australian NPI (Howes 2001b; Murphy 2000; Streets & Di Carlo 1999; Sullivan 1999; Taberner 1999; Greenpeace

1999; Queensland Conservation Council 1999; Hill 1999; National Toxics Network 1998; Fayers 1998; NEPC 1998; QEPA 1999; Slagle 1995; Ernst & Young 1995; Minter Ellison 1995; Gunningham & Cornwall 1994; Gunningham 1993).

The UK has also experienced significant reductions in emissions since the first version of the inventory was introduced (UK EA 2001). The Australian inventory is too recent to provide a reasonable historical trend. Research[1] suggests that NGOs are not as interested as their US counterparts in pursuing polluting firms because of the barriers to using the legal system and a different political culture that encourages them to focus on wilderness issues. There remains some hostility and suspicion regarding the NPI from firms that have to report, making it harder to encourage the adoption of ecological modernisation discourses. This bears out the more general findings on the impact of political culture and institutional contexts on the Internet's ability to encourage greater civic engagement.

Critiques of these inventories indicate that they are not a panacea for the environmental risks generated by industrial society. They do, however, provide an interesting tool of governance in that they seek to use the Internet as a means to redeploy strategically knowledge in a way that prompts NGOs to act as environmental watchdogs. This role is limited to those organisations with Internet access, the ability to interpret the technical data and the resources to undertake some kind of effective response (Howes 2002a, b). In general industry has been uncomfortable with the increased surveillance, while the state appears satisfied with the deflection of criticism from its agencies on to specific polluters. There was some argument between the different levels of Australian government over how the burden of funding should be shared but these inventories are relatively inexpensive because the cost of reporting falls to industry, while the resources for surveillance and confrontation come from NGOs.

Inventories, risk and governance

Pollution is popularly constructed as a risk to both human health and the environment. Studies in the USA, UK and Australia, however, suggest that there is a significant difference in the perception of such risks between experts and the broader community (Scott 2000; Lash 2000; Landy et al. 1994; ANOP Research Services 1993). Online inventories are an attempt by the state to respond by providing more information about potential risks to the public and in so doing encourage better risk management by industry. These features make them a prime subject for analysis using the concepts of discourse, governmentality and risk theory (see Chapter 2).

Rutherford (1994) suggests that EIAs are a tangible manifestation of Foucault's governmentality approach to environmental problems and it is also evident in online pollution inventories, particularly when the risk theory variant is used (Lupton 1999). In this view the polluting firms have been identified as a risky population, high polluters are seen as deviating from the norm, the inventories put them under surveillance and public pressure is used as a normalising mechanism to encourage a cut in emissions. While this is an elegant way of considering environmental governance and pollution inventories in particular, there is a major limitation in that Foucault's approach does not generate an agenda for change. He offers some thoughts on individual resistance to unjust exercises of power (Rabinow 1991) but, having pointed out the flaws in state activities, there is no sense of how to respond. With regards to pollution inventories, for example, Foucault's approach gives a wonderful explanation for the mentality behind their operation, but it does not tell if they are an appropriate strategy for responding to environmental risks, nor does it tell if they will support or undermine democratic decision making. This is where risk theory and reflexive modernisation can assist.

Chapter 2 introduced the idea of reflexive modernisation based on Beck's (1992) concept of the risk society. Basically the idea is that as industrial production has spread it has created environmental risks that seriously threaten the survival of humanity and the planet. This has resulted in a new kind of politics where struggles over the distribution of 'bads' (such as pollution) have overlaid the traditional struggle over the spread of goods (such as wealth). Both Beck (1994) and Giddens (1998a) suggest that the state in industrialised societies has not been very effective in responding to these new risks (some of the difficulties were covered in Chapter 4; see also Beder 2002) so the political and economic system needs to be more open to more public participation. Pollution inventories fit quite neatly into the sorts of reforms being proposed because they at least partly open up business environmental decision making to public scrutiny. They also exhibit all the hallmarks of ecological modernisation because they are designed to encourage industry to make more efficient use of resources and produce less waste.

The stronger versions of ecological modernisation, together with risk society theory, deal with issues of surveillance and governance in very different ways to governmentality. Surveillance is transformed into a stronger notion of confrontation that better represents the purpose of pollution inventories. Internet-based governance is a manifestation of the mentality of both governed and governing, but it is also transformative because it represents a strategic opening up to community scrutiny for reporting firms. Hajer (1995) has shown that it is possible to construct a useful synthesis between the two. He uses discourse analysis to reveal how some narrower versions of ecological modernisation have underpinned the development of environmental policies, such as sustainable development. In the final part of the analysis he supports Beck's reflexive approach to challenging expert decision making. Specifically, he proposes the creation of discursive public forums and laws to increase civic engagement (see also Eckersley 2004; Dryzek et al. 2003). This synthesis draws on the strengths of both risk theory schools: the analytical tools derived from Foucault that expose the workings of power and the agenda for change of Beck and Giddens that can put this knowledge to use.

Clearly online pollution inventories do seem to be a product of the calculations of governmentality in that they seek to quantify and manage pollution risks with the identification of risky firms, surveillance, discipline and normalisation mechanisms. They also open up an opportunity for the re-engagement of the sub-politics of the risk society by increasing the ability of NGOs to confront industry. The whole concept plays upon the discourse of ecological modernisation that is focused on efficiency within companies and so has the potential to construct a perception of a common interest in reducing pollution risks. This is something that has clearly happened in the USA but not so much in Australia. The differences can be explained by the different political and legal institutions that provide varying opportunities for re-engagement. But what are the broader implications of using the Internet on governance in general?

The Internet, knowledge and environmental governance

With regards to online knowledge, industry, the state and NGOs see the Internet as having considerable political importance and have developed various strategies as a consequence. From Seattle to CHOGM, NGOs utilised websites and email to promote their causes, recruit members, network groups, coordinate actions and directly lobby business and state institutions for change (Howes 2001a). But industry has also seen the potential of the Internet. On the one hand it promotes online business transactions and on the other it seeks to counter the negative messages of protesters. Shell, for example, uses its website to give its own version of the social and environmental impacts of its operations in Nigeria as a counter to the international campaign waged by environmental and human rights groups (Howes 1997). The state has also taken up the new technology with parliamentary debates, ministerial media releases, legislation and many reports now available online.

Further, in many states it is now possible for citizens to email their local MP or government agency to communicate their concerns and request information. For all three players (NGOs, business and the state) there is the added attraction of being able to bypass the editorial controls of the media and make direct contact with target audiences.

The good

Broadly speaking studies on the effect of the Internet can be sorted into three main categories: positive, negative and neutral. On the positive side, J. Smith (2001) emphasises how the Internet has increasingly been used by NGOs and suggests that this could lead to more democratic control of government. Hewitt (1998) argues that it may be the historical equivalent to the invention of the printing press and could break down the control of information and allow the formation of direct relations between people and NGOs around the world. There is a note of caution, however, in that online communications could lead to greater surveillance (which makes an interesting link to Foucault's ideas about surveillance and the perception of being watched covered in Chapter 2).

The bad

The risk of surveillance is the point often picked up by the negative camp and several features of this information technology increase this risk. First, all visits to websites and all emails sent and received leave an electronic trail that can be traced. This means that an employer or state agency can see what you have been accessing, who you have been in contact with and read the content of your communications. Second, electronic records of communications persist on the hard drive of a computer and may be retrieved after the visible files have been deleted. Third, software is available that can scan for key words within communications and automatically bring messages that contain them to an observer's notice. These points have led the media to warn of a potential for Orwellian 'Big Brother' surveillance (Foreshew 2001; Correy 1998). In the academic literature, Moore (1999) warns of the need to protect against intrusive surveillance, the hijacking of the web by the extreme right and the development of information monopolies by powerful transnational firms that seek to act as online gatekeepers. Boden (2000) also argues that the Internet introduces a greater instability into financial markets which could increase the risk of capital flight. This adds to the influence of transnational firms where governments anticipate their demands and adjust policies to encourage investment.

The in-between

Between the positive and the negative ends of the spectrum are theorists that approach the Internet with a degree of neutrality. Hague and Loader (1999) suggest that it is neither a panacea for the shortcomings of liberal democracy nor does it spell its downfall, it is simply a useful tool for conducting current interactions in new ways. Hale et al. (1999), for example, studied 290 US municipal websites and identified substantial barriers to greater civic engagement such as a lack of civic education, general apathy and feelings of disconnection between citizens and leaders (an indicator of reflexive modernisation). They concluded that the use of the Internet to date has not overcome these barriers because they are a product of the general US political culture. Wilhelm (1999) also found that the Internet is not being used to its full potential and Bimber (2001) found it had not encouraged a culture of greater participation in the USA.

Magarey (1999) concluded that Australian politicians are generally not enthusiastic about the idea of e-democracy and were sceptical about the effectiveness of email communications with citizens. This was confirmed at a recent conference[2] where politicians from all parties indicated that they paid more attention to handwritten letters from constituents than emails because they required more effort to create and send. Malina (1999) concludes that social networks are the key to improving democracy and argues that the Internet on its own may only entrench current inequalities because of limited access to the necessary technology and training. Milner (1999) compared online public sector initiatives to provide better information to the community in Australia, the USA and UK. While she made favourable comments about the Australian initiatives of the early 1990s, she also raised the issue of the information 'haves' and 'have nots', that is, those who can afford the equipment, resources and training to make use of the Internet and those who cannot. The theme of the possibility of a growing digital divide is picked up by Symmonds (2000), who argues that it may increase the marginalisation of already vulnerable groups. So can the Internet improve democratic decision making?

A case in point

In 1996 an organisation was formed that brought together environmental activists, professionals and academics from across the Australasian region.[3] The membership was small and geographically dispersed, but was able to keep in contact via email and a website with an online newsletter. In early 1998, while exploring the Department of Environment website, it was discovered that the Commonwealth proposed to combine five pieces of separate legislation into a new *Environment Protection and Biodiversity Conservation Act*. The site contained details of the proposed law and called for public submissions. The information was downloaded and circulated by email to the association's executive with a proposal that it make a submission. This idea was approved and a paper was drafted, circulated, revised, approved and submitted, all by email. When the bill came before parliament, emails with the submission attached were sent to the relevant senate committee, the minister and shadow minister of the environment and the leaders of the minor parties. Two email responses were received from non-government parliamentarians and the minister's office sent a two-page letter. The parliamentary debate was then followed online and reported back to the association in the online newsletter.

This experience demonstrates the ability of the Internet to assist the sub-politics of outsider groups with improved networking and it also suggests a new avenue for re-engagement with the formal institutions of government. Having said this, the submission appears to have had little impact on the final shape of the legislation, confirming Beck's point about the difficulty major institutions of the state have in responding to environmental risks. It also suggests that at this stage the state appears to be using the Internet as a means to create the impression only of community consultation in order to diffuse dissent.

Summary

Overall it is apparent that the Internet has not yet led to the democratic transformation of government predicted by the positive theorists, nor does it appear to have established a totalitarian regime of surveillance. There are signs, however, that the web is increasingly being used by the state, business and NGOs, although users constitute only a small proportion of the world's total population. This is true even in industrialised countries where the Internet is reasonably widely available (Bimber 2001; Magarey 1999). There is still considerable potential for a major transformation of governance and this will continue to spill over into the area of environmental regulation.

Conclusions

Knowledge-based interventions offer an interesting contrast to regulations and economic prompts. EIA was one of the first initiatives and sought to shift the state's role from one of reaction to one of prevention in responding to environmental risks. Although there have been some problems, on the whole it is better to have some kind of EIA system than nothing. Online pollution inventories, on the other hand, provide an interesting laboratory in which to test the impacts of both knowledge and the Internet on governance. A comparison of US, Australian and UK inventories suggests that the institutional context still matters in terms of the effectiveness of such programs. Discourse analysis highlights the power of such surveillance and governmentality gives a compelling account of the mindset that influences the design of these inventories. Reflexive modernisation goes further to locate these programs within a broader agenda for reform that would open up decision making to greater public scrutiny. In terms of the implications for democracy, to date there is little empirical evidence on whether the Internet will have a positive, negative or neutral impact. It certainly has the potential to increase the flow of information between NGOs, business and the state and this might make it more difficult for one player to dominate, but there is still substantial resistance to change.

CHAPTER 6

Sustainable development in the UN and Australia

Introduction

Sustainable development, built on the principles of ecological modernis-ation, rapidly became a central feature of governmentality in the 1990s because it offered a solution to the clash between the discourses of neo-liberalism, administrative rationalism and environmentalism. On the one hand, it professed to take environmental risks seriously and incorporate an ecological perspective into institutional decision-making routines. On the other, it suggested that both the existing institutions of power and industry-based economic growth could be sustained if sufficient care was taken. This avoided the anti-technology, anti-industry and anti-economic growth ideas that had begun to appear in environmental discourses of the 1970s. It also created a new means to legitimise both industrial development and state intervention, while offering a coordinated approach to environmental and social issues.

This chapter analyses the progressive redefinition of sustainable develop-ment by successive policy-making processes internationally and in Australia (the responses of the USA and UK are covered in Chapter 7). Despite the potential of the original concept, subsequent official policies have become a means to manage environmental issues so that they don't pose a challenge to the power of existing institutions and this is yet another indication of reflex-ive modernisation. There remains, however, some merit in the broader notion of sustainable development and the policy-making forums through which it passed did serve to re-engage constructively the sub-politics of major community groups.

The origins of sustainable development policies

In 1970 the UN released its *International Development Strategy* which claimed 'the ultimate purpose of development is to provide increasing opportunities to all people for a better life' and this entailed the need to 'safeguard the environment' (US Department of State 1972, pp. 19 and 28). The strategy preceded the 1972 UN Conference on the Human Environment in Stockholm which discussed the perceived environmental danger of a rapidly industrialising Third World.

In 1980 a joint project between the UN and two international green organisations produced the *World Conservation Strategy*. This document brought the label of sustainable development into the international policy arena, defining it as 'the sustainable utilisation of species and ecosystems' (IUCN, WWF and UNEP 1980, p. vi). The overtly anthropocentric and utilitarian approach to environmental issues was more palatable to industrialised states than some of the more radical green critiques that called for zero growth, animal rights, decentralisation or the abandonment of market economies.

World Commission on Environment and Development

In 1983 the UN established the World Commission on Environment and Development. The objective, under the direction of Gro Harlem Brundtland, was to propose ways to reconcile industrial development and environmental concerns. Chatterjee and Finger (1994) suggest that another function of the commission was to use environmental issues as a means to open up a new East–West dialogue that might ameliorate Cold War tensions. In 1987 the commission released its findings under the title *Our Common Future*, but it is commonly referred to as the Brundtland report. This document addressed three main issues. First, it catalogued a long list of environment and development concerns, including poverty, inequality, resource depletion, the loss of biodiversity and pollution. Second, it defined and promoted sustainable development as a solution to these problems. Third, it proposed a broad strategic framework by which sustainable development might be achieved (WCED 1990).

Reconstructing the risk

Prior to the Brundtland report, industry and neo-liberalism constructed environmental risks as an exclusive disjunction: *jobs versus environment protection*. That is, either you allow the exploitation of the environment to create jobs or you protect it and lose jobs, but you cannot have both. Employment generated by a specific project was tallied up by opponents of regulation and weighed against the less tangible environmental benefits of protection. In the background was the concern that jobs may move overseas if environmental regulations get too tight.

The Brundtland report attempted to use sustainable development, underpinned by the emerging discourse of ecological modernisation (although not mentioned by name; Curran 2001; Christoff 1996), to reconstruct the environmental problem so that the exclusive disjunction becomes an inclusive conjunction. The first step was to redefine the elements within the jobs versus environment protection formulation. The term jobs was replaced by the broader notion of development that can embrace economic activity beneficial to the environment (e.g. establishing a recycling industry). Environment protection was replaced by ecological sustainability, which did not seek to maintain pristine ecosystems but merely tried to limit damage to a level and kind that could be borne in the longer term. Environmental issues were then reconstructed as a challenge to achieve both development and ecological sustainability. This inclusive conjunction was an attempt to resolve the clash between neo-liberalism and environmentalism by constructing a perceived common interest in both a healthy economy and a healthy environment (WCED 1990).

Having redefined the risk, the next step was to establish a link between development and ecological sustainability which validates this logical conjunction. The Brundtland report attempted this via two lines of reasoning. First, it argued that development depended on a healthy environment because it requires 'access to resources' in the long term and uses 'the ability of the biosphere to absorb the effects of human activities' (WCED 1990, pp. 8 and 87). The second line of reasoning was that ecological sustainability depended on industrial development. This was a more dubious claim since many risks have arisen directly from industry's use of the environment. The Brundtland report attempted to use poverty as the link by arguing that poverty caused damage by generating an incentive to overexploit the environment for survival. It is suggested that if industrial development alleviates poverty, the pressure on the environment will be reduced (WCED 1990). The alleviation of poverty was therefore constructed as a necessary condition for sustainable development.

Defining sustainable development

One difficulty with this approach is that there are many other causes of environmental damage that need to be taken into account, such as the deployment of harmful technology, economically driven over-consumption, social norms that encourage resource exploitation and inappropriate government policies. The report implicitly acknowledges these in the way it attempts to define sustainable development.

> Sustainable development is development that meets the needs of the present without compromising the ability of future generations to meet their own needs. It contains within it two key concepts:
> — the concept of 'needs', in particular the essential needs of the world's poor, to which overriding priority should be given; and
> — the idea of limitations imposed by the state of **technology** and **social** organisation on the **environment's** ability to meet present and future needs.
> Thus the goals of **economic** and social development must be defined in terms of sustainability in all countries—developed or developing, market-oriented or centrally planned. Interpretations will vary, but must share certain general features and must flow from a consensus on the basic concept of sustainable development and on a broad strategic framework for achieving it.
> Development involves a progressive transformation of economy and society. A development path that is sustainable in a physical sense could theoretically be pursued even in a rigid social and **political** setting. But physical sustainability cannot be secured unless development policies pay attention to such considerations as changes in access to resources and in the distribution of costs and benefits. Even the narrow notion of physical sustainability implies a concern for social equity between generations, a concern that must logically be extended to equity within each generation (WCED 1990, p. 87).

The emphasis on key words has been added to highlight the five dimensions of development that have an impact on society and the environment: technical, economic, social, political and ecological. Together they constitute a comprehensive set of categories that cover both the causes and dimensions of environmental risks (WCED 1990). The first sentence in this passage has become the most cited definition of sustainable development. Meeting the needs of the poor is the most neglected part of the concept, although it re-emerged at the Rio+10 (2002a) conference in Johannesburg.

The report noted the limitations placed on the state's ability to achieve desired policy goals and acknowledged that any strategy will be constrained by the willingness of transnational corporations to cooperate, particularly those that control and deploy new technology (another indication of the ecological modernisation principles on which it is founded). Although decisions about production are largely in private hands, state intervention was still proposed to ensure that companies behave as good corporate citizens (WCED 1990). Overall, the strategy proposed by the Brundtland report consisted of a set of modest reforms that avoid calls for a more radical restructuring of society that promoted more careful national regulation of the market. Although the power of transnational companies was noted, it was assumed that state intervention remains effective. This was why national environment protection institutions are given a key role in the achievement of sustainable development.

The sustainable development legacy

One of the Brundtland report's recommendations was that an international conference should be held by the UN (WCED 1990). This eventually led to the Conference on Environment and Development in 1992 (more popularly known as the Rio Earth Summit) which produced two framework conventions, a statement of principles and a bulky set of development guidelines called *Agenda 21* (UNCED 1992). The Brundtland report recommended a restructuring of UN environment programs, so the Commission for Sustainable Development was established to report on international progress. The Global Environment Facility was also created to collate information and fund sustainable development projects (Chatterjee & Finger 1994). In 1997 the Rio+5 special session of the UN General Assembly found that international progress towards sustainable development was disappointingly slow (Vidal 1997; Flavin 1997). Much of the resource depletion, loss of biodiversity, pollution, poverty and inequality problems listed by Brundtland had worsened. In 2002 a Rio+10 conference was held in Johannesburg to again review progress and develop further programs. The focus of this conference was very much on development and social issues, but there were some moves to make international fisheries more sustainable and partnerships between industry, government and community groups were promoted as a way of tackling many of the issues (see Chapter 1).

Over the last decade, sustainable development has drawn a surprising cross-section of support from industry, environmentalists and the state. This consensus is largely superficial because the different political actors are agreeing to the same label while maintaining different constructions of what it means. For some industries sustainable development is simply a greener marketing image of business as usual, which explains the lack of progress on major environmental issues (Beder 2002; Athanasiou 1996). To radical green groups, true sustainable development may mean abandoning industrial production altogether (see Chapter 2).

Sustainable development and its critics

Sustainable development is not a panacea for the world's environmental woes and there are substantial critiques of the version promoted by Brundtland. Some critics have argued that the Brundtland report overemphasises poverty as a cause for environmental damage, plays down the role of over-consumption by the rich and fails to ask why this poverty and inequality is generated in the first place (Broad 1994). The report does tend to skirt around these issues. Others claim that it tends to focus on industry and economic growth rather than alternative production methods, quality of life, equity or redistribution of wealth (Ekins 1993; Lele 1991). The report mentions that extremes of both wealth and poverty are damaging to the environment but offers only modest proposals for minor wealth redistribution through the provision of welfare funded by taxation. It does assume that industrial development should be universally pursued and this may not be appropriate if alternative productive practices are already sustainable (De La Court 1990).

Another criticism was that the report failed to challenge the power of dominant institutions (De La Court 1990). There were even claims that the Brundtland commission and the Rio Earth Summit were set up simply to protect existing state and business institutions, rather than address environmental issues (Chatterjee & Finger 1994). This may be due to the fact that the document was prepared by political leaders under the influence of strong international business lobbying. On the right, neo-liberals argue that state institutions and intervention are defended too much. They point out that state-run enterprises in Eastern Europe had a worse environmental record than business in the West and conclude that the state is part of the problem, not the solution (DiLorenzo 1993). But in the absence of state intervention serious environmental problems have been generated by private industry. Further, industry has been reluctant to address environmental problems and has actively resisted change. Conversely, critics on the left claim that the Brundtland report does not go far enough in challenging either market or business institutions (Gallopin et al. 1989).

Despite these deficiencies, or perhaps because of them, the Brundtland version of sustainable development set in train a series of processes that have significantly altered the main policy responses to environmental risks at the international, regional, national and local levels. As a consequence, national governments in industrialised states shifted to a new phase of intervention in the 1990s and attempted to construct new policy goals by adapting the Brundtland version to their domestic situation.

From sustainable development to ESD in Australia

By 1987 environmental risk had become a major feature of Australian politics and the ruling Labor party deployed a strategy of selective interventions to win green support during election campaigns (Richardson 1994; Toyne 1994; McEachern 1991). A few months after the Brundtland report's release, the Hawke government sought to curry favour with environmentally concerned voters by adding the Daintree rainforest to the World Heritage list, while mining at Coronation Hill (within stage III of Kakadu National Park in the Northern Territory) was stopped. The election of five Green Independents to the Tasmanian state lower house in 1989 was a further indication of the electoral importance of environmental issues (see the introduction to this book).

The strategy of courting the support of environmentalists did have its negative side (McEachern 1991). The Hawke government began to face strong criticism from industry and conservative politicians, who accused it of being anti-development. The tactical battle over the proposed Wesley Vale pulp mill in 1989 was an attempt by the Commonwealth to appease both sides. On the one hand it wanted the project to go ahead because of the perceived economic benefits. On the other, it was forced to impose tighter environmental conditions on the project than the Tasmanian government wanted in order to appease the Greens. In the end, the developers (Norandra and NBH) pulled out, publicly blaming the Commonwealth government and Greens for the project's failure. Even though the developers later admitted that the decision was an economic one based on the fall in the world price of pulp, the perception of too many wins for the green movement put the government under increasing pressure from the business community (McEachern 1991). It was under these conditions that Prime Minister Hawke (1989) released his response to Brundtland.

Hawke's 1989 statement: the birth of ESD

The Prime Minister's statement on the environment used the Brundtland report and the National Conservation Strategy as a basis for a new rhetoric of Ecologically Sustainable Development (ESD).

Ecologically sustainable development means economic growth that does not jeopardise the future productive base. Renewable resources are managed so that they are not permanently depleted. In some cases the use of particular technologies or processes may be so damaging that they should be banned.

Only rarely will it be necessary to take such pre-emptive action. In most cases it will be sufficient to temper the way in which projects proceed or technologies are applied to ensure that our future productive base is not impaired (Hawke 1989, p. 4).

This passage demonstrates both the vagueness of ESD and the desire of government to encourage development and economic growth. The rest of the document is taken up with reviewing initiatives in the management of eco-systems, water, the atmosphere, the land and the built environment. Industry and manufacturing get several mentions, with commitments to regulate the use of industrial chemicals, promote the recycling of plastics and encourage 'energy-efficient manufacturing'. The reduction of industrial waste is also targeted. Despite the importance of these goals, the statement is careful to note the limitations of government intervention: 'Governments can pass laws which punish inappropriate behaviour or encourage "good" behaviour, but they cannot compel good behaviour' (Hawke 1989, p. 7).

Overall Hawke's statement lacked detail on what was to be achieved and how. It appears to have been more of an attempt to defuse the intensity of dispute that had grown up around environmental issues through two strategies. On the one hand, it sought to draw the greens' attention to the environmental runs on the board. On the other, it attempted to alleviate the growing concerns of industry about increasing intervention. One of the initiatives announced in the statement was the establishment of the Resource Assessment Commission. This was supposed to resolve contentious environmental and development disputes (particularly in the forestry industry) by weighing up the evidence provided by industry and the greens (Hawke 1989).

The ESD discussion paper

After the March 1990 federal election, it was evident that Labor's concessions on environmental risks had helped return it to power (Toyne 1994). The government continued to promote ESD and released a discussion paper for public comment in June of 1990 (Department of the Prime Minister and Cabinet 1990). As with the Prime Minister's statement, the definition was brief and the focus was very much on reconciling economic and ecological goals. As such it tended to be much narrower than the Brundtland report.

There was, for example, no mention of the disadvantage experienced by indigenous people or women in industrial development. These were at least mentioned in passing by Brundtland (WCED 1990). The paper proposed setting up nine working groups to cover agriculture, forestry, fishing, mining, energy production, energy use, manufacturing, tourism and transport (Department of Prime Minister and Cabinet 1990). The arms industry, which had been mentioned by the Brundtland report as a threat to sustainability, was ignored (WCED 1990). The discussion paper was initially the product of several federal departments, but was rewritten by the Department of the Prime Minister and Cabinet to appease the mining industry and resource bureaucracies (Kellow & Moon 1993). Initially only five working groups were proposed. The manufacturing, energy use, energy production and transport working groups were included later. The working groups were actually a repetition of the National Conservation Strategy process, a response to the World Conservation Strategy of 1980 that had already introduced the idea of sustainable development and involved 20 000 people, with 4500 submissions received (Kellow & Moon 1993).

The five dimensions of development present in the Brundtland report (technical, economic, social, political and ecological) were present, but dispersed through various sections of the ESD discussion paper. Technical research was seen as important for 'providing information on the nature and extent of environmental problems, in developing more resource-efficient (resource saving and recycling) rural, mining and manufacturing processes and finally in identifying longer term technological alternatives' (Department of the Prime Minister and Cabinet 1990, p. 19). It was also noted that improvements in technology increase the 'productive capacity' of resources and it was claimed that Australia may already have an advantage in solar energy and energy conservation technology. The discussion paper focused heavily on economic viability. This was evident in the emphasis placed on the need for economic growth and international competitiveness. Social goals, such as the desire for equity within and between generations, were briefly canvassed and the political dimension was acknowledged in discussing the need for cooperation between all levels of government. The need for ecological sustainability was in the background throughout the whole document without being clearly defined. The manufacturing industry had two pages devoted to it, with the aim of setting up issues to be dealt with by the ESD working group. This part of the report again stressed the economic and technical aspects of ESD. It also emphasised the need for government intervention to correct market deficiencies and the need for uniform regulations across state boundaries.

Brundtland's re-release

Other developments in 1990 included the re-release of the Brundtland report in an Australian edition. This new-look volume kept the original report intact but added a chapter by the Commission for the Future. The purpose was to adapt the notion of sustainable development to the Australian situation in a format that would have more popular appeal than a Commonwealth discussion paper. There was little new material in this section and much of the subject matter overlapped with the National Conservation Strategy, the Brundtland report and Hawke's 1989 environment statement. However, there were three points worthy of note. First, it took a broader approach to sustainable development than the ESD discussion paper and included a small section on Aboriginal involvement in eco-tourism, wildlife management and sustainable farming (WCED 1990). Second, it pointed out the benefits of joint ventures between greens, industry and government (such as Landcare). Third, it suggested that there were two different approaches to sustainable development policy making:

> The first seeks to define social, cultural, political, as well as economic and ecological, requirements of biophysical sustainability. The second focuses more narrowly on the economics of sustainable development; that is, incorporating the biophysical environment into economic modelling, accounting and decision making (WCED 1990, pp. 27–8).

It appears that the Brundtland report and the Commission for the Future at least discussed the broader policy goals. The ESD discussion paper was closer to the narrower, economic approach.

ESD working groups

The discussion paper set the tone for the consultative policy working groups. These were established in August 1990 when Hawke appointed three academics to chair nine groups: agriculture, energy use, energy production, fisheries, forest use, manufacturing, mining, tourism and transport. The overall leader was Dr Roy Green, Director of the CSIRO Institute of Natural Resources and Environment. The other two were Professor Stuart Harris from the Australian National University's Department of International Relations and Professor David Throsby from the School of Economic and Financial Studies at Macquarie University. In November, the three chairs set up separate intersectoral issue and greenhouse inquiries that reported in 1992.

The working groups convened in October. There were 144 participants in total, made up of 90 public sector workers (state and federal), eighteen industry representatives, seventeen conservationists, nine union delegates and seven special interest group representatives. The conservationists were drawn from the WWF, the ACF and Greenpeace. All green groups refused to participate in the forest use group. In March 1991, Greenpeace withdrew because of the federal government's pursuit of resource security legislation that would guarantee access to old-growth native forests for logging by industry. A series of meetings and public conferences took place over the next few months and the interim working group reports were released for public comment from June to August of 1991 (ESD Working Groups 1991). The final reports were released in November. In all, the working groups made 405 recommendations and many of the findings were used in Australia's submission to the Rio Earth Summit in 1992 (DASETT 1991).

The manufacturing working group was typical of the process. It was chaired by Stuart Harris and included fifteen other members: one from the ACTU, two from state ministerial councils (in Victoria and Queensland), four from the Commonwealth, one from the CSIRO, three from conservation groups, two from consumer groups and two from industry groups (the BCA and AMC). Their report, like the others, was closer to the narrow economic approach mentioned in the ESD discussion paper. This was to facilitate the development of consensus, given the limited time and resources available to the group (ESD Working Groups—Manufacturing 1991).

The manufacturing report made 93 recommendations on topics such as:

- the structure of industry (international competition, investment, employment, management practices, green goods and services, environmental monitoring, research and development);
- project development (location and approvals);
- pollution control (regions, market mechanisms, contaminated sites and auditing);
- waste minimisation (packaging, recycling and intractable waste);
- conservation of biodiversity;
- energy and climate change (greenhouse emissions); and
- consumer programs (information, education, health and safety) (ESD Working Groups—Manufacturing 1991, pp. 119–86).

It also made several recommendations about reforming and integrating agencies and policies at all three levels of government.

Although the manufacturing report does not attempt to define sustainable development rigorously, the five dimensions are again apparent, as are the principles of weak ecological modernisation. There is considerable emphasis placed on economic viability through competitiveness (recommendations 4–5) and the need for a politically streamlined approval process (recommendations 31–39). The key role of technology is acknowledged by calls for more research and development into environmentally friendly products and processes (recommendations 26–29). The government's role is seen as being supportive of industry by funding research and taking responsibility for the achievement of social and environmental goals. Broader issues such as the impact of development on women and indigenous Australians rate only a brief mention in recommendation 10. These issues are dealt with in a little more detail in the intersectoral issues report, but even then there is no fundamental questioning of the possible structural causes of the disadvantage felt by these groups. The report does attempt to outline an ideal model for sustainable manufacturing. It initially lists fourteen features that manufacturing should acquire for sustainability but later reduces these to five main points.

> In an ideal world manufacturing operations would create no environmental or health problems during the production process or through the use and disposal of products. A more realistic vision of sustainable manufacturing might incorporate manufacturing processes:
> — which use best environmental practices including the best technology from both environmental and economic perspectives;
> — where all opportunities are taken to minimise waste by extracting and collecting useful by-products from wastes where economically and technologically feasible;
> — where every attempt would be made to minimise or eliminate the production of hazardous waste and to dispose of it in ways that minimise environmental damage;
> — which, where possible, use renewable energy forms or less polluting sources of energy and use all energy efficiently; and
> — which contribute to development of environmental technologies and products (ESD Working Groups—Manufacturing 1991, p. 57).

The aim was to create an industry that operates in a 'closed loop' with the environment by considering the whole life cycle of activity (from raw material extraction, through processing, to use and disposal). This meant using resources and energy sustainably, while generating products and either avoiding waste or producing wastes of a type and quantity that could be assimilated by the environment or recycled. Overall, the report draws heavily on the dimensions of Brundtland and enumerates a reasonably detailed framework for policy implementation. It does, however, tend to take a more narrow focus than the Brundtland report, stressing economic issues and the role of the state in supporting a well-regulated market.

There was a mixed response to the ESD working groups. Some environmentalists initially criticised the incremental reform strategy for achieving ESD (Hare 1992) or saw the agenda as too restricted, with inadequate public consultation (Diesendorf & Hamilton 1997). Some of the public seminars, for example, were conducted even before the draft reports were released, which limited the ability for effective public input (Chaney 1991). The selective use of peak body organisations in the working groups was seen by some as too corporatist (Downes 1996; McEachern 1993; Zarsky 1990). Others accepted that the process was a necessary (but limited) step in the right direction (Rae 1991). The Business Council of Australia (BCA 1991b) called the public consultation process 'confused'. It also claimed that the dominance of public servants in the working groups made the proceedings out of touch with the market place and the needs of industry.

ESD and Best Practice Environmental Management

In 1992 the BCA and the Australian Manufacturing Council (AMC) released their own environmental policy documents in response to the ESD reports. The International Chamber of Commerce had already produced a *Business Charter for Sustainable Development* in 1990 which was appended to the ESD manufacturing report. The BCA document made reference to its involvement in the ESD working groups and drew on the Brundtland definition of sustainable development. The five development dimensions were again apparent, but with even narrower emphasis. In particular, the notion of consulting with the community was recast as a need to publicise the environmental policies of business. Further, environment protection initiatives were endorsed only if business considered them affordable (BCA 1992).

The AMC (1992) released a more detailed set of guidelines under the rubric of Best Practice Environmental Management (BPEM). The five Brundtland criteria were apparent but cast in slightly different forms. There was a more explicit reference to the need to adopt management structures that are flexible and participatory (for both the workforce and the community). The report gave the state a role as the means to assist in the development and deployment of green technology, but emphasised the problems that may arise from over-regulation. Overall, BPEM is portrayed as a kind of paradigm shift in corporate culture and can be understood as a weak version of ecological modernisation. There are several examples of BPEM companies; most of them bear some (but by no means all) of the features outlined in the model of sustainable industry. This appears to be a genuine attempt to develop an alternative policy but, given the ongoing poor performance of Australian industry with regards to the environment, it has had little real impact. The reforms promoted by BPEM are too timid in comparison to the scope, scale and seriousness of environmental risks. In any case, a 1994 study by the AMC found that only a minority of firms had achieved best practice (AMC 1994). This falls within the weaker end of ecological modernisation (Christoff 1996; Dryzek 1997).

A national strategy for ESD

The complex nature of the ESD reports led to the establishment of two further cooperative bodies in 1991. One was the joint federal–state ESD Steering Committee. The other was the ESD Roundtable which included government, industry, unions and environmentalists (Toyne 1994). The object was to develop a coherent national response to the extensive ESD recommendations. In 1992, the ESD Steering Committee released the *National Strategy for Ecologically Sustainable Development* (ESD Steering Committee 1992). This document was targeted at a wider audience than the working group reports and was mainly devoted to summarising the outcome of the ESD policy-making process and the significance of the Rio Earth Summit. It did, however, outline a strategic ESD policy goal for Australia.

THE GOAL IS:
Development that improves the total quality of life, both now and in the future, in a way that maintains the ecological processes on which life depends.
THE CORE OBJECTIVES ARE:
— to enhance individual and community well-being and welfare by following a path of economic development that safeguards the welfare of future generations;
— to provide for equity within and between generations;
— to protect biological diversity and maintain essential ecological processes and life support systems.
THE GUIDING PRINCIPLES ARE:
— decision making processes should effectively integrate both long and short-term economic, environmental, social and equity considerations;

— where there are threats of serious or irreversible environmental damage, lack of full scientific certainty should not be used as a reason for postponing measures to prevent environmental degradation;
— the global dimension of environmental impacts of actions and policies should be recognised and considered;
— the need to develop a strong, growing and diversified economy which can enhance the capacity for environmental protection should be recognised;
— the need to maintain and enhance international competitiveness in an environmentally sound manner should be recognised;
— cost effective and flexible policy instruments should be adopted, such as improved valuation, pricing and incentive mechanisms;
— decisions and actions should provide for broad community involvement on issues which affect them (ESD Steering Committee 1992, p. 8).

There was a short section dedicated to the manufacturing industry which recapitulated the conclusions of the ESD working group and the industry response. Governments were committed to supporting environmental audits, BPEM, providing technical support through targeted research, co-ordinating agencies and integrating regulations. The objective for the manufacturing sector was also defined: 'To achieve a robust, internationally competitive, export-oriented manufacturing sector, which contributes to a stronger economy, operates in accordance with the principles of ESD and efficiently uses the renewable and non-renewable resources on which manu-facturing depend' (ESD Steering Committee 1992, p. 33). This demonstrates how environmental issues have undergone a reconstruction in the policy-making process to become matters of efficiency—the main hunting ground of economists.

Both the ALP and the Liberal party initially released policy documents supporting the ESD outcome in the lead-up to the March 1993 federal election (Liberal and National Parties 1993; Keating 1992). Keating initially appeared to be keen to stress his green credentials after taking over as Prime Minister from Hawke, but the policy had already begun losing momentum. Both the working group recommendations and national strategy were passed on to an array of short-lived state and federal government committees, while the Resource Assessment Commission and ESD Roundtable were both disbanded (Toyne 1994). In 1996 the Intergovernmental Committee for ESD, which replaced the ESD Steering Committee, published a report on progress made by all levels of government. It was an unexceptional catalogue of existing environmental legislation, programs and policy statements and the committee was later abolished (ICESD 1996).

By the time the Commonwealth government changed in 1996, ESD had all but disappeared from the national political agenda and the *National Strategy* was out of print. The new conservative Howard government shifted priority to its own green-vote-catching policy: the Natural Heritage Trust. This scheme was popular because it had a strong emphasis on rural employment, conservation, land use and fresh water management programs (Williams 1997). ESD rhetoric, however, continued to be invoked in legislation, policy announcements and the restructuring of departments.

ESD and the Environment Protection and Biodiversity Conservation Act

In 1998 the Howard government began to develop a new *Environment Protection and Biodiversity Conservation Act*. This Act was designed to replace several pieces of Commonwealth legislation and was trumpeted as a major reorganisation of environmental regulation. An amended version finally passed the Senate in 1999 after intense negotiations with the Democrats. The stated goal of the new Act was to promote ESD (s. 3.1(b)), which was embedded in five principles drawn from the *National Strategy*:

(a) decision-making processes should effectively integrate both long-term and short-term economic, environmental, social and equitable considerations;

(b) if there are threats of serious or irreversible environmental damage, lack of full scientific certainty should not be used as a reason for postponing measures to prevent environmental degradation;

(c) the principle of inter-generational equity—that the present generation should ensure that the health, diversity and productivity of the environment is maintained or enhanced for the benefit of future generations;

(d) the conservation of biological diversity and ecological integrity should be a fundamental consideration in decision-making;

(e) improved valuation, pricing and incentive mechanisms should be promoted (*EPBC Act 1998*, s. 3A).

These principles retain a faint echo of the five dimensions of sustainable development implicit within the Brundtland definition: technical, economic, social, political and ecological. They also incorporate a version of the precautionary and intergenerational equity principles. Noticeably absent, however, is the priority given to meeting the needs of the poor. There is also much more emphasis on efficiency than was in the original idea.

The five principles are deployed in later sections of the Act with regards to Environmental Impact Assessment (s. 28A.2(c)) decisions by the Commonwealth Minister of Environment (s. 131.2(b); s. 136.2(a)) and conservation actions (s. 270.3(c); s. 271.3(c); s. 287.3(c)). A unique provision towards the end of the Act requires all Commonwealth institutions to report annually on how their actions correspond to the ESD principles (s. 516A.6(a)).

Implementing ESD

In February 2000 the Productivity Commission report on the progress that Commonwealth institutions had made towards ESD was released (Productivity Commission 2000). It found that while those departments and agencies dealing directly with the environment or natural resources had incorporated ESD principles into their operations, many other parts of the state were more haphazard. Further, the report noted that environmentalist, farmer and forest industry groups were concerned about the lack of implementation and the risk that ESD was simply rhetoric. The report remained optimistic, however, that the situation was improving. Even so, it did admit upfront that some of the implementation problems were due to the lack of clarity in defining ESD and framed the policy in terms of correcting market failures.

In 1999 the Commonwealth published *Our Community, Our Future: A Guide to Local Agenda 21*, which had been developed through ANZECC from an APEC response to the Rio Earth Summit in 1997. It cited definitions of sustainable development from both the Brundtland report and the *National Strategy for ESD* (Environment Australia 1999). The principles are repeated in various forms with an emphasis on business and community consultation processes and it was noted that some 140 councils (out of 750) had adopted some sort of sustainable development policy by 1997.

Conclusions

Sustainable development emerged from an international policy-making process that was in large part an attempt to resolve tensions between industry and the environment movement, the rich North and the poor South, the capitalist West and socialist East and neo-liberalism and environmentalism. It culminated in the Rio Earth Summit and *Agenda 21*, which helped to infuse ecological modernisation into subsequent international responses to environmental risks. While the underlying discourse of ecological modernisation remained consistent, Australian ESD policies were much more narrowly defined and emphasised the economic rather than the ecological dimension. This is despite the wide-ranging consultations of the ESD working groups and the subsequent intergovernmental negotiations. This less comprehensive approach was preferred by industry but despite more than a decade of ESD policies Australia does not appear to be much closer to a sustainable society (see Chapter 8).

CHAPTER 7

Sustainable development in the USA and UK

Introduction

As in the Australian case, the USA and UK responded to UN initiatives by creating their own national variants of sustainable development policy. The processes were remarkably similar in that they involved cross-sectoral and interdisciplinary committees, community forums and public submissions and produced a series of documents that attempted to create some sort of shared vision or goal. This chapter will review the processes and outcomes, drawing parallels with the UN and Australian experience outlined in Chapter 6. The US experience will be dealt with first, followed by the UK. The influence of neo-liberalism, its clash with environmentalism and the compromises offered by ecological modernisation are again apparent.

Sustainable development and the USA

The creation of the US EPA in 1970 preceded the rise of sustainable development policies in American domestic politics by two decades. The Stockholm Conference and the *World Conservation Strategy* left the agency largely unaffected and it was not until 1990 (three years after the Brundtland report) that the state really began to take notice. By that stage the US EPA's legislation, programs and responsibilities had been independently developing for two decades.

The US EPA's initial reaction

In late 1990, US EPA administrator William Reilly began to adopt some of the rhetoric of the Brundtland report. He suggested that the agency needed to move beyond its traditional functions to encourage pollution prevention and sustainable development, but tempered these statements with recognition of the need for sustainable economic growth (Reilly 1990a, b). In 1993, after the Rio Earth Summit, Congress asked the US EPA to outline its role in achieving sustainable development. The response was a report from the US EPA Office of Policy, Planning and Evaluation. This document cited Brundtland but went on to point out the lack of a clearly agreed definition, stressed the need for economic growth to pay for environmental protection and proposed three tenets for institutionalising sustainability: long-term planning perspectives; recognition that the economy and ecology are interdependent; and 'new, integrative approaches to achieve economic, social and environmental objectives' (US EPA 1993, p. 2).

The report addressed the role of the agency in achieving sustainable development. This subject was approached with some defensiveness and it was argued that many of the agency's programs were already in accord with the new policy goal. Four factors inhibiting the ability of the US EPA to pursue sustainable development were discussed. First, it was argued that the agency was limited by the fact that sustainable development was not at that time a stated goal of any legislation for which the US EPA had responsibility. Second, it was stated that sustainable development entailed a broad set of ideas that were difficult to apply to specific decisions. Third, it was suggested that any new program would have to fit in with existing projects to avoid duplication. The final point was perhaps the most pertinent one for this study and is worth quoting in some length.

> [T]he full scope of planning and implementation of sustainable development policies extends well beyond the purview of EPA. Objectives often associated with sustainable development, such as sustainable management of natural resources, sustainable agricultural practices, improved energy efficiency, improved economic and environmental equity and a competitive U.S. economy, can only be addressed through the cooperative efforts of multiple federal agencies, the Congress, state and local governments, businesses and non-government organizations. Similarly, cooperation among many government agencies will be needed to develop useful measures of sustainability and to assess the sustainability of environmental and economic trends on a variety of temporal and

geographic scales. As the lead national agency for environmental protection, EPA can exercise an important role in developing inter-governmental and public-private coalitions to accelerate progress toward sustainability, but progress will depend on the contributions of many institutions (US EPA 1993, pp. 3–4).

This statement is based on the agency's experience trying to respond to environmental risk and the reflexive resistance it encountered from industry and other state agencies (Beder 2002). Many times in the past the US EPA had been blamed for failing to find a quick fix for chronic risks that were inherent within conventional industrial development and that had accumulated over centuries. Given the limited resources and restricted jurisdiction, it would be unreasonable to expect the US EPA alone to make the profound changes required for US industry to become sustainable.

The rest of the report was taken up with a list of existing programs that seemed to be in accord with the tenets of sustainable development. These included: information programs such as the Environmental Monitoring and Assessment Program and the National Human Exposure Assessment Survey; social science research focused on why humans behave as they do towards the environment; and pollution prevention and energy conservation programs. There was also: the Toxics Release Inventory; tradable permits under the *Clean Air Act*; green technology transfer programs; the move to regional and multi-media regulation; environmental education programs; and community right to know legislation associated with the Superfund policy. The report discussed the US EPA's ability to promote sustainable development in international forums and mentioned the need to include environmental concerns in inter-national trading arrangements. Although the agency was initially slow to pick up the policy and was a little defensive early on, it did see a major role for itself in promoting sustainable development. Adapting sustainable development to the US fell to two consultative forums: the National Commission on the Environment (NCE) and the President's Council on Sustainable Development.

National Commission on the Environment

The NCE was a group of ex-bureaucrats (from local, state and federal author-ities), along with environmentalists, industry leaders and financiers. This commission was the initiative of the World Wide Fund for Nature and was designed to raise the environment as an issue during the 1992 presidential campaign. It was in this election that Presidential candidate Bill Clinton, supported by the environmentally sympathetic Vice-Presidential candidate Al Gore, led the Democrats to victory over the incumbent Republican

President George Bush senior. Of the nineteen NCE members, four were former US EPA administrators: Russell Train, William Ruckelshaus, Douglas Costle and Lee Thomas. The group met eight times during 1992 and produced a report in 1993 called *Choosing a Sustainable Future* (NCE 1993).

Overall the group was critical of the piecemeal approach to environmental regulation and suggested that the federal government create a long-term strategy for sustainable development. The NCE favoured economic prompts over regulations and pollution prevention over 'end of pipe' solutions. There were several proposals to get the market price of goods to reflect their true environmental and economic costs. There were also calls for environmental problems to be sorted into various levels of priority and the promotion of sustainable technology (NCE 1993). Both these elements indicate some influence by neo-liberalism and the weaker version of ecological modernisation.

The US EPA got several mentions as a key player. It was proposed that the agency be remade into part of a larger department of the environment, although this has not occurred. Other suggestions about the US EPA included: getting more involved in environmental education, implementing the proposed national sustainable development strategy, helping reduce pollution at its source and setting up a long range forecasting information clearinghouse. Several programs run by the agency were mentioned and recommended for expansion: sulphur dioxide tradable permits and emission bubbles created by the Clean Air Act, the Toxics Release Inventory and the Green Lights program (that encouraged firms to install energy efficient lighting). The most interesting proposition was for senior environmental managers to be placed in every federal department and agency (NCE 1993). This is comparable to the UK's deployment of junior environment ministers for every portfolio and Australia's requirement that all Commonwealth departments report annually on their contribution to sustainable development.

The President's Council on Sustainable Development

After the NCE had reported in 1993 the newly elected President Clinton created the President's Council on Sustainable Development to develop an appropriate national strategy. It was similar in structure to the NCE only this time current federal and state bureaucrats were included, with industry leaders, environmentalists and a union representative (PCSD 1996). The total membership was twenty-five, Carol Browner (then US EPA administrator) was one of the participants and Vice-President Gore took an active interest. A series of public meetings and conferences were held across the country over three years in order to collect ideas (much like the Australian ESD Working Group process). The final report was due to be released in November 1995, but was side-tracked by the budget wrangling between Congress and the White House. The report was eventually leaked to the *New York Times* in February 1996, prompting its formal release (Cushman 1996).

The most surprising aspect of the report was that the industry representatives supported a continuance of federal regulations as a 'safety net', albeit with substantial improvements to the current system. This was in direct contradiction to Republican moves to reduce federal regulation but it may be due to firms using the investment in pollution abatement technology as a cost barrier to new firms thinking of entering their markets, rather than a genuine greening of attitudes. The report concluded that: 'Pollution is waste, waste is inefficient and inefficiency is expensive' (Cushman 1996, p. C11). This was in accord with the US EPA's pollution prevention policy and a clear, but unacknowledged, element of ecological modernisation.

The report constructed a set of broad goals under the rubric of sustainable development: a healthy environment and a prosperous economy for the US; the conservation of nature and natural resources; promoting a sense of stewardship towards the environment; developing sustainable communities; encouraging 'civic engagement' in decision making; stabilising the US population; taking the lead in international forums; and promoting environmental education. The report did mention the Australian ESD Roundtable as a forerunner, but did not give details or draw any links with its own work (PCSD 1996).

Overall, the environmental participants accepted the need for economic growth in return for industry acknowledging the ecological limits on their activities. More specific lessons were drawn from the US experience in environmental regulation. While some benefits from regulations were acknowledged, there was a call to move beyond this safety net and develop more flexible approaches.

> The experience of the last 25 years has yielded the following lessons, which would be wise to heed in developing a new framework to achieve the objectives of sustainable development:
> — Economic, environmental and social problems cannot be addressed in isolation. Economic prosperity, environmental quality and social equity need to be pursued simultaneously.
> — Science-based national standards that protect human health and the environment are the foundation of any effective system of environmental protection.
> — The adversarial nature of the current system precludes solutions

that become possible when potential adversaries cooperate and collaborate.
- Technology-based regulation can sometimes encourage tech-nological innovation, but it can also stifle it; pollution prevention is better than pollution control.
- Enhanced flexibility for achieving environmental goals, coupled with strong compliance assurance mechanisms—including enforcement—can spur private sector innovation that will enhance environmental protection at a substantially lower cost both to individual firms and to society as a whole.
- Science, economics and societal values should be considered in making decisions. Quality information is essential to sound decision making.
- Many state governments have developed significant environ-mental management capacity. Indeed, many of the most creative and lasting solutions arise from collaborations involving federal, state, local and tribal governments in places problems exist—from urban communities to watersheds (PCSD 1996, p. 26).

This passage includes the five dimensions of sustainable development (tech-nical, economic, social, political and ecological) with most emphasis being placed on technology and economics. It is yet another manifestation of the way neo-liberalism shaped policy-making responses by the state to environmental risks and is also increasingly influenced by ecological modernisation, although the term is never used. The report stresses the need to make changes to the current regulatory system, develop greater flexibility, get firms to consider their responsibility for their end products, make more use of economic prompts, develop partnerships with the community and business and help develop better technology. The report also suggests that the US federal government should 'set boundaries for and facilitate place-based policy dialogues' between business and communities (PCSD 1996, p. 8). It also proposes that the tax system be restructured to encourage sustainable development and promote the environment in international forums.

The US EPA is mentioned specifically several times and is given the role of: setting performance based standards for industry; coordinating different agencies and levels of government; identifying opportunities for industry to improve its environmental performance; and providing critical data about the environment. It was recommended that the US EPA's demonstration projects be expanded and the Common Sense Initiative, Project XL, the Toxics Release Inventory and the Eco-Industrial Park program were all applauded (PCSD 1996).

The report does attempt to apply the broader concept of sustainable development specifically to industrial production. It suggests a whole life-cycle approach to minimise the environmental impacts of extraction, production, use and disposal of goods. The ideal objective is a zero waste system. This is remarkably similar to the 'closed loop' ideal promoted by the Australian ESD Working Group—Manufacturing (1991). It is suggested that progress towards sustainable industry should be indicated by more efficient material, water and energy use, as well as less waste generation and the deployment of more innovative technology (PCSD 1996).

After the President's Council

After the report, the council was asked by President Clinton to continue its work as a federal advisory committee and a revised charter was adopted in 1997 for a further three years (PCSD 1999a). Several task forces were established to try to find ways to implement the policy goal, including: the Innovative Local, State and Regional Approaches Task Force; the New National Opportunities Task Force; the International Leadership Task Force; the Climate Change Task Force; the Environmental Management Task Force; and the Metropolitan and Rural Strategies Task Force. The council also hosted a series of 'Town Meetings' across the USA in 1999 to encourage business, communities and interested organisations to undertake sustainable development projects (PCSD 1999b).

The National Opportunities Task Force reported in April 1997 on collaborative approaches to sustainable development (PCSD New National Opportunities Task Force 1997). Several of the US EPA's programs were evaluated, including: the Common Sense Initiative; Project XL; and the National Environmental Performance Partnership System. The report suggested that although it was too early to assess the first two programs, in general the US EPA's collaborative projects have 'had some successes' although it is difficult to quantify their effectiveness because of a lack of baseline data and monitoring. It was suggested that the US EPA should translate its vision of goals into specific objectives and provide strong leadership in collaborative projects.

The US EPA and sustainable development

Under Carol Browner's administration, the US EPA continued to explore the possibilities for its role in sustainable development. The rhetoric of the 1994–99 strategic plan suggested that the Agency's executive has embraced the policy (US EPA 1994b). Again there was the emphasis on shared responsibility, economic growth, appropriate technology and the need to provide effective information to decision makers and the public. The idea of targeting US EPA programs to address high priority areas first appears to have been included to counter anticipated criticisms about how the US EPA has functioned in the past.

The strategic plan summarises the goals and programs of the agency with regards to: ecosystem protection; environmental justice (particularly for lower income communities that seem to be exposed to more forms of environmental problems); pollution prevention; the development of better science and data; partnerships (with industry, community groups and other authorities); improving US EPA management; and environmental accountability through better enforcement and compliance (US EPA 1994b).

The strategy goes through the different offices within the US EPA and summarises what each is doing and how this relates to the stated policy goals. Sustainable development is often mentioned but never defined. The Office of Policy, Planning and Evaluation talks about its attempts to restructure the economy and measures of 'economic wellbeing' to include environmental factors to get around the economy versus environment dilemma. It gives three undertakings to:

— Promote policies that improve the functioning of markets through legal and institutional structures, thus encouraging the more efficient deployment of production capital . . .
— Develop regulatory and non-regulatory policies, such as market incentives, to promote environmental protection and economic growth . . .
— Bring environmental considerations into economic decisions (US EPA 1994b, p. 86).

There is a sustainable industries program where the office works with selected firms and industries over five years to 'help them satisfy their customer demand through non-polluting or less polluting production processes'(US EPA 1994b, p. 89). The final section of the report outlines the programs of the ten regional offices. About half of these have program summaries that use the term sustainable development. Although it is noted that Region 10 has adopted a specific sustainable development program, not much is explained about what this is supposed to achieve.

Pollution prevention appears to have become a way for the US EPA to begin to respond to the rise of sustainable development ideas. Carol Browner took up this initiative from the previous administrator, William Reilly, and continues to promote it as a better way to deal with environmental problems because it seeks to avoid damage in the first place. The idea is to encourage firms to audit their operations and find ways to make adjustments to production that reduce both their pollution and running costs (Browner 1993).

Industry and sustainable development

At first glance it would be reasonable to expect that industry would be very keen to join these programs, however, the US EPA continues to face a major struggle against some recalcitrant corporations (see Chapter 8 and Beder 2002). Even though pollution prevention programs have been cost effective and profitable many senior executives still perceive them as an unnecessary cost that complicates decision making. The environmental, economic and technical complexity of such schemes requires the deployment of effective cross-disciplinary teams that need the backing of senior management. It is difficult to get management to do this, but several success stories suggest that it is not impossible (see Chapter 9 and Cebon 1993).

The question still remains as to whether this type of state intervention is enough to achieve even a modest version of sustainability. Underwood (1993) suggests that the rate of depletion of fossil fuel reserves remains unsustainable, which is a fundamental problem for all industrialised economies. Despite the substantial reductions of chemicals under the Toxics Release Inventory, the level of emission of hazardous pollutants is still too high. Any effective attempt to promote sustainable development will therefore involve more substantial restructuring of the market and business institutions to reduce the externally constructed interest in consuming more non-renewable resources and polluting. Further, perceived interests will need to be reassessed through more sustainable corporate attitudes and better knowledge of the extent of environmental problems. The US EPA's programs have only just begun to address these factors and the lack of implementation of sustainable development policies in the later years of the Clinton administration was disappointing. The change of government in 2000 led to the further sidelining of sustainable development policies, although much of the sustainable development rhetoric has infused the US EPA's revised goals (see Chapter 3).

The UK and sustainable development

In the UK, the early 1980s was a time of hostility towards the environment movement by the Thatcher government (Dryzek et al. 2003). This changed in the late 1980s, just as the concept of sustainable development was on the rise and pressure from the EU was increasing (Garner 2000).

This Common Inheritance *1990*

The government issued an initial response to the Brundtland report in 1988 and then released *This Common Inheritance: Britain's Environmental Strategy* in 1990 (UK Government 1990). Like Australian Prime Minister Hawke's 1989 statement, the strategy set out some general principles, then went on to point to the improvements already achieved across different sectors of society. While there is reference to the Stockholm Conference, the then approaching Rio Earth Summit and the Brundtland report, the strategy only briefly defines the concept of sustainable development.

> The Government therefore supports the principle of sustainable development. This means living on the earth's income rather than eroding its capital. It means keeping the consumption of renewable resources within the limits of replenishment. It means handing down to successive generations not only man-made wealth (such as buildings, roads and railways) but also natural wealth, such as clean and adequate water supplies, good arable land, a wealth of wildlife and ample forests (UK Government 1990, p. 47).

The five dimensions (technical, economic, social, political and ecological) are again apparent, although the emphasis is on the need for economic development and growth. Responsibility for achieving sustainable development was portrayed as a cooperative effort between industry, all levels of government and the public. This indicates the influence of neo-liberalism and ecological modernisation. It specifically mentioned the importance of integrated pollution control, Her Majesty's Inspectorate of Pollution and the *Environment Protection Act 1990* as playing key roles in addressing environmental risks. The idea of creating a new environment agency, however, was dismissed, as the previous reorganisation of pollution inspectorates had only recently been achieved (UK Government 1990).

Sustainable development: The UK Strategy 1994

A second major UK policy statement appeared in 1994, after the Rio Earth Summit, called *Sustainable Development: The UK Strategy* (UK Government 1994). As with both the Australian and US policies, this document was produced after considerable public consultation. In 1992 the Department of Environment called for a national debate and asked for public submissions on a framework strategy. A series of discussions followed with all levels of government, business, NGOs and academia, culminating in a three day seminar at Oxford in March 1993. A consultation paper was then released in July and circulated to 6000 organisations, from which 500 responses were received. There was also a series of media articles and a newspaper question-naire produced 8000 responses. A further 40 meetings with some 100 organisations were conducted from July to October 1993 and three consul-tative bodies were established: the Advisory Committee on Business and the Environment; the Central and Local Government Environment Forum; and the Voluntary Sector Environment Forum.

The basic assumptions that underpin this version of sustainable develop-ment include: the desire for economic growth; the belief that some environ-mental damage is inevitable; the assertion that human health should remain a major focus; and the acceptance of the need to conserve some resources. This led to a set of principles that guided the governmentality of the strategy.

> Because in many ways the environment is shared, collective action is necessary. There are certain specific principles to take into account in pursuing this:
> — Decisions should be based on the best possible scientific infor-mation and analysis of risks.
> — Where there is uncertainty and potentially serious risks exist, precautionary action may be necessary.
> — Ecological impacts must be considered, particularly where resources are non-renewable or effects may be irreversible.
> — Cost implications should be brought home directly to the people responsible—the 'polluter pays' principle (UK Government 1994, p. 7).

Again the implicit technical, economic, social, political and ecological dimen-sions are apparent, with the emphasis firmly on the economic. Integrated pollution control is still seen as an important part of the government response, but unlike the 1990 strategy, the idea of a new environment agency is now being supported. Interestingly, there is a statement by the Secretary of State for the Environment in the introduction that appears to implicitly accept that modernisation has become reflexive.

> Our successes were themselves the cause of many of our new fears . . . We began to see that growth and development demanded a

price and that price was increasingly beyond our ability to pay. Effects we could ignore when they were confined to the actions of a few, became intolerable when they were spread more and more widely (UK Government 1994, p. 5).

This statement is quickly tempered by a commitment to ongoing industrial development and economic growth, but the fact that such an idea is acknowledged is interesting. Ecological modernisation also makes an appearance throughout in the way the report constructs environmental risk and responses. There is the assertion that industrialised economies can achieve both economic growth and reduced pollution, for example, demonstrating the idea of material delinking of the economy. Direct reference to the manufacturing and service industries reinforce this point.

> Government must concentrate on:
> — protecting or maintaining essential environmental standards by regulation, if necessary, although the preferred mechanism is the more efficient economic instrument;
> — promoting environmental management and such schemes as BS 7750, Eco-Management and Audit and Responsible Care in the chemicals industry;
> — raising consumer awareness through measures such as eco-labelling and environmental reporting;
> — encouraging energy efficiency in the workplace;
> — encouraging the development of new products and processes to increase and minimise pollution and waste;
> — encouraging the development of new technologies to assist in more effective, efficient and innovative pollution prevention (UK Government 1994, p. 13).

There are many parallels here with the Australian and US policies. Local Agenda 21 and environmental management systems, for example, are promoted as a means of getting local authorities to play their role in achieving sustainable development. As in Australia, the UK has included sustainable development as the main goal of recent environmental legislation such as the Environment Act 1995 (Duxbury & Morton 2000). There were also several committees established to help implement the concept. Achieving or even defining the goal still remains a problem and some critics have suggested that the concept is still too broad to be practical (Helm 1998).

A Better Quality of Life *1999*

In 1999 the Blair government released its own policy statement entitled: *A Better Quality of Life: A Strategy for Sustainable Development in the UK* (UK Government 1999). This restated many of the principles from the two previous strategies.

> Our Strategy for sustainable development has four main aims. These are:
> — social progress which recognises the needs of everyone;
> — effective protection of the environment;
> — prudent use of natural resources; and
> — maintenance of high and stable levels of economic growth and employment.
> For the UK, priorities for the future are:
> — more investment in people and equipment for a competitive economy;
> — reducing the level of social exclusion;
> — promoting a transport system which provides choice and also minimises environmental harm and reduces congestion;
> — improving the larger towns and cities to make them better places to live and work;
> — directing development and promoting agricultural practices to protect and enhance the countryside and wildlife;
> — improving energy efficiency and tackling waste;
> — working with others to achieve sustainable development internationally (UK Government 1999, p. 1).

Again the technical, economic, social, political and ecological dimensions of the Brundtland report are present. There is a commitment to Local Agenda 21 and principles like the 'polluter pays'. As with the other strategies it is anthropocentric and utilitarian in nature with the emphasis on economic growth. Progress towards this latest strategy is reviewed each year. In 2002 the review claimed that some advances were being made towards the government's economic, social and ecological goals set (UK Government 2002). The Blair government also established an independent Sustainable Development Commission to review progress. It is currently chaired by Jonathan Porritt, a long-term environmental activist in the UK. The 2003 report of the commission covered a great deal of ground, from Johannesburg to local government. Overall the assessment concluded that only slow and patchy progress had been made (a point considered in more detail in Chapter 8) (UK Sustainable Development Commission 2003).

Conclusions

The initial concept of sustainable development, although far from perfect, had the potential to generate a comprehensive policy to address the technical, economic, social, political and ecological problems associated with industrial development. It also offered a way to abate the clash between neo-liberalism and environmentalism by generating a new governmentality based on ecological modernisation. The fact that governments were prepared to host policy-making forums that included environmental groups is tacit acknowledgment that modernisation has become reflexive and these were attempts to re-engage with the sub-politics generated. National policies, however, have systematically narrowed the concept to suit a pre-existing political and economic agenda. Despite clearly unsustainable trends in the use of the environment, the overriding emphasis has been to find ways to protect industrial development and economic growth rather than ecosystems. This again is an indication of the difficulty of getting nineteenth-century institutions to respond to twentieth-century risks. In the current institutional context it is clearly very difficult to take such a broad-ranging concept and produce concrete outcomes, but at least a start has been made.

PART C

Has it worked?

CHAPTER 8

Has government intervention worked?

Introduction

The previous chapters have reviewed what three national governments have done in response to environmental risk, in particular the creation of new institutions, new regulations, new economic prompts, new knowledge-based initiatives and new policy goals. This chapter assesses the overall effectiveness of these responses. The first section briefly outlines the difficulties associated with measuring success. The remaining sections then work through four different methods of more detailed assessment: meeting the goals set; tracking changes in selected environmental indicators; the level of enforcement and resistance; and redirecting the flow of resources. It is suggested that the choice of method will not only be influenced by the discourses under which the assessment is conducted but also affect the outcome of the analysis. Together, however, these methods can be triangulated to allow a composite picture of the effectiveness of government responses to emerge. Overall it is argued that while no state has achieved a sustainable society, significant progress has been made.

The problem of measuring success

How can the effectiveness of an agency, regulation, program or policy be measured? This is a simple question, but finding an answer is quite difficult.

It is obviously important because governments need to know if progress is being made towards some goal or if further changes are needed. The periodic review of state actions is a normal part of the process of governance (Bridgman & Davis 2002), yet there are significant barriers to finding a single metric to measure success.

The performance of industry can be fairly easily measured by a number of key indicators, such as the level of profit, the return on investment, the share price, the ratio of debt to equity and the percentage of market share. Further, tracking these factors over time will give a reasonable picture of whether the firm is improving its performance. Political parties can track their success based on the number of votes cast for them at the last election, the number of seats held in the legislature, the number of policies or laws put into effect, the current number of party members and recent opinion polls. Many other social institutions, such as community groups, can measure their success by the size of their membership, the number of active members and the total amount of revenue brought in through fees or fundraisers.

None of these options are really useful for measuring the success of government responses to environmental risk. The proportion of the budget directed towards an agency, the number of staff employed and the range of powers delegated might be considered (as in Chapter 3). But these factors are more an indication of the priority assigned by the government of the day, or the perceived size of the risk, which are in turn generally the products of prevailing discourses. By comparing a cross-section of methods, however, a clearer picture of the impact of interventions can be constructed.

Method 1: Meeting the goals set

One of the first things that can be done to assess the effectiveness is to consider whether the goals that were stated at the outset have been achieved. Key players in addressing environmental risk have been environment agencies and these have usually been established with a clear set of aims (see Chapter 3). Further, individual pieces of environmental legislation have created some very specific targets, while national sustainable development polices have delineated some broader goals.

The initial objective of the US EPA was heavily weighted towards improving environmental quality by reducing pollution (Nixon 1971). This was later qualified to include a requirement that broader economic and social goals should also be met (US EPA 1993) and more recently the statement to 'safeguard the natural environment—air, land and water—upon which life depends'—was added (US EPA 2002, p. I–1). The goals of the UK Environment Agency, on the other hand, include improvements in environmental quality, waste minimisation, conservation and communication (UK EA 1997, 2002). The Australian Environment Protection and Heritage Council includes in its aims improving environmental quality, eco-efficiency, conservation and heritage protection, while the Commonwealth's Department of Environment and Heritage seeks to protect and conserve the environment (NEPC 2002; DEH 2002).

Chapter 4 outlined how these goals were to be achieved via specific regulations and economic initiatives that had their own targets. The US federal *Water Pollution Control Act 1972*, for example, required the US EPA to make all waters 'fishable' and 'swimmable' by 1985. Further, the USA, UK and Australia also developed national sustainable development policy goals in the 1990s. These national policies were discussed in some detail in Chapters 6 and 7 and the overall goal was to attempt to continue economic growth while limiting the associated environmental damage to a scale or type that the environment could bear in the long term. So how well have all these goals been met?

Chapter 1 outlined a cross-section of incidents and ongoing problems that give an indication of the scope and seriousness of environmental risk. It also mentioned a range of international reports and conferences over the last three decades that have attempted to assess the progress made. Running parallel to this process have been several attempts to measure the performance of individual states. Two such reports are considered in a little more detail below.

Human and ecological wellbeing

One analysis, undertaken by Prescott-Allen (2001), is called *The Wellbeing of Nations: A Country-by-Country Index of Quality of Life and the Environment* and covered 180 countries. This report was prepared in cooperation with the International Development Research Centre, the International Union for the Conservation of Nature, the International Institute for Environment and Development, the United Nations Food and Agricultural Organisation, Mapmaker Limited and the United Nations Environment Program. The aim of the study was to quantify the wellbeing of people and ecosystems, as well as measure how they were affecting each other.

The report used several indices as a measure of how close each state was to sustainable development. The human wellbeing index considered the economic, social and political dimensions of each country. It included ratings for health (e.g. life expectancy, infant mortality), population (e.g. density and growth), wealth (e.g. average income), knowledge (e.g. level of education achieved), community (e.g. level of freedom, crime, peace) and equity (e.g.

distribution of wealth). The ecological wellbeing index was an aggregate measure of quality of land, water and air (based on levels of degradation and pollution), species/genes (e.g. diversity and proportion under threat from extinction) and resource use (e.g. energy consumption, food and timber production). The average of these two indices was taken as the overall wellbeing index and all of the countries were then ranked on the basis of their score.

Each index had a maximum of 100 and was divided into five bands:

1   80–100 was a good score and indicated sustainable development;
2   60–80 was a fair score which meant the country was almost sustainable;
3   40–60 was the medium score;
4   20–40 indicated a poor performance which meant the country was almost unsustainable; and
5   0–20 meant a bad rating and the country was unsustainable.

The key scores for the USA, UK and Australia have been extracted and presented in Table 8.1 for ease of reference. These results indicate that while all three states have a fair record on the human side, they were all almost unsustainable with regards to ecological wellbeing. This dragged their overall ratings down into the medium performance band. Of the three, Australia scored the highest on the human side but lowest on the ecological, yet retained the highest overall ranking (with the USA second and UK third). It should be noted that no country achieved a score above 80 in the ecological wellbeing index. (To put the rankings in context: Sweden came 1st, Germany was 12th, Japan was 24th, the Russian Federation was 65th, China was 160th and Iraq was 180th.) The scores for the various components that made up the ecological wellbeing index are given in Table 8.2.

In terms of land, the UK has the lowest rating in part because of its high population density, small landmass and high proportion of area under development (see Chapter 3, Figure 3.1). Australia and the USA rate badly for

Table 8.1 Ratings of wellbeing

	USA	UK	Australia
Human wellbeing index	73	73	79
Ecological wellbeing index	31	30	28
Overall wellbeing index	52.0	51.5	53.5
Ranking out of 180 countries	27	33	18

Source of data: Prescott-Allen, R. 2001, *The Wellbeing of Nations: A Country-by-Country Index of Quality of Life and the Environment*, Island Press, Washington.

air quality in part because of their high per capita emission of carbon dioxide. This index also encompasses measures of pollutants that have been strongly regulated by all three states, including sulphur dioxide, nitric oxide, ozone, carbon monoxide, particulate matter and atmospheric lead. This is significant because these are factors that have attracted considerable attention and regulation in all three countries (see Chapter 4). It is clear, however, that they all need to perform much better across the areas of environmental risk if they are to meet their goals to protect the environment and achieve the overall aim for sustainable development.

Table 8.2 Comparison of ecological index components

	USA	UK	Australia
Land	51	38	55
Water	46	21	21
Air	6	30	11
Species and genes	23	41	25
Resources use	35	20	42

Source of data: Prescott-Allen, R. 2001, *The Wellbeing of Nations: A Country-by-Country Index of Quality of Life and the Environment*, Island Press, Washington.

The OECD Environmental Performance Review 1993–2000

Other international organisations have taken an interest in monitoring environmental risk and performance. The Organisation of Economic Cooperation and Development (OECD Working Party on Environmental Performance 2000) recently undertook a review of the performance of its 32 member states which covered the period 1993–2000. This report did not attempt to formulate a single rating for countries but included both numerical data and discursive assessments of its members. Table 8.3 summarises some of the key data for the USA, UK and Australia.

This data confirms Prescott-Allen's (2001) findings that no country has a perfect record on environmental protection nor are any close to sustainable development. The UK is the heaviest user of fertilisers and pesticides and has the highest proportion of species under threat of extinction. By comparison, the USA produces the most solid waste per head of population but spends the largest proportion of its GDP on pollution abatement and control. Australia has the highest per capita emission of sulphur oxides and the smallest percentage of land protected. A comparatively small population, relatively large mining/smelting sector and heavier reliance on coal-fired power stations is probably a major contributor to the higher sulphur figure. There are, however, some positive signs of decoupling economic growth from

Table 8.3 Selected OECD environmental data 1993–2000

	USA	UK	Australia
% GDP change 1990–2000	+38.9	+24.3	+42.7
% total land area protected	21.2	20.4	7.7
Nitrogen fertiliser use (tonnes/km² of arable land)	6.3	20.1	1.7
Pesticide use (tonnes/km² of arable land)	0.21	0.58	0.23
% known mammal species under threat	10.5	22.2	14.9
% known bird species under threat	7.2	6.8	6.4
Annual emission of sulphur oxides (kg/person)	68.9	34.5	100.6
% change (1990–late 1990s)	−14	−46	−3
Annual emissions of carbon dioxide (tonnes/person)	20.0	9.3	16.6
% change (1990–98)	+12	−4	+20
Municipal waste (kg/person/year)	720	480	690
Pollution abatement and control expenditure (% GDP)	1.6	1.0	0.8

Source of data: Working Party on Environmental Performance OECD (2000), *Environmental Performance Reviews (1st Cycle) 32 Countries (1993–2000)*, Paris, OECD. Annexes: 1.A & 1.B.

environmental damage during the 1990s with all three states recording substantial increases in GDP but decreases in sulphur emissions per person. The UK was also able to reduce its per capita carbon dioxide emissions. Such trends would have to continue if industry is to modernise ecologically (see Chapter 2). The large rise in carbon dioxide emissions per person for both the USA and Australia during the 1990s may have discouraged both governments from ratifying the Kyoto protocol on greenhouse gas reductions.

The OECD report gave a discursive summary of the past performance of each member state, with proposals for improvement (OECD Working Party on Environmental Performance 2000). It acknowledged that the USA was quick to take up environmental regulation in the 1970s and that many improvements in environmental quality had resulted. The Toxics Release Inventory was given a special mention as a positive initiative. Attention was also drawn, however, to the fact that many of the targets set on water and air quality have not been met. The report on the UK applauded the introduction of Integrated Pollution Control, Best Available Technology Not Entailing Excessive Cost (BATNEEC), Best Practicable Environmental Option (BPEO) and the creation of the Environment Agency. It was critical of the lack of progress in reducing air pollutants such as oxides of nitrogen, carbon monoxide and volatile organic substances. Improvements in Australian air quality, the rapid removal of ozone-depleting substances and the establishment of the Natural Heritage Trust were all applauded. There were criticisms of the lack of environmental monitoring and public information as well as problems with coordination and enforcement between the different state and

Commonwealth jurisdictions. The newly established National Environment Protection Measure process and the National Pollutant Inventory were seen as improvements. Efforts by the USA, UK and Australia to create national sustainable development policies were seen as positive, but it was pointed out that they were all having difficulty with implementation, coordination and integration (particularly with economic policies). Overall the report was keen to promote economic instruments that were seen as under-utilised.

These reports can be used by the first method of analysis to give some indication of where society is now (still a long way from sustainable development), identify areas of progress (some reduction in specific pollutants) and points for improvement (the need for more coordinated and integrated governance). But focusing solely on meeting the goals set will tend to underestimate the effectiveness of government responses to environmental risks because often the goals initially set were unrealistic. Common understanding during the early years of regulation simply underestimated the scale, scope and seriousness of environmental risks. Further, given that these risks have been developing over several centuries around the globe, it is simply unreasonable to expect that a handful of agencies and laws could provide some miracle cure. It is clearly going to take a much more concerted effort by all parts of the state, business and community to have a significant impact, a point that is tacitly acknowledged by recent attempts to encourage all areas of them to become involved in sustainable development. The tendency to understate the effectiveness of this method may be why many critics of environmental regulation tend to focus on the failure to meet goals. Understanding how effective each state's response to environmental risk has been will therefore require more detailed analysis.

Method 2: Tracking changes in selected indicators

Another method is to track the changes in specific pollutants, unsustainable practices or quality indicators. This method is often used by the environmental agencies themselves to demonstrate the positive impact they are having and fits in with the governmentality that encourages a programmable approach to risk (see Chapter 2). The OECD report offered a comparison of progress on some aspects of environmental quality since 1993 but what evidence is there for the longer-term trends? Fortunately national agencies have been tracking indicators well before this period. By the mid-1990s, after 25 years in operation, the US EPA had released an impressive list of gains (see Figure 8.1).

Figure 8.1 Changes in US environmental quality

1970 to mid-1990s:

- Average airborne particulates were reduced by 63%.
- SO_2 was reduced by 27%.
- NO_x increased only 7% (instead of a projected 28% if there had been no regulation).
- Volatile organics were reduced by 26%.
- CO down by 40%.
- Atmospheric lead reduced by 97%.
- Lake Eerie fishing industry returned.
- The Potomac River and 60% of all US surface waters were 'swimmable' by 1994.
- Dumping wastes in the sea 'virtually stopped'.
- Untreated waste dumping on land has 'largely stopped'.
- Over 5000 waste water and sewerage treatment plants had been constructed by 1994.
- Lead in petrol, asbestos, DDT, PCBs, CFCs were banned (average level of DDT in humans had dropped from 8 ppm in 1970 to 2 ppm in 1983).
- The number of contaminated sites identified under Superfund laws grew from 418 to 1207 between 1982 and 1990; sites cleaned up rose from 52 to 200 between 1989 and 1994, with 1700 emergency waste removal actions.

Source: This list compiled from the figures cited in Browner (1996a, b); US EPA (1994a, b); US Goverment (1992); Habitch (1990); Reilly (1990); Ettlin (1990).

Several sources within the UK report similar historical trends in environmental quality (Figure 8.2). The first report by the Royal Commission on Environmental Pollution (RCEP 1971) noted that the *Clean Air Act* had had a major impact on urban environmental quality with a 33 per cent drop in ground-level sulphur dioxide and 50 per cent fall in smoke for the period 1958–68 despite steady GDP growth.

These are similar historical results to the USA and, as was mentioned in Chapter 5, pollution inventories in both the UK and USA have indicated a downwards trend in the emission of 150 and 320 core toxic chemicals respectively. This was of the order of 40 per cent from the late 1980s to the late 1990s. Historical data for Australia is more difficult to find, as was noted in the OECD report, and the National Pollutant Inventory has only been running for a few years with increases in the number of reporting facilities and listed substances making trend comparisons difficult. There has been some data collected for the 1980s and 1990s and this is summarised in Figure 8.3.

Figure 8.2 Changes in UK environmental quality

- Particulate matter fell 90% between 1960 and 1990.
- Lead in air fell by 50% between 1985 and 1988.
- SO_2 fell 45% between 1970 and 1994.
- NO_x is estimated to fall 50% between 1980 and 2003.
- CO is estimated to fall 50% between 1980 and 2000.
- 90% of potable water was good or fair quality by 1990.
- Bathing waters meeting EU standards rose from 55% to 74% between 1987 and 1989.
- Dumping of waste at sea stopped in 1992.
- Thirteen local area action plans were completed by 2000.
- 40% of local authorities were working on adopting Local Agenda 21 by 1997.

Source: UK Government (1990, 1994, 2002); UK Local Government Management Board (1997).

Figure 8.3 Changes in Australian environmental quality

- Consumption of leaded petrol fell by 67% between 1984 and 1998.
- CO levels for the six largest cities were halved during 1979–99, with four of the six cities falling below the NEPM of 9 ppm.
- One-hour ground-level ozone concentrations for the six largest cities were cut by approximately 30%, with three cities falling below the NEPM of 10 ppm.
- Airborne lead in the six largest cities fell by approximately 80% during 1985–99; all are now below the NEPM of 0.5 ug/m^3.
- One-hour NO_2 concentrations in six major cities fell from a peak in 1986 to approximately two-thirds of that peak by 1999.
- 24-hour particulate matter (PM10) fell by approximately 10% for four major urban areas.
- Per capita waste recovery rose by more than 150% for the ACT and Victoria in the period 1993 to 2000.

Source: Estimates extracted from Environment Australia (2001b) charts.

Interpreting environmental quality indicators

On the surface, these results suggest that all the government responses (covered in Chapters 3 to 7) are starting to have some very positive impacts on the environmental performance of industry and are helping to reduce the level of risk from pollution. Further, the fact that these results have been achieved during substantial economic growth suggests that society may be starting to see the kind of decoupling that ecological modernisation predicts is possible with the deployment of more efficient production technology. But caution should be taken so as not to read too much into the meaning of these results for several reasons. First, the figures are based mainly on estimates and the actual magnitudes may be open to challenge. Second, the choice of indicators is highly selective and so can say little about the factors not monitored. Third, although there is a conjunction between the environmental interventions and a reduction in specific risks, there may be other factors at work that have contributed to this trend.

Consider the first point—the accuracy of the figures cited for the US EPA, for example. Although the general trends are agreed, the size of the claimed pollutant reductions are disputed and alternative estimates vary substantially (Rosenbaum 1991). Further, the creation, monitoring and enforcement of standards for a particular pollutant is by its very nature selective and runs the risk of neglecting other potentially damaging substances. This approach requires decisions to be made about acceptable risk, urgency and policing, all of which are influenced by discourses. While the US EPA's activities are probably responsible for the lion's share of these changes, it is possible that factors other than agency initiatives have led to improvements in environmental quality (Freeman 1990; US Department of Commerce 1985). The US steel industry reduced the number of older integrated mills and opened cleaner mini-mills in response to changes in technology and the world market. This contributed to significant reductions in air pollution that were not due to US EPA programs. Similar economic shifts have occurred in both the UK and Australia, with a general trend of heavily polluting industry shifting to developing countries.

In summary, method 2 indicates that selected pollutants are decreasing, while some aspects of the environment, such as water quality, are improving. It is this sort of data that the agencies like to use to illustrate their performance, but at least part of these improvements may be due to factors beyond their control. Measuring trends in environmental quality may therefore tend to overstate the effectiveness in government intervention. Taken together methods 1 and 2 offer a coarse range of adjustment on the analytical microscope. This sets the boundaries with method 1 understating effectiveness and method 2 slightly overstating it (which is why critics of government action will often use the first approach, while supporters and the regulators themselves take the second). What is needed now is to refine the focus of the analysis and look at why these changes were or were not achieved and, in particular, how difficult it was for them to be made. This is where the third method becomes useful.

Method 3: Enforcement and resistance

Evaluating the effectiveness of environmental interventions requires an understanding of the factors affecting their development, implementation and degree of success. The history of agency creation, regulation, intervention and policy making covered in Chapters 3 to 7 reveals that two related factors have been at work: the resistance to change and the political will to implement or enforce interventions. Both of these are products of competing discourses that influence how humans construct the nature of environmental risks, their cause and responses that are perceived to be appropriate. As pointed out in Chapter 2, neo-liberalism and the Promethean response can underpin substantial resistance and a lack of enforcement which will undermine the effectiveness of any intervention. Some variants of environmentalism, on the other hand, can help to reduce barriers to change and increase the political will to take action, hence increasing effectiveness. As has been demonstrated in the foregoing chapters, resistance has been generated by several different institutions: industry; competing state organisations; recalcitrant groups within environment agencies; and some elements within the broader community. This combined resistance has often sapped the political will of governments to intervene.

Industry has been one of the key players in efforts to address environmental risks (see Chapter 4). US steel manufacturers, for example, were able to delay and water down *Clean Air Act* regulations by falsely blaming job losses on the US EPA and dramatically overestimating the cost of compliance (OECD 1984, 1996a; NCEP 1995; Landy et al. 1994; US Department of Commerce 1985; Ford 1977; Crenson 1971). The automobile industry was also caught out in the 1970s when Japanese manufacturers pointed out that their vehicles were already meeting emission standards that the US industry had claimed were technologically impossible to achieve (Hoberg 1992). A large proportion of the money allocated to the Superfund program has been spent fighting legal challenges from industries that don't want to accept liability for contaminated sites (Rosenbaum 1991). In Australia, resistance from the manufacturing sector led to such liability being left out of the ESD working group recommendations, despite the objection of participating environmental groups (ESD Working Group—Manufacturing 1991). Other research[1] has uncovered resistance by industry to the introduction of pollution inventories, yet the predictions of dire economic consequences have not come true (see Chapter 5).

Beder (2002) recounts several strategies industry has adopted to resist regulations and influence the policy development process. Some firms set up 'front groups' that pose as concerned citizens in consultation forums but push the industry line. Others created the 'wise use movement' to promote brands of conservatism or neo-liberalism to counter the rising tide of environmentalism. There were lawsuits filed against activists in an attempt to silence their criticisms. Conservative think-tanks were established to conduct research that stressed the costs of regulation and questioned the seriousness of environmental risks. Several public relations strategies were developed to soften the image of industry and win over moderate environmentalists (Beder 2002).

Resistance from within the state can also be a major stumbling block (see Chapters 3 and 4). The US EPA has fought an ongoing battle with the Office of Management and Budget (OMB) and sceptics within the Congress who believed environmental regulation was bad for the economy. It had to overcome stiff resistance and engage in economic arguments via cost–benefit analyses to implement bans on lead in petrol and the use of asbestos (Percival 1991; Fraas 1991). A congressional inquiry found that the OMB had even been deliberately leaking proposed regulations to industry in order to help generate arguments against their implementation (US House of Representative Committee on Energy and Commerce 1984). In Australia, tensions between the different levels of government led Western Australia temporarily to pull out of the new national environmental protection system during its formative years (West Australian Government 1994). In the UK the Thatcher government's brand of neo-liberalism resulted in environmental organisations being sidelined in the policy-making processes of the early 1980s (Dryzek et al. 2003). Beder (2002) suggests that at least part of the problem stems from the close links between industry and key politicians in many industrialised countries that encourage some to support industry resistance.

Resistance can even come from inside an environment agency (see Chapter 4). When the US EPA, for example, was created in 1970 the pesticide regulation unit was transferred directly from the Department of Agriculture (Hoberg 1992). This group saw their role as assisting farmers with advice in how to use pesticides and they resisted moves to restrict or ban products like DDT and fought with the Office of General Council (Williams 1993; Lazarus 1991). This internal dissent added to the external industry resistance and made effective responses to risks difficult.

The political will to create and enforce interventions is very much affected by the resistance to change from all these sources (Beder 2002). The USA, UK and Australia have gone through phases where the government, environment agency or both have been extremely reluctant to take action. As was pointed out in Chapter 3, even President Nixon, who established the US EPA, was reluctant to give it more comprehensive environmental powers and actively withheld funds for specific projects. Enforcement actions during the Reagan administration fell dramatically and eventually both the head of the US EPA and Superfund were forced to resign over the lack of enforcement and program spending (Landy et al. 1994; Fraas 1991; Percival 1991; Lazarus 1991; Johnson 1991; Schrecker 1990; Portney 1990; Amy 1990; Burford & Greenya 1986; Dallek 1984). The current US and Australian administrations have also demonstrated a lack of political will to take tough action on climate change with both refusing to ratify the Kyoto Protocol (Beder 2002). Even the UK government was slow in addressing environmental risks and often had to be prompted by EU directives, particularly during the 1970s and early 1980s (Dryzek et al. 2003; Hawke 2002).

Method 3, using case studies to gauge resistance to change, is a favourite of social scientists studying the effect of institutions on society. Pluralist scholars are particularly fond of this approach because it allows them to highlight cases where small pressure groups have defeated large firms in some contested issues. Although the pluralist model is overly simplistic (as indicated in the introduction to this volume), the fact that even large transnational firms do not always get what they want suggests that their power over policy making is not absolute (Eckersley 2004; Dryzek et al. 2003; McEachern 1991). This suggests that state institutions do have at least some room to manoeuvre in the area of environmental governance, particularly if they are motivated by the constant pressure of the green movement.

By putting these results together, a clearer picture of the effectiveness of government responses to environmental risk emerges. Method 1 indicated that the rather ambitious goals of many agencies, regulations, programs and policies have at best only partially been met. Method 2 suggested that some patchy progress has been made with regards to selected aspects of environmental quality. Finally, method 3 revealed that these gains have been achieved despite considerable resistance. All of this needs to be related back to the original theoretical framework developed in Chapter 2 in order to generate some context by which effectiveness can be understood.

Method 4: Redirecting the flow of resources

The first three methods have been used to criticise, support or explain state actions and comparing them enables the construction of a broad-brush view of the effectiveness of responses. A fourth method is possible that relates back to the nature of environmental risk and the governmentality of such institutions (as described in Chapter 2). It is also concordant with the reflexive history of environmental governance (covered in chapters 3 to 7).

Consider Foucault's insight that society is a dynamic web of shifting force relations with associated discourses that can clash, overlap or reinforce. Institutions, such as industry or state agencies, emerge when sets of discourses reinforce and begin to prevail over competing discourses. These institutions accumulate into more complex sets, such as the market or the state, which influence the trajectory of historical development, such as modernisation or globalisation. In much of the Western world, for example, Keynesian economics led to a rapid expansion of welfare state institutions from the 1930s. Perceived crises in the 1960s–1970s then encouraged a challenge from neo-liberalism which has since predominated public policy, leading to privatisation and deregulation of the economy. The history of attempts to respond to the growing perceptions of environmental risk has also been highly influenced by this change in prevailing governmentality. Note the shift in focus over the last two decades from regulations towards economic prompts, voluntary programs, information-based systems and consultative policy-making forums.

The purpose of industrial production, guided by the process of modernisation, is to utilise resources to create goods and services that enhance the quality of life. In the market place the aim is to perform this function in a way that will both make a profit for shareholders and satisfy consumer demand. As McEachern (1991) puts it, the purpose of industry is to take raw materials out of the environment and put waste back (see also Doyle & McEachern 2000). The problem, as Beck (1992, 1994) has highlighted, is that the negative side effects of this process have now grown to the point where they threaten the very environment on which humanity depends. In response, governments have created new environmental institutions (agencies, laws, programs and policies). The aim is not to shut down industry but to exert some power over it in order to limit collateral damage and steer it into a more sustainable form.

In the model derived in Chapter 2, state environment institutions try to redirect the flow of resources through the web of relations/discourses that make up a society. Resources are anything that can be utilised by humans and can be divided into four main groups: raw materials, money, labour and knowledge. Knowledge is defined as information derived from sensory data that is causally connected to the external world and has been interpreted through discourses. Perceived interests emerge from both external institutional imperatives created by the shape of the web and internal discourses. At the individual level, power is experienced as the pull and push of the web of personal relations/discourses in which people are enmeshed. Applying this to assessing the effectiveness of state interventions requires some indication that the flow of natural resources, money, labour or knowledge has been redirected through society by an environmental institution.

In terms of raw materials, analytical methods 1 and 2 demonstrate that there has been some change in the flow of raw material waste back into the environment, a point confirmed by pollution inventories (Chapter 5). The imposition of Environmental Impact Assessment procedures, the establishment of conservation areas and the promotion of cleaner production methods have also had some impact on the way new industrial developments take raw materials out of the environment. Together, these constitute an alteration in the flow of raw materials through industrial institutions and therefore constitute evidence of an effective exercise of institutional power. The problem of industry resistance and an inconsistent political will, discussed in method 2, suggests that this power is uneven in its strength, but still appears to have a significant effect on raw material resource flows.

In terms of money, Table 8.3 indicates that the UK, USA and Australia have redirected part of their GDP into pollution abatement and environment protection. Australia is perhaps the least successful by this relative measure, with only 0.8 per cent compared to 1.0 per cent for the UK and 1.6 per cent for the USA (OECD Working Party on Environmental Performance 2000). Since the creation of all the interventions covered in Chapters 3 to 7, expenditure on pollution abatement measures by US industry rose from US$26 billion in 1972 to over US$160 billion in 1994 (OECD Working Party on Environmental Performance 2000; NAPA 1995; US EPA 1994a; Underwood 1993; Richman 1992; Rosenbaum 1991; Fraas 1991). The fact that this has happened despite the resistance from industry and other parts of the state suggests that this is a net measure of success. Further, the apparent reluctance of US state and local authorities to intervene suggests that national initiatives have played a key role in inducing this expenditure (Anderson & Howitt 1995; Ruckelshaus 1993; Petulla 1987). In fact the US EPA's budget averaged 13 per cent of the total of all money spent on the environment by all three levels of government (US EPA 1990). A similar reluctance to intervene has been demonstrated by various levels of government in the UK and Australia (Dryzek et al. 2003; Hawke 2002; Briody & Prenzler 1998; Toyne 1994).

It should also be noted that the increased expenditure by industry on the environment has been achieved without having a negative impact on overall employment levels and economic growth, despite the claims of neo-liberal critics (Goodstein 1999; OECD 1984, 1996a; NCEP 1995; US Department of Commerce 1985). As was acknowledged in Chapter 4, however, not all interventions have led to the most efficient economic outcome and the burdens have been unevenly distributed (Moran 1995; Thompson 1995; Howard 1994). In general the cost of compliance imposed on individual firms is lower than the economic costs imposed on the community by the environmental damage done (Eckersley 1995; Jacobs 1995; Kinrade 1995). It is also apparent that industry tends to overstate the costs of environmental regulation and understate its benefits (Beder 2002; Landy et al. 1995).

A notable redeployment of labour to the pollution abatement and environment protection sector has occurred in all developed countries, while employment in some older sectors of the economy has declined (Goodstein 1999; OECD 1984, 1996a; NCEP 1995; US Department of Commerce 1985). In the USA, for example, it has been estimated that 38 899 jobs were lost due to environmental regulation from 1970 to 1984, but 105 000 created by the water treatment construction program and a further 43 900 in pollution equipment industries in 1983 alone (OECD 1984). It was even calculated in 1995 that environmental regulations had actually saved industry money in reduced raw material wastage, created 68 000–90 000 jobs and added about US$3.7 billion to GDP (NCEP 1995). Efficiency gains from cleaner production, improved employment opportunities and increased competitiveness have been highlighted in case studies from both the developed and the developing world (Suzuki & Dressel 2002; AtKisson 1999; Hawken et al. 1999). This suggests that more jobs have been created by the stimulus provided to the economy by environmental regulation that led to the development of pollution abatement industries than have been lost due to the extra costs imposed on polluting firms.

The final element in this model of the redirection of resources should be knowledge. This is the most difficult factor to assess. As indicated in Chapter 5, Environmental Impact Assessment procedures and online pollution inventories have forced firms to provide information about their activities that they were previously reluctant to release. These programs redirect information to the community and business executives as well as construct an external incentive for change through public or consumer pressure and the corporate awareness of waste. Despite the limitations of such interventions they have been successful in putting pressure on industry to reduce its use and emission of toxic substances. Both the US Toxics Release Inventory and the UK Pollution Inventory indicate a reduction of more than 40 per cent in reported releases (see Chapter 5).

In summary, method 4 suggests that changes actions by government, such as creating new environment agencies, laws, programs and policies, have been able to redirect the flow of resources (raw materials, money, labour and knowledge). The net impact, however, has been patchy and relatively small in comparison to the overall size of the economy.

Conclusions

The assessment of the effectiveness of government environmental interventions is very difficult and heavily influenced by the choice of method.

Overall it is reasonable to suggest that the state has not done as badly as neo-liberal critics and method 1 (meeting the goals set) suggest, nor has it done as well as the agencies and method 2 (selected indicators) imply. The somewhat patchy gains that have been made were achieved despite concerted resistance from industry and parts of the state (method 3) and considerable resources have been redirected (method 4). These, however, constitute a small part of a much larger economy. No country has achieved sustainable development nor have they succeeded in making their industry sustainable.

CHAPTER 9

Has industry changed the way it operates?

Introduction

All the state interventions discussed so far have been directed at exerting some influence on industry to make it more sustainable, but as was pointed out in the introduction to this book, the relationship between industry and the state is complex. There are both visible contests and hidden dimensions to the power relations that have supported or challenged these institutions and their responses to environmental risks. Further, the rise of the environment movement has generated a three-way tussle between neo-liberalism, administrative rationalism and environmentalism. These power struggles have been played out in the history of successes and failures in environmental governance recounted in the preceding chapters. This chapter now turns attention to how industry has responded.

While every firm has responded differently to environmental risk and increased government intervention, McEachern (1991) suggests that these responses can be grouped into three broad categories (see also Doyle & McEachern 2000):

1 those firms that rejected the seriousness of the risk or the need for change;
2 those firms that sought to accommodate the rising tide of concern and regulation with modest reforms; and

3 those firms that attempted to create genuinely sustainable industries independently of the actions taken by the state.

Each is dealt with in turn in the sections that follow. The first section considers the neo-liberal rejection of the seriousness of environmental risk (Dryzek 1997). This has strong links to the kinds of barriers to change that were discussed in previous chapters. The second section looks at the way some firms have attempted to accommodate environmentalism by adopting the weaker version of ecological modernisation to varying degrees. The third section then considers how a few industries have adopted an environmental approach that goes beyond simply responding to the prompts of state intervention or community activism and is built on the stronger version of ecological modernisation. The final section considers whether the changes in industry behaviour have been enough to provide an adequate basis for responses to environmental risk.

Rejecting environmental risk

In rejecting the need for environmental intervention, industries may adopt a number of, often inconsistent, strategies. The first is usually to deny the reality of an environmental risk (the 'Promethean response'; Dryzek 1997). When this position becomes difficult to sustain in the face of mounting evidence to the contrary, there is often a switch to more subtle neo-liberal stances, particularly in the face of scientific debate regarding the level of risk. One argument often used is that no action should be taken until incontrovertible scientific proof is found because otherwise costs might be needlessly imposed on firms, or it might be argued that there is no viable alternative. Another strategy is to admit that a problem exists, but claim it is only minor and that firms need to keep operating to earn the money that could fund remedial action or develop better technology. Some opponents take this one step further and admit that a risk is serious but argue that either the cost of change is far too high and it would be cheaper simply to adapt to the environmental impacts, or that humanity will eventually develop technology that will fix the problem (Beder 2002; Doyle & McEachern 2000; DiLorenzo 1993; Hoberg 1992; McEachern 1991).

All these strategies were deployed with regards to climate change and they appear in various guises in Lomborg's *Sceptical Environmentalist* (discussed in Chapter 1). This was evident with the US steel industry overestimating the cost of implementing the *Clean Air Act*. It was also apparent with the reluctance of Australian industry to accept the National Pollutant Inventory. The overall aim is to play down the risks and shore up the power of industry over government. In the process, the industries further undermine the faith of the community in the ability of mainstream institutions to address environmental risk. This means that neo-liberal rejection is further evidence of reflexive modernisation at work because it is apparent that these productive institutions find it difficult to acknowledge and respond effectively to the risks they have created.

Moving away from rejection

On the bright side, some firms do not remain stuck in rejection and later move on to address environmental concerns despite their initial recalcitrance. One good example is 3M, which fought hard to stop the introduction of the US Toxics Release Inventory. Once the firm was forced to conduct an audit of its operations, however, the executive was shocked by how much raw material was being wasted in inefficient plant processes. They began a Pollution Prevention Pays program that continues to this day and has substantially reduced their pollution per tonne of product. Many of the changes implemented were quite simple, such as improving batch monitoring to catch problems before they resulted in spoilage or switching to water-based adhesives to replace petrochemical solvents (Gottlieb et al. 1995; Porter & van der Linde 1995). But not all changes are so easy to make and in 2002 the company announced that it would stop making Scotchguard because it couldn't change the product formulation or process to make them less environmentally damaging (Fieweger 2000).

Such positive stories are encouraging, but they need to be viewed with some caution (Underwood 1993). Firms may begin a process of improvement but backslide years later. Also, despite reducing its waste per tonne of product, 3M grew so rapidly that it still produced more pollution overall (Athanasiou 1996). If society is to achieve ecological modernisation, the efficiency gains need to outstrip the growth in production. Finally, even the new 3M is still a long way from being sustainable and still relies heavily on non-renewable resources and a greenhouse-gas-intensive energy supply. The ability of the firm to move away from the position of rejection, however, is still a very positive sign and gives some hope for powerful firms that still remain recalcitrant.

Barriers to change

Several studies of industry in the USA, UK and Australia over the last dozen years have touched on the barriers that discourage industry from taking up cleaner production, pollution prevention programs, best practice or other initiatives based on the range of ideas from various versions of ecological modernisation. (See, for example, Eckersley 1995, 2004; Dryzek et al. 2003; Suzuki & Dressel 2002; Beder 2002; Van Berkel 2000; AtKisson 1999; Clayton et al. 1999; Goldfarb 1999; Weale 1998; NCEP 1995; AMC 1994; Cebon 1993; UK Department of Trade and Industry 1991). Such studies offer some insight into the institutional context that encourages rejection among some firms that seek to subordinate the environment movement, while shoring up their position of power over government. While each study has focused on different aspects of the issue, there are some common themes that emerge which can be grouped into two categories: factors external to the firm and factors internal to the firm.

External factors include regulation, economics and information (the three modes of intervention adopted by the state, as discussed in Chapters 4 and 5), as well as the availability of cleaner technology. Regulatory barriers to change include: regimes that do not encourage firms to go beyond compliance, that do not provide a constant long-term direction for change or are not backed up with a consistent political will of enforcement. In short if the state is not persistent, consistent and committed to change, industry sees no need for investing in new technology. Economics, on the other hand, is a double-edged sword. If a firm is operating in a sector with low profit margins or if the perceived economic gains of change are low, improvement in environmental performance is unlikely. A crisis, however, can provide a catalyst for change if the firm sees its future threatened by a do nothing response. Information plays a role in a number of ways. If there is little awareness of cleaner production options among executives, or if there is no risk to the public reputation of the firm from poor performance, change is unlikely. Finally, change will be impeded if cleaner technology is not readily available, if there are some doubts over its reliability or if there is a shortage of skilled labour able to install, operate and maintain new equipment.

Internal factors include the institutional structure, corporate culture and capacity for learning inherent within a firm. Firms that have a 'top-down' hierarchical decision-making structure tend to be more resistant to change than those that adopt some form of industrial democracy. Consulting a workforce with a hands-on knowledge of the production process allows for the harnessing of local knowledge and gives employees some sense of ownership of the change. Overall, the executive corporate culture is of paramount importance. A commitment to consult and innovate is more likely to lead to change than more insular or anti-change attitudes. Finally, a capacity for the institution to learn by investing in research, development and deployment of new technology will increase the uptake of cleaner production.

The author's experience as an industrial chemist and technical manager in the manufacturing sector bears out the findings of these studies. Time and again individuals were met who were uncomfortable with the behaviour of the firm they were working for but were forced to override their concerns by the role the institutional structure forced upon them. Some got frustrated at having their proposals for improvement rejected or deferred, while others found ways to make small modifications that led to waste reduction. In another case, a one-day professional training seminar[1] on the National Pollutant Inventory and cleaner production was run in conjunction with the Queensland Environmental Protection Agency and a local engineering consulting firm. As with the 3M example, at first the industry managers and technicians present appeared to be quite hostile to the imposition of the inventory, but by the end of the day many had warmed to the idea of using it to identify and eliminate waste.

Knowledge is a key resource in the discourses adopted by industry, government and the community. If industries know that there are alternatives and that cleaner production can increase profits while reducing waste, they will be more likely to change. If governments know that environmental regulations do not cause job losses, but merely shift resources between different sectors of the economy and may even stimulate the growth of new industries, they will be less reluctant to intervene. If the community is aware of the risks to their health and future, they will be more likely to demand improvements. Many of the firms that started by rejecting environmental risks have since moved towards a more accommodating position, but it is clear that a baseline of regulation is necessary to keep the recalcitrant industries from backsliding into a high-polluting position.

Accommodating environmental concern

Firms that attempt to accommodate concerns about environmental risks come in a number of different shapes and sizes. What separates them from rejection is that they are more willing to acknowledge publicly that environmental risks exist, although a number of caveats are attached to this admission (Doyle & McEachern 2000; McEachern 1991). First, it is assumed that the seriousness of these risks has been overstated, a point that is in accord with the views of Lomborg (2001). Under accommodation, the risks do not threaten the survival of the planet but simply pose another set of issues that can be adequately addressed with minor changes to the normal process of established decision-making procedures. Second, it is argued that the most appropriate response is improved management of resources by industry. If firms are more careful about the way they produce things, it is assumed that the problems will be solved. Third, it is argued that strict government regulation is no longer needed because industry has now recognised the problem and is working on solutions. Further, as the main developer and user of productive technology, it is assumed that industry is in a better position to solve the problems. Finally, the role that governments are allocated is one of facilitation. They are there simply to help clean up past mistakes, assist industry to develop better technology and explain to the public why there's no need to worry.

This accommodation is underpinned by the weaker version of ecological modernisation that emerged in the 1980s in Western Europe (see Chapter 2; Weale 1998; Dryzek 1997; Christoff 1996). It has manifest itself in institutional reforms such as the adoption of environmental management systems. Many European firms, for example, have adopted the Eco-Management and Audit Scheme (EMAS), some Australian industries took up Best Practice Environmental Management (BPEM) and firms in the USA have created Pollution Prevention Pays (PPP) programs. Internationally, a new environmental management regime has emerged from the International Standards Organisation 14 000 series (ISO 14000) which enables firms to gain accreditation for their commitment to monitor and continuously improve their environmental performance.

On the positive side, accommodation and the change of management practices that it entails can lead to significant improvements in environmental quality. This has obviously contributed to the improvements in urban environmental quality and reductions in pollution (as outlined in Chapter 8). The US EPA, UK Environment Agency and Environment Australia have even released positive case studies on their websites in which the agencies have used their expertise to help individual firms adopt cleaner production practices. These agencies have also created economic incentives through grants, tax breaks and pollution charges to encourage such changes in other firms (see Chapter 4).

On the negative side, some firms have adopted the rhetoric of accommodation, but have done little to change their actual practices or impacts. Shell, for example, was praised for adopting sustainable development as a key goal in the mid-1990s and the senior executive even went so far as to say that in the long term the firm would have to get out of fossil fuels and into renewable energy. At the same time, however, their operations in Nigeria were being heavily criticised for their impacts on the ecology and communities of the Niger delta. The situation was so bad that the company's senior environmental engineer resigned and blew the whistle on what was happening. This apparent contradiction has led to the questioning of the company's commitment to sustainable development (Yearley & Forrester 2000; Howes 1997; Catma Films 1994).

Greenwashing

Similar cases where a firm's actions don't meet its rhetoric have led critics to coin the term 'greenwashing' (Beder 2002; Athanasiou 1996). This is where firms see an opportunity to use environmental concern as a marketing tool but fail to make substantial changes to their operations to meet their market claims. A classic example is a firm in Australia which released a new range of cleaning products under an environmentally friendly name, in green bottles and with silhouettes of dolphins on the label. The products were in fact the same as they had always made, only the packaging and marketing had changed. One claim, for example, was that the dishwashing liquid was environmentally friendly because it contained no phosphate. Phosphates can wash into waterways, act as a fertiliser and lead to algal blooms that reduce the oxygen content of the water and kill other aquatic life (a process called eutrophication). This issue had been widely publicised at the time, hence the marketing strategy. The problem is that phosphates are not normally used in dishwashing liquids, so this was no better than any other product. (The strategy failed and the brand name was taken over by a different firm in the 1990s that actually did improve its formulation.) Such actions, however, are often exposed and lead to a general cynicism among consumers, even those who want to adopt green purchasing strategies to encourage firms to change.

Accommodation is therefore a double-edged sword. While it can lead to improvements, the risk of greenwashing is high. When dubious practices are exposed, both the individual firm and general reputation of industry suffer, adding to the reflexive sub-politics of groups that are disaffected with the mainstream institutions of power. Firms that might adopt improvements, however, would be more likely to respond to economic prompts provided by governments, but is it possible for industry to be sustainable?

Environmental industry as an agent of change

When McEachern (1991) first proposed the three types of industry responses he noted that the environmental category was almost empty. More than a decade on, the number of firms in this group remains very small. Environmental industries accept that environmental risks are serious and include social responsibility as a core principle. This means that they go beyond a narrow focus on technical solutions at the weaker end of the ecological modernisation spectrum (Mol & Spaargaren 2000; Dryzek 1997; Christoff 1996) to incorporate wider internal institutional change. Such firms:

- are committed to the sustainable use of renewable resources, so that the firm can continue to operate in the long term;
- avoid hazardous chemicals or animal testing;
- seek to eliminate, reduce, reuse or recycle waste;
- attempt to design genuinely green products and processes;
- undertake to be honest in the way they advertise their products and practices;
- aim to treat their employees fairly in terms of working conditions, health and safety and remuneration;
- establish a less hierarchical decision-making structure to provide a higher level of internal industrial democracy; and
- adopt a partnership approach to local communities and their organisations.

These features break down some of the barriers to change that are prevalent in firms that reject environmental risk. Unlike the accommodation, they adopt a new institutional structure rather than attempting to adopt slightly different management practices within a pre-set hierarchy. This makes the adoption of greenwashing strategies less likely.

Case study: The Body Shop

One of the best examples of an industry of this kind to date has been The Body Shop, started by Anita Roddick in the 1970s as a single shop selling toiletries. Products were made from plant extracts, were not tested on animals and were sold in plastic bottles that were refilled or recycled. The business expanded rapidly and by the end of the 1980s the company had been floated on the stock exchange with a franchise network of stores that extended around the world. Suppliers of raw materials were often community cooperatives in developing countries that were paid a fair return and controlled their own production. Advertising was kept to a minimum but the company did support campaigns for human rights and the environment (Suzuki & Dressel 2002; Roddick 1991, 2000; Doyle & McEachern 2000; McEachern 1991). Although the products were more expensive, the growth in environmental concern and green consumerism enabled the business to thrive.

It was not all plain sailing and some problems did emerge (Beder 2002). Roddick (2000) herself admits that there was at least one situation where one of the indigenous South American communities that agreed to supply the company suffered some serious negative social impacts. The firm also had difficulty in breaking into the US market and suffered some economic losses during the 1990s. In recent years Roddick lost control of the company and has criticised it for moving away from her original principles (Suzuki & Dressel 2002; Cropley 2001). Further, there is some question as to whether all the products produced are really necessary, whether the use of packaging like disposable shrink-wrap is sustainable and whether transporting the products and ingredients over long distances around the world is a good idea. With these provisos in mind, over the last three decades The Body Shop has still provided one of the best examples of an environmental industry, although many other firms have also transformed themselves (see, for example, Suzuki & Dressel 2002; AtKisson 1999; Hawken et al. 1999).

Examples such as these are the embodiment of the stronger version of ecological modernisation and fit the broader notion of sustainable development which includes technical, economic, social, political and ecological dimensions. These examples also suggest that it is possible for industry to move beyond the first phase of reflexive modernisation (i.e. the initial inability to address environmental risk) and towards some of the prescriptions for transforming society outlined by Beck and Giddens. If all industries operated like The Body Shop, the environmental risks generated and the need for regulation would be greatly reduced. The free flow of knowledge about the impacts of decisions and alternative technologies, however, will remain something that governments could certainly assist. Perhaps, just as many firms have moved from rejection to accommodation over the last two decades, so the transition may continue and the number of environmental firms may eventually become the largest group.

From reflexive to ecological modernisation

These three responses of industry yet again demonstrate the power of discourse in environmental governance and the difficulty that nineteenth-century institutions of power have in addressing risks when modernisation becomes reflexive. The neo-liberalism that underpins rejection not only puts the entire planet at risk, it is actually bad for the firms operating under its influence. Industries of rejection construct environmental risk as a threat to profitability, whereas the alternative of ecological modernisation would allow them to see it as an opportunity for increased efficiency. As a result the firm misses opportunities to cut costs, fails to improve its public relations and stays with older, more polluting practices that are in decline instead of diversifying its investments into new growth areas. If rejection prevails among a senior executive their decisions will work against the material interests of the firm in the global market place.

Firms that have moved to the position of accommodation, apart from those that have simply adopted a strategy of 'greenwashing', have generally adopted weaker versions of ecological modernisation via some environmental management system. Environmental risk and increased governance are constructed as a business opportunity to capture a new market, or a challenge to find improvements in production efficiency. There is a strong focus on the development of better technology and the economic benefits of efficiency gain (Dryzek 1997; Christoff 1996). This approach clearly has benefits for the environment, in terms of reduced pollution, and for the firm, by lowering production costs. It tends, however, to work within established business practices, taking a technocratic and managerial approach, rather than opening up the firm to more flexible or democratic control.

The example of 3M previously cited is a case in point. There are also many other examples, such as Interface carpet manufacturers in the USA, which eliminated all toxic chemicals, redesigned their product to enable recycling and offered a floor covering service where they would supply, maintain, replace and recycle carpet squares for their customers (AtKisson 1999). Another example is Collins Pine, which has sustainably harvested timber from the same tract of forest for 150 years by using selective logging and good land management techniques (Suzuki & Dressel 2002). The key to all three of these cases is the mindset of the executives who control the firm.

Environmental firms take one step further and move into the strong version of ecological modernisation. They move beyond the focus on technology and simple economics, to apply the principles of ecology to their institutional structure and operating routines. This gives them a more democratic and deliberative structure, where workers, suppliers, customers and the broader community are treated as partners to be consulted in the venture (Dryzek 1997; Christoff 1996). Again, The Body Shop is one of the best examples and it has been dealt with in some detail above.

Both the strong and weak versions of ecological modernisation are certainly an improvement on neo-liberal rejection in terms of the risk management strategy developed in Chapter 2. They still, however, leave the main institutions of reflexive modernisation largely intact, although they do encourage them along a more sustainable development trajectory. They do not, for example, address the issue of mass poverty nor do they seek to challenge the power of industry over government and its ability to create a bounded democracy.

Is it enough?

Overall it does appear that industry has been improving its environmental performance, although the change is very patchy and has been due in large part to prompting by the environment movement and government. The question still remains as to whether this is enough to address adequately the kinds of environmental risks outlined in Chapter 1. Will it allow society to avoid incidents like Bhopal or ongoing problems like climate change? Will it prevent unexpected risks like the depletion of the ozone layer due to seemingly innocuous products like CFCs? The answers will depend on which of the three discourses prevail.

If the majority of firms stick with rejection, humanity faces a problematic future given the seriousness of environmental risks that have been generated by their past practices. This would lock society into using up non-renewable resources at an ever-increasing rate, increasing levels of pollution, higher risks from the use and release of hazardous chemicals and continued high levels of resource waste in disposable products and packaging. It would also entail a risk management strategy that refuses to take action until there is unequivocal scientific certainty about the seriousness of ongoing environmental risks like climate change, land and water degradation and the loss of biodiversity. If most firms move to accommodate environmental concerns, there should be at least a patchy improvement in environmental quality of the kind noted in Chapter 8. This would attenuate to some extent, but not solve, the risks outlined above. The result would be a reduction in the number of incidents and more time to develop better responses.

If most firms go environmental society might actually get industry on to a sustainable development trajectory. This would be modelled on the 'closed loop' production model discussed in Chapters 6 and 7 and would give rise to the kinds of industries discussed in the previous section. But the state will have to continue to enforce regulations to bring rejecting industries up to an acceptable standard, create economic prompts to encourage accommodating firms to do better and provide essential knowledge to both industry and the community. It will also be necessary for community groups to continue to act as watchdogs to prevent firms backsliding. On top of this, making production sustainable does not necessarily improve the distribution of goods or services and humans may still face the risks posed by poverty, the threat of violence, discrimination, restricted access to health care, stunted educational opportunities and a failing social infrastructure. In the past the market has failed to provide these things so the state and community groups have had to step in to provide such public goods. This will continue to be the case even under the strong version of ecological modernisation and the environmental firms it would create.

Conclusions

Industry is the main productive interface between society and the environment; it is the immediate point where many of the risks are generated and it has the potential to play a major role in their solution. Up to the end of the 1970s most firms adopted neo-liberal rejection that denied or played down the significance of environmental risks. Since then, many have moved into accommodation, which has encouraged some to make improvements, while others have done little more than change their public relations and marketing strategies. A few firms, some independently of government interventions, have adopted a stronger version of ecological modernisation that has taken them close to the idea of a sustainable industry. The battle between these discourses will determine the collective ability to respond to environmental risks. Even if society achieves the most positive outcome, however, people will still need the state to provide public goods and community groups to act as watchdogs.

CONCLUSIONS

Greening democracy?

Thus far, with rough and all-unable pen,
Our bending author hath purs'd the story;
In little room confining mighty men,
Mangling by starts the full course of their glory.

William Shakespeare, *Henry V* (1599)

This book has been about change—understanding the historical changes of modernisation that delivered so many benefits but also created serious environmental risks; examining the recent changes made by governments in response to those risks; and considering further changes to put society on a more sustainable branch of development. Inevitably this has required some attempt to 'in little room confine mighty' issues and there is some risk of 'mangling by starts the full course of their glory'. The task was attempted using a comparative cross-section of selected case studies in three stages. First, it considered whether the planet really needed saving and why. Second, it reviewed how governments responded. Finally, it sought to discover whether this was enough. Throughout, the author 'with rough and all-unable pen' has attempted to demonstrate how this history of environmental governance bears the hallmarks of reflexive modernisation and the clash of discourses.

172

Does the planet need saving?

While there are many competing discourses on the nature and causes of environmental risks, it has been argued that there is evidence that modernisation has become reflexive (i.e. the historical process of modernising change is being undermined by its own success because of the spread of negative side effects). Although there are uncertainties, the bulk of the scientific evidence suggests that industrial development has contributed to serious environmental incidents and ongoing problems, with significant social, economic and political impacts. Even if there are sceptics, it is still not a good risk management strategy to ignore warnings of even greater problems emerging. Dissatisfaction with the responses of the state and industry has generated a sub-politics of environmentalism that is constantly challenging the prevailing administrative rationalism and neo-liberalism. All this is evidence of reflexive modernisation and suggests that the planet does indeed need saving.

What has government done?

One of the key things to consider in understanding how government has responded is the way discourses shape whether environmental risks are acknowledged or ignored, how they are understood or constructed and how the institutional response is bounded or directed. So far governments have acted within the space created by the institutions inherited from the nineteenth century, yet they are trying to address twentieth- and now twenty-first-century risks. They have established new organisations, passed new laws and regulations, developed economic prompts, deployed new knowledge-based programs and created new policy goals. While these actions have been piecemeal, the emerging policy goal of sustainable development has the potential to coordinate and integrate efforts to better effect, but attempts at implementation have often been impeded by the fragmented and contradictory nature of the mainstream institutions of power (i.e. industry and the state). As a consequence, governments have made only a patchy start in addressing environmental risks.

Has it worked?

The effectiveness of environmental governance should be indicated by the achievement of set goals, improvements in specific environmental indicators, the ability to enforce decisions and overcome resistance to change and the redirection of resources through society and the environment. There has been a reduction in selected urban air pollutants, a few major bodies of water have been cleaned up, some contaminated land has been rehabilitated and several conservation areas have been established. Overall, however, the world is still a long way from sustainable development or ecological and social well-being. Non-renewable resources are being used at an increasing rate, biodiversity is still being lost, hazardous chemicals are still being released, climate is being altered, too many people are living in poverty and too many are being killed or injured by environmental incidents. Further, many environmental goals have not been achieved while pockets of resistance continue to operate within industry and the state. Some progress has been made, but something more is needed.

In a nutshell

The argument is twofold. First, that humanity needs to take action, even though knowledge is imperfect. Second, the risks faced are structural in nature—having been generated by a path of industrial development gone astray. At the very least the state must consistently intervene using a range of regulatory and economic tools to make industry sustainable. Actions to date are necessary but not sufficient, particularly if the majority of firms continue to reject the seriousness of environmental risks. This is why the prompt of the environment movement is still necessary to apply continuous pressure for improvement. Overall, it has become apparent that knowledge is playing an increasingly important role for all political actors and institutions. If government is to save the planet, it will have to be restructured to overcome the prevailing administrative rationalism of the state and become more receptive to discourses developed by the sub-politics of various social and environmental movements. Further, to succeed, it will need to have the cooperation of an ecologically modern industry and an empowered community.

Where to from here?

So what might this new kind of government look like? Several models of ecological democracy, a green state and environmental business have been proposed (Eckersley 1995, 2004; Dryzek et al. 2003; Dryzek 1987, 1990, 1992, 1995, 1997; AtKisson 1999; Hawken et al. 1999; Gore 1992; Partridge 1987). Usually these propose opening up the state and business to the community through establishing bodies for consultation and decision making within each institution (like multiple, mini-versions of the sustainable development groups convened in the USA, UK and Australia). Sometimes it is proposed that these include people elected to represent future generations or other species. Often it involves challenging the prevailing economically rational discourses with ecologically rational ones. These proposals often mesh quite well with the stronger versions of ecological and reflexive modernisation (Mol & Spaargaren 2000; Giddens 1998b; Weale 1998; Hajer 1995; Christoff 1996). More recently, there have been proposals that increased use of the Internet may lead to more community empowerment, information and networking which may assist in the transformation of governance (Howes 2002b; Hewitt 1998). All these changes would help to create political, economic and social feedback loops that could help warn of potential hazards and push society towards sustainable development.

'Reasons to be cheerful'[1]

Is such an institutional transformation possible? The answer from recent history in other areas of politics is definitely yes. Consider the situation in the mid-1980s after Gorbachev had taken control of the USSR. At this time the Cold War appeared to have no end in sight, with many people growing up under the threat of a nuclear holocaust. US President Reagan had even upped the ante with his proposal for a missile defence shield. Gorbachev made a range of offers on restricting nuclear weapons and began a modest set of domestic political reforms (called *Glasnost* and *Perestroika*). These reforms unexpectedly combined with underlying anti-Soviet discourses that had remained hidden among the population and eventually rose to overthrow USSR institutions. The result was the 1989 revolution which gave rise to a set of newly independent democratic states. No one foresaw this collapse because no one expected that the entrenched socialist government elite would be prepared to give up their power. While there are still considerable problems with the ensuing restructuring, the change happened very quickly. Perhaps the same is true for the creation of a green democracy. It is hard to see why people who benefit most from activities that generate environmental risk and hold considerable power would be prepared to allow change, but the USSR case demonstrates that this can happen. Modest reforms already implemented may be the environmental equivalent of *Glasnost* and *Perestroika*, and might already be catalysing the transformation to come.

There are many other cases from recent history which can give some hope for positive change. The fact that governments didn't destroy the planet with a nuclear war despite 40 years of political brinkmanship is a good sign. The fact that many dictatorships, both right and left, have fallen and race-based systems such Apartheid have been abandoned is also positive. With regards to the environment, the fact that effective action was eventually taken on ozone-depleting substances, despite industry resistance and inadequate first steps, is obviously a positive sign. Further, there are now so many people so concerned about environmental risks, mobilised in a network of groups around the globe, that it has become increasingly difficult for decision makers to get away with damage as they did in the past. Even some formerly recalcitrant industry leaders are starting to talk about the risks seriously.

Reflexive modernisation suggests that global problems stem from the tendency to ignore the negative side effects of industrialisation and treat them as localised or isolated. This has led to the systematic risks that are now faced. Had the problems of pollution and wastage of resources been dealt with before spreading industrial production around the globe, they would not threaten the survival of the planet. Environmental scientists and the green movement have provided a small nagging voice which might help avoid future risks. At the very least society should internalise the negative environmental and social externalities into microeconomic and macroeconomic accounting systems. Imagine if someone within Union Carbide or Shell Nigeria had raised concerns about the impact of operations and been listened to by the senior executive—thousands of people could have been saved and large parts of the environment spared degradation. Further, the firms themselves would not have suffered economically from the ensuing consumer backlash. In short, by ignoring the small risks larger ones were created.

So can government save the planet?

A pessimist may look at this history of environmental governance and point to all the failures as an indicator of the inability to address risks. An optimist would see the failures as something to learn from and draw heart from the successes. While past actions have bought more time, society still operates within the context of a democracy bounded by powerful entrenched interests that reject the seriousness of the problems. This makes comprehensive and effective responses difficult. Switching to a more sustainable branch of development will require an ecologically modern industrial sector, a green economy and an ecological democracy. The first tentative steps have been taken towards this transformation, but a more rapid uptake of environmental business practices, a major restructuring of the state, an expanded watchdog role for empowered environmental or community groups and the broader support of the public is needed in order to achieve sustainable development. A transformed government that can constructively engage with an ecologically modern market and a revitalised civil society could indeed save the planet.

Notes from chapters

Introduction

1   US and UK elections are dominated by single-member electorates (i.e. one person is elected to represent a constituency) where whoever receives the most votes wins the seat, even if they don't have 50 per cent of the support. This system has some significant consequences. First, the more candidates that run, the more the vote is divided so that fewer votes are available for the leading candidates. If two candidates enter the race from the same side of politics, their vote will be split and their main rival from the other side would win. For example, if a poll attracts 40 per cent left-of-centre voters and 30 per cent right-of-centre voters, a single left-of-centre candidate would win. If there are two candidates with left-of-centre platforms, however, the vote might be split so that 25 per cent goes to one and 15 per cent goes to the other. In this case the right-of-centre candidate would win because their 30 per cent is the highest. Hence the Greens are caught in the dilemma of wanting to put pressure on politicians from both sides, but risk undermining the election of sympathetic front-runners if they put up their own candidate. The second consequence of the first-past-the-post system is that it is very difficult for smaller parties, such as the Greens, to get elected because successful candidates have to be the most popular to attract the largest share of the vote. To date there have been no Green party candidates elected to the US Congress or Westminster parliament.

2   In this situation, constituencies each elect several candidates. If there is a full-Senate election in Australia, for example, each state is treated as a single constituency and elects twelve senators. A quota is set for election of 7.7 per cent (calculated by 100 per cent divided by the number of people to be elected plus one). Each voter must number all candidates in order of preference. If a candidate reaches the quota with first preferences, they are elected and the votes they receive in excess of the quota are

distributed according to their second preferences. The preferences from the most unpopular candidates are also distributed until twelve candidates are elected. Hence it is easier for Green candidates to get elected because they need fewer votes and there have been Green senators ever since the late 1980s.

3   The most effective use of proportional representation has been in the state of Tasmania, where the House of Assembly has five multi-member constituencies. Until 1998, each constituency elected seven representatives, each requiring 12.5 per cent of the vote. The system was changed to five per constituency for the 1998 election, requiring 16.7 per cent. The Greens have had members in the Tasmanian House of Assembly since 1983 and have twice held the balance of power.

4   The Tasmanian Green–Labor Accord is an interesting case study because it represents a period when environmentalists theoretically had the maximum level of influence over policy and regulation. It also had major implications for other governments that later formed alliances with the Greens in New Zealand and Germany. For further information on this case see Crawford (1992), Diwell (1992), Lester (1992), *The Sunday Tasmanian* (1992), *The Examiner* (1991), Bates (1990), Flanagan (1990), Green (1981), Harries (1990), Haward (1990), Lowe (1985, 1990), Lynch (1990), McGee (1989), Darby (1989) and Prismall (1989).

5   In part this is due to who will control the Senate, but the preferential voting system used in the Commonwealth House of Representatives also gives the Greens some influence. Under this system successful candidates must obtain more than 50 per cent of the preferred vote. This is how it works. When each voter casts their ballot they number all candidates in order of their preference (i.e. 1 is their most preferred, 2 is their second choice, 3 their third and so on). If no candidate wins more than 50 per cent of the first preferences, the second preferences of the least popular candidates are distributed until one person has more than 50 per cent of the total ballots. For example, consider a poll where the Greens get 10 per cent, the Labor Party gets 42 per cent and the Liberal Party gets 43 per cent. If the Greens tell their supporters to direct their second preferences to Labor (and they follow this suggestion), then the Labor candidate would win with 52 per cent of the preferred vote. If they direct their preferences to the Liberals, they would win with 53 per cent of the vote. This system places the Greens in a very powerful position because even though they may not win, they can still register a protest and may determine which party wins the seat or, ultimately, government. As a consequence, both major parties have to develop policies to please the Greens in order to court their preferences. At the Commonwealth level, Green preferences

helped the Labor government retain power in the 1987 and 1990 polls after a series of pro-environment policy decisions designed to win their support (Doyle & Kellow 1995; Toyne 1994; Richardson 1994; McEachern 1991). In 1996 the Liberal Party's Natural Heritage Trust policy was deliberately designed to help it win government (in coalition with the Nationals) by siphoning off some of these Green preferences (Williams 1997). So the Greens can exert considerable power over policy without actually being elected.

Chapter 1

1   This information is based on an interview conducted by the author.
2   This observation is based on the author's experience studying science from within and without, working as a scientist in industry and working with other scientists.
3   The author attended the meeting in Adelaide, Australia.
4   While these theories have been applied to the study of international relations to explain why states often cheat on agreements (Brown 1997), the author has not seen them used with regard to the sceptic's dilemma and environmental policy.

Chapter 2

1   There is a small group of free-market environmentalists who would disagree with the need for more state intervention but these are very much in the minority within the environmental movement (see Eckersley 1993; DiLorenzo 1993).

Chapter 3

1   The term 'state' is used in two different senses in this book. To avoid confusion the following convention has been adopted. When referring to the total set of national institutions that constitute the public sector, rule a territory known as a country and represent all citizens contained within that country the term 'the state' will be used. When referring to the subnational, second tier of government institutions in federal systems such as the USA (e.g. California) or Australia (e.g. New South Wales), the term 'states' or 'the state government' will be used.

2   The author visited the agency in 2001 and interviewed two senior administrators working in the area of pollution regulation. One of them stressed the importance of integrated pollution control, the other mentioned the significance of the EU directive on integrated pollution prevention and control. Both tended to play down the resistance of industry.

3   The author interviewed senior people involved in setting up the NEPC secretariat in 1994 and later spoke to one of the administrators after the formation of the EPHC in 2002. One of the people helping to establish the NEPC from the Commonwealth side said that the goal of the new body was to 'epitomise and distil progress ... concerted progress into the standards that are set and protocols and goals and guidelines'. These would 'reflect best practice, best available technology' but would 'take into account economic and social factors'.

4   The author visited the Commonwealth department in 1994 and 2002 to conduct interviews with some of the people involved in coordinating parts of their environment protection and pollution regulation regime. One senior executive pointed out that countries adopt the system of environment protection that best suits their history, culture, 'structures of government' and 'structures of law'. He suggested that the early work of both the US EPA and the Commonwealth was to bring the worst polluting and most dangerous firms into line with regulations. By the 1990s, however, he believed that they had moved beyond just maintaining minimum standards and adopted other tools to encourage industry to 'be smart, save money, save energy, save on the environment'.

Chapter 4

1   These are sometimes referred to as 'command and control' regulations because opponents claim they are authoritarian (DiLorenzo 1993). They have also been referred to as 'end-of-pipe' solutions (Clayton et al. 1999). To avoid becoming bogged down in a dispute over terminology this book will simply use the term 'regulations' to refer to this kind of intervention.

2   The author visited the UK Environment Agency in 2001 and two of their senior managers explained how IPPC works in practice.

Chapter 5

1   Conducted by the author.

2   The Australasian Political Studies Association 2000 Conference, 3–6

October, Australian National University, Canberra, attended by the author.

3 The author was a member of this organisation's executive, was elected convenor for the period 1998–99 and was the main protagonist in this case study (i.e. he prepared the submission and reported back to the organisation). This analysis is therefore offered from the point of view of a participant-observer.

Chapter 8

1 By the author.

Chapter 9

1 That the author helped to organise and run in 2001.

Conclusions

1 This subtitle was inspired by the song 'Reasons to be cheerful, part 3' by Ian Dury and the Blockheads, Papillon Music.

Bibliography

Adam, B., Beck, U. & Van Loon, J. eds 2000, *The Risk Society and Beyond: Critical Issues for Social Theory*, Sage, London.

AMC (Australian Manufacturing Council) 1992, *The Environmental Challenge: Best Practice Environmental Management*, Australian Manufacturing Council, Melbourne.

——1994, *Leading the Way: A Study of Best Manufacturing Practices in Australia and New Zealand*, AMC, Melbourne.

Amy, D. J. 1990, 'Decision techniques for environmental policy: A critique' in *Managing Leviathan: Environmental Politics and the Administrative State*, eds R. Paehlke & D. Torgerson, Belhaven Press, London, pp. 59–79.

Anastapolo, G. 1989, *The Constitution of 1787: A Commentary*, John Hopkins University Press, Baltimore.

Anderson, J. & Howitt, A. 1995, 'Clean Air Act SIPs, sanctions and conformity', *Transportation Quarterly*, vol. 49, no. 3, pp. 67–79.

ANOP Research Services 1993, *Community Attitudes to Environmental Issues*, Department of Environment, Sport and Territories, Canberra.

Athanasiou, T. 1996, 'The Age of Greenwashing', *Capitalism, Nature, Socialism*, vol. 7, no.1, March, pp.1–36.

AtKisson, A. 1999, *Believing Cassandra: An Optimist Looks at a Pessimist's World*, Scribe, Melbourne.

Baker, R. 2002, 'The Lomborg file: When the press is lured by a Contraria's tale', *Columbia Journalism Review*, vol. 40, no. 6, March–April, pp. 78–80.

Bates, G. 1990, 'The Greening of Politics' in *The Greening of Government: The Impact of the Labor/Green Accord on Government in Tasmania*, ed. P. Lamour, Royal Australian Institute of Public Administration and Wombat Publishing, Hobart, pp. 13–15.

——1992, *Environmental Law in Australia*, 3rd edn, Butterworths, Sydney.

BCA (Business Council of Australia) 1991a, 'A Federal Environment Protection Agency: The question remains', *Business Council Bulletin*, vol. 79, pp. 36–8.

——1991b, 'Ecologically sustainable development: A truly heroic quest', *Business Council Bulletin*, vol. 79, September, pp. 6–11.

——1992, *Principles of Environmental Management*, Business Council of Australia, Melbourne.

Beattie, C., Longhurst, J. & Woodfield, N. 2002, 'Air Quality Action Plans: Early indicators of urban local authority practice in England', *Environmental and Science Policy*, vol. 5, pp. 463–70.

Beck, U. 1992, *Risk Society: Towards a New Modernity*, Sage, London.

——1994, 'The reinvention of politics: Towards a theory of reflexive modenization' in *Reflexive Modernization: Politics, Traditions and Aesthetics in the Modern Social Order*, eds U. Beck, A. Giddens & S. Lash, Polity Press, Cambridge, pp. 1–55.

——1998a, 'Politics of risk society' in *The Politics of Risk Society*, ed. J. Franklin, Polity Press, Cambridge, pp. 9–22.

——1998b, 'From industrial society to the risk society: Questions of survival, social structure and ecological enlightenment' in *Debating the Earth*, eds J. Dryzek & D. Schlosberg, Oxford University Press, Oxford, pp. 327–46.

——2000, 'Risk society revisited: Theory, politics and research programs' in *The Risk Society and Beyond: Critical Issues for Social Theory*, eds B. Adam, U. Beck & J. Van Loon, Sage, London, pp. 211–29.

Beck, U., Giddens, A. & Lash, S. 1994, *Reflexive Modernization: Politics, Tradition and Aesthetics in the Modern Social Order*, Polity Press, Cambridge.

Beder, S. 2002, *Global Spin: The Corporate Assault on Environmentalism*, revised edn, Green Books, UK.

Beetham, D. 1992, 'Liberal democracy and the limits of democratisation' in *Prospects for Democracy*, ed. D. Held, Blackwell, Oxford.

Bell, S. 1995, 'The environment—a fly in the ointment', *Chain Reaction*, vol. 73/74, pp. 30–3.

Bell, S. 1997, *Ball and Bell on Environmental Law*, Blackstone, London.

Benedick, R. 1998, *Ozone Diplomacy: New Directions in Safeguarding the Planet*, 2nd edn, Harvard University Press, Cambridge, Massachusetts.

Berger, S. 1972, *Peasants Against Politics*, Harvard University Press, Cambridge, Massachusetts.

——1981, *Organising Interests*, Cambridge University Press, Cambridge.

Bimber, B. 2001, 'Information and political engagement in America: The search for the effects of information technology at the individual level', *Political Research Quarterly*, vol. 54, no.1, pp. 53–67.

Blowers, A. 1997, 'Environmental policy: Ecological modernisation or the risk society?', *Urban Studies*, vol. 34, no. 5–6, pp. 845–71.

Boden, D. 2000, 'Worlds in action: Information, instantaneity and global futures trading' in *The Risk Society and Beyond: Critical Issues for Social Theory*, eds B. Adam, U. Beck & J. Van Loon, Sage, London, pp. 183–97.

Bongaarts, J. 2002, 'Population: Ignoring its impact', *Scientific American*, vol. 286, no. 1, pp. 67–9.

Bookchin, M. 1982, *The Ecology of Freedom*, Cheshire Books, California.

——1987, 'Social ecology versus deep ecology', *The Raven*, vol. 1, no. 3, November, pp. 219–50.

——1990, *Remaking Society: Pathways to a Green Future*, South End Press, Boston.

——1994, *Which Way for the Ecology Movement?*, AK Press, Edinburgh.

Bradbury, J. & Mitchell, J. 2001, 'Devolution: New politics for old?', *Parliamentary Affairs*, vol. 54, no. 2, pp. 257–75.

Bridgman, P. & Davis, G. 2002, *Australian Policy Handbook*, 3rd edn, Allen & Unwin, Sydney.

Briody, M. & Prenzler, T. 1998, 'The enforcement of environmental protection laws in Queensland: A case of regulatory capture?', *Environmental and Planning Law Journal*, vol. 15, no. 1, pp. 54–71.

Broad, R. 1994, 'The poor and the environment: Friends or foes?', *World Development*, vol. 22, no. 6, pp. 812–13.

Brogan, H. 1985, *Longman History of the United States of America*, Guild Publishing, London.

Brown, A. 1998, 'Asymmetrical devolution: The Scottish case', *The Political Quarterly*, vol. 69, no. 3, pp. 215–23.

Brown, B. 1990, 'Ecology, economy, equality, eternity' in *The Rest of the World is Watching*, eds C. Pybus & R. Flanagan, Pan Macmillan, Sydney.

——1991, 'First address concerning the first "No Confidence" motion in the Field Government', *Parliamentary Debates (Hansard), Tasmanian Parliament, House of Assembly*, 41st Parliament, Third Session 1991, No. 15, Hobart, pp. 4635–86.

Brown, C. 1997, *Understanding International Relations*, Macmillan, London.

Browner, C. 1993, 'Pollution prevention takes center stage', *EPA Journal*, vol. 19, no. 3, July–September, pp. 6–8.

——1996a, *Statement to Congressional Democrats' Hearing on FY 1996 EPA Budget*, 26 February, US Congress, Washington DC.

——1996b, *Statement to the Organization for Economic Cooperation and Development*, Environment Policy Committee Meeting, 20 February, Paris.

Bulleid, P. 1997, 'Assessing the need for EIA' in *Planning and Environmental Impact Assessment in Practice*, ed. J. Weston, Longman, London, pp. 26–41.

Burford, A. & Greenya, J. 1986, *Are You Tough Enough?*, McGraw-Hill, New York.

Callus, A. 2000, 'Analysis—investors with hearts bend corporate ears', *Planet*

Ark, <http://www.planetark.org/dailynewsstory.cfm?newsid=6623>, [accessed 11 May 2000.]

Cardwell, D. 1994, *The Fontana History of Technology*, Fontana, London.

Carson, R. 2000 [1962], *Silent Spring*, Folio Society, London.

Case, K. & Fair, R. 1989, *Principles of Economics*, Prentice-Hall, New Jersey.

Catma Films 1994, *The Drilling Fields*, BBC Channel 4, London.

Cebon, P. 1993, 'Corporate obstacles to pollution prevention', *EPA Journal*, vol. 19, no. 3, p. 20.

Chaney, F. 1991, 'The alternatives—the Opposition view on ESD', *The Australian Quarterly*, vol. 63, no. 4, Summer.

Chatterjee, P. & Finger, M. 1994, *The Earth Brokers: Power, Politics and World Development*, Routledge, London.

Chemical Week 2003, 'Lawmakers want more EPA Funds', vol. 265, no. 38, 22 October, p. 35.

Christoff, P. 1996, 'Ecological modernisation, ecological modernities', *Environmental Politics*, vol. 5, no. 3, pp. 476–500.

CIA (Central Intelligence Agency) 1996, *The World Factbook 1995*, Washington DC, <http://www.cia.gov/cia/publications/factbook>, accessed 1996.

——2003, *The World Factbook 2002*, Washington DC, <http://www.cia.gov/cia/publications/factbook>, accessed 2003.

Clark, M. 1980, *A Short History of Australia*, 2nd edn, Mentor, New York.

Clayton, A., Klemmensen, B. & Williams, R. 1999, *Policies for Cleaner Technology: A New Agenda for Government and Industry*, Earthscan, London.

Cohen, M. 1997. 'Risk society and ecological modernisation', *Futures*, vol. 29, no. 2, pp. 105–19.

Colebatch, H., Prasser, S. & Nethercote, J. eds 1997, *Business–Government Relations: Concepts and Issues*, Nelson, Melbourne.

Commonwealth EPA (Environment Protection Agency) 1994, *Public Review of the Commonwealth Environment Impact Assessment Process: Main Discussion Paper*, Australian Government Publishing Service, Canberra.

Consumer Reports 2001, 'Pesticides, food and you', vol. 66, no. 3, March, pp. 6–7.

Cooley, M. 1987, *Architect or Bee? The Human Price of Technology*, Hogarth Press, London.

Correy, S. 1998, 'The E-Files', *Radio National Background Briefing*, Australian Broadcasting Commission, Sydney, <http://www.abc.net.au/rn/talks/bbing/stories/s19072.htm>, accessed 1998.

Crawford, W. 1992, 'Labor–Liberal accord: Beat the Greens', *The Mercury*, 4 January, p. 9.

Crenson, M. 1971, *The Un-Politics of Air Pollution*, John Hopkins Press, Baltimore.

Crommelin, M. 1987, *Commonwealth Involvement in Environment Policy: Past, Present and Future*, Intergovernmental Relations in Victoria Program, University of Melbourne Law School, Melbourne.

Cropley, E. 2001, 'Body Shop has lost its soul—Founder Roddick', *Planet Ark*, <http://www.planetark.org/dailynewsstory.cfm/newsid/12155/story.htm>, accessed 27 August 2001.

Curran, G. 2001, 'The Third Way and ecological modernization', *Contemporary Politics*, vol. 7, no. 1, pp. 41–55.

Cushman, J. 1996, 'Adversaries back the current rules curbing pollution', *New York Times*, 12 February, pp. 1 and C11.

Dahl, R. 1967, *A Preface to Democratic Theory*, Chicago University Press, Chicago.

Dallek, R. 1984, *Ronald Reagan: The Politics of Symbolism*, Harvard University Press, Massachusetts.

Darby, A. 1989, 'Spirit of Accord offended, say Greens', *The Age*, 6 September.

DASETT (Department of Arts, Sport, the Environment, Tourism and Territories) 1991, *Australian National Report to the United Nations Conference on Environment and Development*, Australian Government Publishing Service, Canberra.

DEH (Department of the Environment and Heritage) 2002, *Annual Report 2001–02*, Canberra.

——2003, *Annual Report 2002–03*, Canberra, <www.deh.gov.au/about/annual-report/02–03/outcome–1-resources.html>, accessed 2003.

De La Court, T. 1990, *Beyond Brundtland: Green Development in the 1990s*, Zed Books, London.

Department of the Prime Minister and Cabinet 1990, *Ecologically Sustainable Development: A Commonwealth Discussion Paper*, Australian Government Publishing Service, Canberra.

Devall, B. & Sessions, G. 1985, *Deep Ecology*, Smith, Salt Lake City.

Diamond, J. & Quinby, L. 1988, *Feminism and Foucault: Reflections on Resistance*, Northeastern University Press, Boston.

Diesendorf, M. & Hamilton, C. 1997, 'The ecologically sustainable development process in Australia' in *Human Ecology, Human Economy*, eds M. Diesendorf & C. Hamilton, Allen & Unwin, Sydney.

DiLorenzo, T. 1993, 'The mirage of sustainable development', *The Futurist*, September–October, pp. 14–19.

DiMaggio, P. & Powell, W. eds 1991, *The New Institutionalism in Organisational Analysis*, University of Chicago Press, Chicago.

Diwell, S. 1992, 'Policy switch for investment boom', *The Mercury*, 22 September, p. 9.

Dobson, A. 2000, *Green Political Thought*, 3rd edn, Routledge, London.

Doggett, T. 2000, 'EPA, oil firms reach record deal to fix refineries', *Planet Ark*/Reuters, <http://www.planetark.com/dailynewsstory.cfm?newsid=7611 &newsdate=27-Jul-2000>, accessed 2004.

Douglas, M. 1972, 'Environments at risk' in *Ecology: The Shaping Enquiry*, ed. J. Benthall, Longman, London, pp. 129–45.

Dower, R. 1990, 'Hazardous waste' in *Public Policies for Environmental Protection*, ed. P. Portney, Resources for the Future, Washington DC, pp. 151–97.

Downes, D. 1996, 'Neo-corporatism and environmental policy', *Australian Journal of Political Science*, vol. 31, no. 2, July, pp. 175–90.

Doyle, T. 1998, 'Sustainable development and Agenda 21: The secular bible of global free markets and pluralist democracy', *Third World Quarterly*, vol. 19, no. 4, pp. 771–86.

——2000, *Green Power: The Environment Movement in Australia*, University of New South Wales Press, Sydney.

Doyle, T. & Kellow, A. 1995, *Environmental Politics and Policy Making in Australia*, Macmillan, Melbourne.

Doyle, T. & McEachern, D. 2001, *Environment and Politics*, 2nd edn, Routledge, London.

Dreyfus, D. & Ingram, H. 1985, 'The National Environmental Policy Act: A view of intent and practice' in *Enclosing the Environment: NEPA's Transformation of Conservation into Environmentalism*, ed. C. Kury, *Natural Resources Journal* 25th Anniversary Anthology, University of New Mexico School of Law, Albuquerque, pp. 49–67.

Dreyfus, H. & Rabinow, P. 1983, *Michel Foucault: Beyond Structuralism and Hermeneutics*, University of Chicago Press, Chicago.

Dryzek, J. 1987, *Rational Ecology: Environment and Political Economy*, Basil Blackwell, Oxford.

——1990, 'Designs for environmental discourse: The greening of the administrative state?' in *Managing Leviathan: Environmental Politics and the Administrative State*, eds R. Paehlke & D. Torgerson, Belhaven Press, London, pp. 97–111.

——1992, 'Ecology and discursive democracy: Beyond liberal capitalism and the administrative state', *Capitalism, Nature, Socialism*, vol. 3, no. 2, issue 10, June, pp. 18–24.

——1997, *The Politics of the Earth: Environmental Discourse*, Oxford University Press, Oxford.

Dryzek, J., Downes, D., Hunold, C. & Schlosberg, D., with Hernes, H.-K. 2003, *Green States and Social Movements: Environmentalism in the United States, United Kingdom, Germany and Norway*, Oxford University Press, Oxford.

Dryzek, J. & Schlosberg, D. eds. 1998, *Debating the Earth*, Oxford University Press, Oxford.

Dunleavy, P., Gamble, A., Heffernan, R., Holliday I. & Peele, G. eds 2002, *Developments in British Politics*, revised edn, Palgrave, Hampshire.

Duxbury, R. & Morton, S. 2000, *Blackstone's Statutes on Environmental Law*, 3rd edn, Blackstone, London.

Easterbrook, G. 1995, *A Moment on Earth: The Coming of Age of Environmental Optimism*, Viking, New York.

Eckersley, R. 1992, *Environmentalism and Political Theory: Toward an Ecocentric Approach*, State University of New York Press, Albany.

——1993, 'Free market environmentalism: Friend or foe?', *Environmental Politics*, vol. 2, no. 1, pp. 1–19.

——ed. 1995, *Markets, the State and the Environment*, Macmillan, Melbourne.

——2004, *The Green State: Rethinking Democracy and Sovereignty*, MIT Press, Massachusetts.

Eckersley, R. & Hay, P. 1993, 'Tasmania's Labor–Green Accord 1989–1991: Lessons from Lilliput', *Environmental Politics*, vol. 2, no. 1, pp. 88–93.

Economist, The (UK) 2003, 'Science and technology: Thought control; Bjørn Lomborg', vol. 366, no. 8306, 11 January, p. 72.

Economist, The (USA) 2002, 'Defending science; The environment', 2 February.

Economou, N. 1992, 'Problems in environmental policy creation: Tasmania's Wesley Vale Pulp Mill dispute' in *Australian Environmental Policy*, ed. K. Walker, University of New South Wales Press, Sydney, pp. 41–56.

Ehrlich, P. 1969, *The Population Bomb*, Pan, London.

Ehrlich, P. & Ehrlich, A. 1990, *The Population Explosion*, Simon and Schuster, New York.

Ekins, P. 1993, '"Limits to growth" and "sustainable development": Grappling with ecological realities', *Ecological Economics*, vol. 8, pp. 274–80.

Elliott, L. 1998, *The Global Politics of the Environment*, Macmillan, London.

English, J. 1997, 'The truth about toxins', *E Magazine*, November/December, pp. 21–2.

Environment Australia 1996, *State of the Environment Report*, Department of Environment and Heritage, Canberra, <http://www.ea.gov.au/soe/soe96/index.html>, accessed 2003.

——1999, *Our Community, Our Future: A Guide to Local Agenda 21*, <http://www.environment.gov.au/psg/igu/local/manual.pdf>, accessed 2001.

——2000, *Budget Initiatives and Explanations of Appropriations 2000–01 Budget Related Paper No. 1.7*, Canberra, <http://www.ea.gov.au/about/budget/budget2000/pbs/envher/index.html>, accessed 2003.

——2001a, *Environment Australia Achieves Investors in People Recognition*, Media Release, 11 December, <http://www.ea.gov.au/media/dept-mr/dp11dec01.html>, accessed 2002.

——2001b, *State of the Environment Report*, Department of Environment and Heritage, Canberra, <http://www.ea.gov.au/soe/2001/index.html>, accessed 2002.

——2003, *Eco-efficiency and Cleaner Production Database*, <http://www.ea.gov.au/industry/eecp/index.html>, accessed 2003.

Ernst & Young 1995, *Analysis of Public Comment on the National Pollutant Inventory Public Discussion Paper of February 1994*, Commonwealth Environment Protection Agency, Canberra.

ESD Steering Committee 1992, *National Strategy for Ecologically Sustainable Development*, Australian Government Publishing Service, Canberra.

ESD Working Group Chairs 1992, *Intersectoral Issues Report*, Australian Government Publishing Service, Canberra.

ESD Working Groups 1991, *Final Report—Executive Summaries*, Australian Government Publishing Service, Canberra.

ESD Working Groups—Manufacturing 1991, *Final Report*, Australian Government Publishing Service, Canberra.

Ettlin, R. 1990, 'Facts to reflect on', *EPA Journal*, vol. 16, no. 5, September/October, p. 29.

Everett, J. & Neu, D. 2000, 'Ecological modernization and the limits of environmental accounting', *Accounting Forum*, vol. 24, no. 1, pp. 5–29.

Examiner, The 1991, 'Turmoil will harm state', 11 April, Launceston.

Fairley, P. 1996, 'TRI: Growing pains', *Chemical Week*, 12 June, pp. 18–20.

Fayers, C. 1998, 'Environmental reporting and changing corporate environmental performance', *Accounting Forum*, vol. 22, no. 1, pp. 74–94.

Fieweger, K. 2000, 'Update—3M to stop making many Scotchgard products', *Planet Ark*, <http://www.planetark.org/dailynewsstory.cfm?newsid=6706>, accessed 17 May 2000.

Finer, E. 2000, 'Accounting for pollution', *Chemistry and Industry*, 16 October, pp. 668–9.

Fisher, R. 2002, 'Skeptical about the skeptical environmentalist', *Skeptical Inquirer*, vol. 26, no. 6, November–December, pp. 49–51.

Flanagan, R. 1990, 'Return the people's Pedder!' in *The Rest of the World is Watching*, eds C. Pybus & R. Flanagan, Pan Macmillan, Sydney.

Flannery, T. 1995, *The Future Eaters: An Ecological History of the Australasian Lands and People*, Reed Books, Sydney.

Flavin, C. 1997, 'The legacy of Rio' in *State of the World 1997*, Worldwatch Institute, Washington DC, <http://www.worldwatch.org/pubs/sow/sow97/ch01.html>, accessed 1997.

Ford, G. 1977, 'The President's News Conference of May 3, 1976' in *Public Papers of the Presidents of the United States: Gerald R. Ford, 1976–77*, Vol. II, National Archives and Record Service, Washington DC, pp. 1434–46.

Foreman, D. 1998, 'Putting the Earth first' in *Debating the Earth*, eds J. Dryzek & D. Schlosberg, Oxford University Press, Oxford, pp. 358–64.

Foreshew, J. 2001, 'Privacy the biggest e-government hurdle', *The Australian*, <http://australianit.news.com.au/common/storyPage/0 3811 1973192%255E9768 00.html>, accessed 2001.

Formby, J. 1986, 'Environmental policies in Australia—climbing the down escalator' in *Environmental Policies: An International Review*, ed. C. Park, Croom Helm, London, pp. 183–222.

Fosnot, C. ed. 1996, *Constructivism: Theory, Perspectives and Practice*, Teachers College Press, New York.

Foucault, M. 1977, *Discipline and Punish*, Penguin, London.

——1980, *Power/Knowledge*, ed. C. Gordon, Routledge, London.

——1985, *The History of Sexuality*, Vol. 2: *The Use of Pleasure*, Viking, London.

——1990, *The History of Sexuality*, Vol. 1: *An Introduction*, Penguin Books, London.

——1991, 'Governmentality' in *The Foucault Effect: Studies in Governmentality*, eds G. Burchell, C. Gordon & P. Miller, University of Chicago Press, Chicago, pp. 87–104.

Fox, W. 1984a, 'Deep ecology: A new philosophy in our time', *Ecologist*, vol. 14, no. 5–6, pp. 194–200.

——1984b, 'On guiding stars to deep ecology', *Ecologist*, vol. 14, no. 5–6, pp. 203–4.

Fraas, A. 1991, 'The role of economic analysis in shaping environmental policy', *Law and Contemporary Problems*, vol. 54, no. 4, Autumn, pp. 113–26.

Franklin, J. ed. 1998, *The Politics of Risk Society*, Polity Press, Cambridge.

Freeman, A. 1990, 'Water pollution policy' in *Public Policies for Environmental Protection*, ed. P. Portney, Resources for the Future, Washington DC, pp. 97–150.

Fullerton, T. 2004, 'The Lords of the Forests', *Four Corners*, Australian Broadcasting Corporation, Sydney, <http://www.abc.net.au/4corners/content/2003/transcripts/s1046232.htm>, accessed 16 February 2003.

Gallopin, G., Gutman, P. & Maletta, H. 1989, 'Global impoverishment, sustainable development and the environment: A conceptual approach', *International Social Science Journal*, vol. 41, August, pp. 377–95.

Garner, R. 2000, *Environmental Politics: Britain, Europe and the Global Environment*, Macmillan, London.

Garrett, G. & Weingast, B. 1991, 'Ideas, Interests and Institutions: Constructing the EC's Internal Market', paper presented to the NBER Conference on Political Economics, 15–16 November.

Gibson, R. 1990, 'Out of control and beyond understanding: Acid rain as a political dilemma' in *Managing Leviathan: Environmental Politics and the Administrative State*, eds R. Paehlke & D. Torgerson, Belhaven Press, London, pp. 243–57.

Giddens, A. 1994, 'Living in a post-traditional society' in *Reflexive Modernization: Politics, Traditions and Aesthetics in the Modern Social Order*, eds U. Beck, A. Giddens & S. Lash, Polity Press, London, pp. 56–109.

——1998a, 'Risk society: The context of British politics' in *The Politics of Risk Society*, ed. J. Franklin, Polity Press, Cambridge, pp. 23–34.

——1998b, *The Third Way: The Renewal of Social Democracy*, Polity Press, Cambridge.

Gilpin, A. 1980, *Environment Policy in Australia*, University of Queensland Press, Brisbane.

Ginsberg, B. & Shefter, M. 1990, 'After the Reagan revolution: A postelectoral politics' in *Looking Back on the Reagan Presidency*, ed. L. Berman, The John Hopkins University Press, Baltimore, pp. 241–67.

Goldfarb, T. ed. 1999, *Taking Sides: Clashing Views on Controversial Environmental Issues*, 8th edn, Dushkin/McGraw-Hill, USA.

Goldstein, T. 1988, *Dawn of Modern Science*, Houghton Mifflin, Boston.

Goodstein, E. 1999, *The Trade-Off Myth: Fact and Fiction About Jobs and the Environment*, Island Press, Washington DC.

Gore, A. 1992, *Earth in the Balance: Ecology and the Human Spirit*, Houghton Mifflin, New York.

Gorz, A. 1994, *Capitalism, Socialism, Ecology*, Verso, London.

Gottlieb, R., Smith, M., Roque, J. & Yates, P. 1995, 'New approach to toxics: Production design, right to know and definition debates' in *Reducing Toxics: A New Approach to Policy and Industrial Decision Making*, ed. R. Gottlieb, Island Press, Washington DC.

Green, R. 1981, *Battle for the Franklin*, ACF/Fontana, Melbourne.

Greenpeace 1999, *Greenpeace Rejects Flawed Law*, Media Release, 23 June, <http://www.greenpeace.org.au/press/releases/1998/230398.html>, accessed 2002.

Greenweek 1993a, 'Booklet tells how to make environmental tax claims', 6 July, p. 6.

——1993b, 'CEPA to help develop green products', 24 August, p. 6.

Greer, L. & van Loben Sels, C. 1999, 'When pollution prevention meets the bottom line' in *Taking Sides: Clashing Views on Controversial Environmental Issues*, ed. T. Goldfarb, 8th edn, Duchkin/McGraw-Hill, Guilford, pp. 267–74.

Gunningham, N. & Cornwall, A. 1994, 'Legislating the right to know', *Environmental and Planning Law Journal*, vol. 11, no. 4, pp. 274–88.

Gunningham, N. 1993, 'Empowering the public: Information strategies and environment protection', *Environmental Crime*, Australian Institute of Criminology Conference Proceedings, Hobart, pp. 225–45.

Gunningham, N., Grabosky, P. and Sinclair, D. 1998, *Smart Regulation: Designing Environmental Policy*, Clarendon Press, Oxford.

Guruswamy, L. 1991, 'The case for integrated pollution control', *Law and Contemporary Problems*, vol. 54, no. 4, Autumn, pp. 41–56.

Haas, E. 1990, *When Knowledge is Power: Three Models of Change in International Organisations*, University of California Press, Berkeley.

Habitch, F. 1990, 'Strategies for meeting our goals', *EPA Journal*, vol. 16, no. 5, September/October, pp. 8–11.

Hague, B. & Loader, B. 1999, 'Digital democracy: An introduction' in *Digital Democracy: Discourse and Decision Making in the Information Age*, eds B. Hague & B. Loader, Routledge, London, pp. 2–22.

Hague, R., Harrop, M. & Breslin, S. 1998, *Comparative Politics: An Introduction*, 4th edn, Macmillan, London.

Hahn, R. 1995, 'Economic prescriptions for environmental problems: Lessons from the United States and Continental Europe' in *Markets, The State and the Environment*, ed. R. Eckersley, Macmillan, Melbourne, pp. 129–56.

Hajer, M. 1995, *The Politics of Environmental Discourse: Ecological Modernization and the Policy Process*, Clarendon Press, Oxford.

Hale, M., Musso, J. & Weare, C. 1999, 'Developing digital democracy: Evidence from Californian municipal web pages' in *Digital Democracy: Discourse and Decision Making in the Information Age*, eds B. Hague & B. Loader, Routledge, London, pp. 96–115.

Hamilton, J. 1993, 'Pollution as news: Media and stock market reactions to the Toxics Release Inventory data', *Journal of Environmental Economics and Management*, vol. 28, pp. 98–113.

Harcourt, W. 1994, *Feminist Perspectives on Sustainable Development*, Zed Books, London.

Hardin, G. 1998 [1968], 'The tragedy of the commons' in *Debating the Earth*, eds J. Dryzek & D. Schlosberg, Oxford University Press, Oxford, pp. 23–34.

Hardin, R. 1982, *Collective Action*, The John Hopkins University Press, Baltimore.

Harding, R. ed. 1998, *Environmental Decision-Making: The Role of Scientists, Engineers and the Public*, Federation Press, Sydney.

Hare, B. 1992, 'Where to now?', *Habitat Australia*, vol. 20, no. 1, pp. 12–13.

Harries, C. 1990, 'Meet the Greens', *Habitat Australia*, vol. 18, no. 2, pp. 16–19.

Harris, S. 1993, *Environmental Regulation, Economic Growth and International Competitiveness*, Department of International Relations Research School of Pacific Studies Working Paper, Australian National University, Canberra.

Haward, M. 1990, 'The 1989 Tasmanian election: The Green Independents consolidate', *Australian Journal of Political Science*, vol. 25, no. 2, pp. 196–217.

Haward, M. & Larmour, P. eds 1993, *The Tasmanian Parliamentary Accord & Public Policy: Accommodating the New Politics?*, Federalism Research Centre, Australian National University Press, Canberra.

Hawke, N. 2002, *Environmental Policy: Implementation and Enforcement*, Ashgate, Aldershot.

Hawke, R. 1989, *Our Country, Our Future*, Australian Government Publishing Service, Canberra.

Hawken, P., Lovins, A. & Hunter, L. 1999, *Natural Capitalism: Creating the Next Industrial Revolution*, Little, Brown, USA.

Hay, P. 2002, *Main Currents in Western Environmental Thought*, University of New South Wales Press, Sydney.

Hearne, S. 1996, 'Tracking toxics: Chemical use and the public's "right-to-know"', *Environment*, July/August, pp. 4–34.

Helm, D. 1998, 'The Assessment: Environmental policy—objectives, instruments and institutions', *Oxford Review of Economic Policy*, vol. 14, no. 4, pp. 1–19.

Hewitt, P. 1998, 'Technology and democracy' in *The Politics of Risk Society*, ed. J. Franklin, Polity Press, Cambridge, pp. 83–9.

Hill, R. 1999, *Annual Report to the National Environment Protection Council on the Implementation of the National Environment Protection (National Pollutant Inventory) Measure for the Commonwealth*, NEPC Annual Report 1998–99, Adelaide, < http://www.nepc.gov.au, pp. 143–5>, accessed 2002.

Hindess, B. 1996, *Discourses of Power*, Blackwell, Oxford.

Hoberg, G. 1992, *Pluralism by Design: Environmental Policy and the American Regulatory State*, Praeger, New York.

Holdren, J. 2002, 'Energy: Asking the wrong question', *Scientific American*, vol. 286, no. 1, pp. 65–7.

Holland, I. & Fleming, J. eds 2003, *Government Reformed: Values and New Political Institutions*, Ashgate, Aldershot.

House of Commons Select Committee on the Environment, Transport and Regional Affairs 2000, *The Environment Agency*, HMSO, London.

Howard, P. 1994, *The Death of Common Sense: How Law is Suffocating America*, Random House, New York.

Howes, M. 1997, 'Shell's corporate citizenship in Nigeria', *Environment SA*, vol. 6, no. 3, p. 37.

——1998a, 'Has business won the "policy contest" and does it matter?' in *Green Politics in Grey Times: Ecopolitics XI Conference Proceedings*, ed. C. Star, 4–5 October 1997, University of Melbourne, Ecopolitics Association of Australasia, Hobart, pp. 6–16.

——1998b, 'Environment protection, sustainable industry and federal government: lessons for Australia from the USA' in *Ecopolitics X Conference Proceedings*, ed. Lorraine Elliott, 26–29 September 1996, Australian National University, Canberra, pp. 213–23.

——2000, 'A brief history of Commonwealth sustainable development policy discourse', *Policy, Organisation and Society*, vol. 19, no. 1, pp. 65–85.

——2001a, 'Globalisation and environmental protest: A case of reflexivity?', *Policy, Organisation and Society*, vol. 20, no. 2, pp. 77–96.

——2001b, 'What's your poison? The Australian National Pollution Inventory v. the US Toxics Release Inventory', *Australian Journal of Political Science*, vol. 36, no. 3, pp. 529–52.

——2001c, 'Digital disclosures: Environmental governance and the Internet' in *New Natures, New Culture, New Technologies Conference*, International Sociological Association, Research Committee on Environment and Society, Cambridge University, Fitzwilliam College.

——2002a, 'Reflexivity or governmentality? The curious case of on-line pollution inventories', paper presented at the XVth International Sociological Association World Congress of Sociology, 7–13 July 2002, Brisbane.

——2002b, 'Reflexive modernisation, the Internet, and democratic environmental decision-making', *Organization and Environment*, vol. 15, no. 3, pp. 323–6.

Hulsberg, W. 1988, *The German Greens: A Social and Political Profile*, Verso, London.

Hutton, D. ed. 1987, *Green Politics in Australia*, Angus and Robertson, Sydney.

Hutton, D. & Connors, L. 1999, *A History of the Australian Environment Movement*, Cambridge University Press, Cambridge.

ICESD (Intergovernmental Committee for Ecologically Sustainable Development) 1996, *Report on the Implementation of the National Strategy for Ecologically Sustainable Development (1993–1995)*, Department of Environment, Sport and Territories, Canberra.

IPCC (Intergovernmental Panel on Climate Change) 1995, IPCC Second Assessment—*Climate Change 1995*, United Nations, New York, <http://www.ipcc.ch/pub/reports.htm>, accessed 2004.

——2001a, *Climate Change 2001: Working Group I—The Scientific Basis*,

United Nations, NewYork, <http://www.grida.no/climate/ipcc_tar/wg1/index.htm>, accessed 2003.

——2001b, *Climate Change 2001: Working Group II—Impacts, Adaption, and Vulnerability*, United Nations, New York, <http://www.grida.no/climate/ipcc_tar/wg2/005.htm>, accessed 2003.

ITV (Independent Television) 1996, *The Price of Petrol: Shell in Nigeria*, London.

IUCN, WWF and UNEP (International Union for the Conservation of Nature and Natural Resources, the World Wildlife Fund and the United Nations Environment Programme) 1980, *World Conservation Strategy*, UN Publications, Geneva.

Jacobs, M. 1991, *The Green Economy: Environment, Sustainable Development, and the Politics of the Future*, Pluto Press, London.

——1995, 'Sustainability and "the market": A typology of environmental economics' in *Markets, The State and the Environment*, ed. R. Eckersley, Macmillan, Melbourne, pp. 46–70.

——ed. 1997, *Greening the Millennium? The New Politics of the Environment*, Blackwell Publishers, Oxford.

Jaensch, D. 1997, *The Politics of Australia*, 2nd edn, Macmillan, Melbourne.

Johnson, C., Tyson, L. & Zysman, J. eds 1989, *Politics and Productivity*, Ballinger, USA.

Johnson, H. 1991, *Sleepwalking Through History: America in the Reagan Years*, W. W. Norton and Co., New York.

Jordan, A. 2002, 'Environmental policy' in *Developments in British Politics*, eds P. Dunleavy, A. Gamble, R. Heffernan, I. Holliday & G. Peele, Palgrave, Houndmills, pp. 257–75.

Keating, P. 1992, *Australia's Environment: A Natural Asset—Prime Minister's Statement on the Environment*, Australian Government Publishing Service, Canberra.

Kellow, A. 1999, *International Toxic Risk Management: Ideals, Interests and Implementation*, Cambridge University Press, Cambridge.

Kellow, A. & Moon, J. 1993, 'Governing the environment: Problems and possibilities' in *Governing in the 1990s: An Agenda for the Decade*, ed. I. Marsh, Longman Cheshire, Melbourne.

Kellow, A. & Niemeyer, S. 1999, 'The development of environmental administration in Queensland and Western Australia: Why are they different?', *Australian Journal of Political Science*, vol. 34, no. 2, pp. 205–22.

Khanna, M., Quimio, W. & Bojilova, D. 1998, 'Toxics release information: A policy tool for environment protection', *Journal of Environmental Economics and Management*, vol. 36, pp. 243–66.

Kinrade, P. 1995, 'Towards ecologically sustainable development: The role and shortcomings of markets' in *Markets, The State and the Environment*, ed. R. Eckersley, Macmillan, Melbourne, pp. 86–109.

Klee, H. 1990, 'The industry perspective: Refining EPA/Amoco Yorktown project' in *Responding to Environmental Challenge: A Discussion Among People from Industry, Government and Environmental Groups*, The American Petroleum Industry Conference on Health and Environment, Washington DC, pp. 11–12.

Landy, M., Roberts, M. & Thomas, S. 1994, *The Environmental Protection Agency—Asking the Wrong Questions: From Nixon to Clinton*, expanded edn, Oxford University Press, New York.

Lash, S. 1994, 'Reflexivity and its doubles: Structure, aesthetics, community' in *Reflexive Modernization: Politics, Traditions and Aesthetics in the Modern Social Order*, eds U. Beck, A. Giddens & S. Lash, Polity Press, Cambridge, pp. 110–73.

——2000, 'Risk Culture' in *The Risk Society and Beyond: Critical Issues for Social Theory*, eds. B. Adam, U. Beck & J. Van Loon, Sage, London, pp. 47–62.

Lazarus, R. 1991, 'The neglected question of congressional oversight of EPA: *Quis Custodiet Ipsos Custodes* (Who shall watch the watchers themselves)?', *Law and Contemporary Problems*, vol. 54, no. 4, Autumn, pp. 205–20.

Lee-Wright, M. 1997, 'Taking charge of the environmental team' in *Planning and Environmental Impact Assessment in Practice*, ed. J. Weston, Longman, London, pp. 42–59.

Lele, S. 1991, 'Sustainable development: A critical review', *World Development*, vol. 19, no. 6, pp. 613–15.

Lester, M. 1989, 'Power to Parliament', *The Mercury*, Hobart, 30 May.

——1990, 'Leading ministers shafting greens to wreck accord', *The Mercury*, Hobart, 16 January.

——1992, 'Lib forest policy cops both barrels', *The Mercury*, Hobart, 13 January, p. 2.

Levitas, R. 2000, 'Discourses of risk and Utopia' in *The Risk Society and Beyond: Critical Issues for Social Theory*, eds B. Adam, U. Beck & J. Van Loon, Sage, London, pp. 198–210.

Liberal and National Parties 1993, *Environment Policy: A Better Environment—and Jobs*, Liberal and National Parties, Canberra.

Lindblom, C. 1977, *Politics and Markets*, Basic Books, New York.

Lomborg, B. 2001, *The Skeptical Environmentalist: Measuring the Real State of the World*, Cambridge University Press, Cambridge.

Lovejoy, T. 2002, 'Biodiversity: Dismissing scientific process', *Scientific American*, vol. 286, no. 1, pp. 69–71.

Lowe, D. 1985, 'A government changes' in *Battle for the Franklin*, ed. R. Green, ACFG/Fontana, Melbourne.

Lowe, E. 1996, 'Industrial ecology: A context for design and decision' in *Design for Environment: Creating Eco-Efficient Products and Processes*, ed. J. Fiksel, McGraw-Hill, New York, pp. 437–71.

Lowe, I. 1990, 'Global crisis: danger and opportunity' in *The Rest of the World is Watching*, eds C. Pybus & R. Flanagan, Pan Macmillan, Sydney.

Lukes, S. 1974, *Power: A Radical View*, Macmillan, London.

Lupton, D. 1999, *Risk*, Routledge, London.

Lynch, M. 1990, 'Uncharted territory' in *The Rest of the World is Watching*, eds C. Pybus & R. Flanagan, Pan Macmillan, Sydney.

McEachern, D. 1991, *Business Mates: The Power and Politics of the Hawke Era*, Prentice-Hall, Sydney.

——1993, 'Environmental policy in Australia 1981–91: A form of corporatism?', *Australian Journal of Public Administration*, vol. 52, no. 2, June, pp. 173–86.

McGarity, T. 1991, 'The internal structure of EPA rulemaking', *Law and Contemporary Problems*, vol. 54, no. 4, Autumn, pp. 57–112.

McGee, C. 1989, 'Union outcry over accord with Greens', *The Australian*, 31 May.

McLennan, W. 1999, *Environment Protection Expenditure: Australia*, Australian Bureau of Statistics, Canberra, <http://www.ausstats.abs.gov au/ausstats/subscriber.nsf/Lookup/CA25687100069892CA2568880028F 848/$File/46030_1995–96+and+1996–97.pdf>, accessed 2003.

Macpherson, C.B. 1966, *The Real World of Democracy*, Clarendon Press, Oxford.

Magarey, K. 1999, 'The Internet and Australian parliamentary democracy', *Parliamentary Affairs*, vol. 52, no. 3, pp. 404–28.

Malina, A. 1999, 'Perspectives on citizen democratisation and alienation in the virtual public sphere' in *Digital Democracy: Discourse and Decision Making in the Information Age*, eds B. Hague & B. Loader, Routledge, London, pp. 23–38.

Marcus, A. 1991, 'EPA's organizational structure', *Law and Contemporary Problems*, vol. 54, no. 4, Autumn, pp. 5–40.

Maslin, D. 2000, 'Are you efficient?', *Energy and Environmental Management*, July, pp. 32–4.

May, J. 1978, 'Defining democracy: A bid for coherence and consensus', *Political Studies*, vol. 26, no. 1, pp. 1–14.

Megalogenis, G. 1994, 'Economy no worse off with no GST', *The Australian*, 24 June, p. 4.

Meister, M. & Japp, P. 1998, 'Sustainable development and the global economy: Rhetorical implications for improving the quality of life', *Communication Research*, vol. 25, no. 4, pp. 399–421.

Merchant, C. 1992, *Radical Ecology: The Search for a Livable World*, Routledge, New York.

Mies, M. & Shiva, V. 1993, *Ecofeminism*, Spinifex, Melbourne.

Miliband, R. 1970, *The State in Capitalist Society*, Weidenfeld and Nicholson, London.

Miller, P. & Rose, N. 1993, 'Governing economic life' in *Foucault's New Domains*, eds M. Gane & T. Johnson, Routledge, London, pp. 75–105.

Milner, E. 1999, 'Electronic government: More than just a "good thing"? A question of "ACCESS"' in *Digital Democracy: Discourse and Decision Making in the Information Age*, eds B. Hague & B. Loader, Routledge, London, pp. 63–72.

Minter Ellison 1995, *Development of Legislative Modelling for the National Pollutant Inventory and Associated Community Right-to-Know in Australia*, Commonwealth Environment Protection Agency, Canberra.

Mol, A. & Spaargaren, G. 2000, 'Ecological modernisation theory in debate: A review', *Environmental Politics*, vol. 9, no. 1, pp. 17–49.

Moore, B. 1967, *Social Origins of Dictatorship and Democracy*, Penguin, London.

Moore, M. 1992, 'February 1 showdown', *The Mercury*, 3 January, pp. 1–2.

Moore, R. 1999, 'Democracy and cyberspace' in *Digital Democracy: Discourse and Decision Making in the Information Age*, eds B. Hague & B. Loader, Routledge, London, pp. 39–59.

Moran, A. 1995, 'Tools of environmental policy: Market instruments versus command-and-control' in *Markets, The State and the Environment*, ed. R. Eckersley, Macmillan, Melbourne, pp. 73–85.

Morgenstern, R., Pizer, W. & Shih, J. 1998, *The Cost of Environment Protection*, US EPA, Washington DC, <http://www.yosemite.epa.gov/EE/epa/wpi.nsf/7e8e12c2a0e34c0585256c2c00577d69/7e24bf9279f975bf852566c7005c0480?OpenDocument>, accessed 1999.

Murchison, K. 1994, 'Environmental law in Australia and the United States: A comparative overview', *Environmental and Planning Law Journal*, Part I, vol. 11, no. 3, pp. 179–92 and Part II, vol. 11, no. 5, pp. 254–73.

Murphy, S. 2000, 'European countries ban sphygmomanometer', *7:30 Report*, 15 February, Australian Broadcasting Commission, Sydney, <http://abc.net.au/7.30/stories/s100543.htm>, accessed 2001.

Naess, A. 1974, 'The shallow and the deep, long-range ecology movement: A summary' in *The Politics of the Environment*, ed. R. Goodin, Elgar, Aldershot.

——1984, 'Intuition, intrinsic value and deep ecology and guiding stars to deep ecology', *Ecologist*, vol. 14, no. 5–6, pp. 201–4.

NAPA (National Academy of Public Administration) 1995, *Setting Priorities, Getting Results: A New Direction for EPA*, Report to US Congress, Washington DC.

National Toxics Network 1998, *Community Right To Know About Pollution 'Gutted'*, press release, <http://www.spirit.com.au/~biomap/>, accessed 2002.

NCE (National Commission on Environment) 1993, *Choosing a Sustainable Future*, Island Press, Washington DC.

NCEP (National Commission for Employment Policy) 1995, *Environment and Jobs: The Employment Impact of Federal Environmental Investments*, NCEP Research Report No. 95–02, US Government Printing Office, Washington DC.

NEPC (National Environment Protection Council) 1998, *National Pollutant Inventory: Summary of Submissions Received by the National Environment Protection Council in Relation to the National Environment Protection Measure and Impact Statement for the National Pollutant Inventory and National Environment Protection Council's Response to those Submissions*, NEPC Corporation, Adelaide.

——2002, *Annual Report 2001–2002*, NEPC Corporation, Adelaide.

Newton, T. 1998, 'Theorising subjectivity in organisations: The failure of Foucauldian studies', *Organisational Studies*, vol. 19, no. 3, pp. 415–47.

Nicholson, M. 1987, *The New Environmental Age*, Cambridge University Press, Cambridge.

Nixon, R. 1971, 'Special message to the Congress about reorganisation plans to establish the Environmental Protection Agency and the National Oceanic and Atmospheric Administration' in *Public Papers of the Presidents of the United States: Richard Nixon*, Item No. 215, National Archives and Record Service, Washington DC, pp. 578–86.

North, R. 1995, *Life on a Modern Planet: A Manifesto for Progress*, Manchester University Press, Manchester.

OECD (Organisation for Economic Cooperation and Development) 1984, *Environment and Economics. Results of the International Conference on Environment and Economics*, OECD, Paris.

——1993, Industrial Policy in OECD Countries: Annual Review 1993, OECD, Paris.

——1996a, 'Environmental policies and employment' in *Report to the Meeting of OECD Environment Policy Committee at Ministerial Level*, Paris, 19–20 February, <http://www.oecd.org/news_and_events/reference/nw96–15a.htm>, accessed 1997.

——1996b, *Control of Hazardous Air Pollutants in OECD Countries*, OECD, Paris.

OECD Working Party on Environmental Performance 2000, *Environmental Performance Reviews (1st Cycle) 32 Countries (1993–2000)*, OECD, Paris.

Paehlke, R. ed. 1995, *Conservation and Environmentalism: An Encyclopaedia*, Garland Publishing, New York.

Paehlke, R. & Torgerson, D. eds 1990, *Managing Leviathan: Environmental Politics and the Administrative State*, Belhaven Press, London.

Palmer, J. ed. 2001, *Fifty Key Thinkers on the Environment*, Routledge, London.

Papadakis, E. 1984, *The Green Movement in West Germany*, Croom Helm, England.

——1993, *Politics and the Environment: The Australian Experience*, Allen & Unwin, Sydney.

——1996, *Environmental Politics and Institutional Change*, Cambridge University Press, Cambridge.

Partridge, M. 1987, 'Building a sustainable green economy: Ethical investment, ethical work' in *Green Politics in Australia*, ed. D. Hutton, Angus and Robertson, Sydney.

Passell, P. 1994, 'For utilities, new clean air plan', *New York Times*, November, pp. 18 and C1.

Patchak, R. & Smith, W. 1999, 'So long! command and control … hello! ISO 14000' in *Taking Sides: Clashing Views on Controversial Environmental Issues*, ed. T. Goldfarb, 8th edn, Dushkin/McGraw-Hill, Guilford, pp. 260–6.

PCSD (President's Council on Sustainable Development) 1996, *Final Report*, Washington DC, <http://www.whitehouse.gov/WH/EOP/pcsd/Council_report>, accessed 1997.

——1999a, *Historical Overview of the President's Council on Sustainable Development*, April, <http://www.whitehouse.gov/PCSD/history.htm>, accessed 1999.

——1999b, *National Town Meeting for a Sustainable America*, April, <http://www.whitehouse.gov/PCSD/ntm/index.htm>, accessed 1999.

PCSD New National Opportunities Task Force 1997, *Lessons Learned from Collaborative Approaches*, April, <http://www.whitehouse.gov/PCSD/Publications/Lessons_Learned.htm>, accessed 1998.

Pepper, D. 1993, *Eco-socialism: From Deep Ecology to Social Justice*, Routledge, New York.

Percival, R. 1991, 'Checks without balance: Executive office oversight of the Environmental Protection Agency', *Law and Contemporary Problems*, vol. 54, no. 4, Autumn, pp. 127–204.

Petulla, J. 1987, *Environmental Protection in the United States: Industry, Agencies, Environmentalists*, University of San Francisco, San Francisco.

Piore, M. & Sabel, C. 1984, *The Second Industrial Divide: Possibilities for Prosperity*, Basic Books, New York.

Plumwood, V. 1986, 'Ecofeminism: An overview and discussions of positions and arguments', *Australasian Journal of Philosophy*, vol. 64, June, pp. 120–38.

Porter, M. & van der Linde, C. 1995, 'Green and competitive: Ending the stalemate', *Harvard Business Review*, September–October, pp. 120–34.

Portney, P. ed. 1990, *Public Policies for Environmental Protection*, Resources for the Future, Washington DC.

Poster, M. 1984, *Foucault, Marxism and History*, Polity Press, Cambridge.

Postman, N. 1993, *Technopoly: The Surrender of Culture to Technology*, Vintage Books, New York.

Powell, S. 2001, 'New challenges: Residential pesticide exposure assessment in the California Department of Pesticide Regulation', *The Annals of Occupational Hygiene*, vol. 45, no. 1001, April, p. 119.

Pratt, R. & Phillips, P. 2000, 'The role and success of UK waste minimisation clubs in the correction of market and information failures', *Resources, Conservation and Recycling*, vol. 30, pp. 201–19.

Prescott-Allen, R. 2001, *The Wellbeing of Nations: A Country-by-Country Index of Quality of Life and the Environment*, Island Press, Washington DC.

Prismall, B. 1989, 'Green campaign over boundaries', *The Examiner*, Launceston, 6 September.

Productivity Commission 2000, *Implementation of Ecologically Sustainable Development by Commonwealth Departments and Agencies—Final Report*, <http://www.pc.gov.au/inquiry/esd/finalreport/index.html>, accessed 2000.

Pusey, M. 1991, *Economic Rationalism in Canberra: A Nation Building State Changes its Mind*, Cambridge University Press, Melbourne.

Pybus, C. 1991, 'For Napoleon, there's nowhere to go but down', *Australian Society*, vol. 10, no. 11, pp. 20–3.

Pybus, C. & Flanagan, R. 1990, *The Rest of the World is Watching*, Pan Macmillan, Sydney.

QEPA (Queensland Environmental Protection Agency) 1999, *Coming Clean in South East Queensland—A Trial of the National Pollutant Inventory*, Queensland Department of Environment and Heritage, Brisbane.

Queensland Conservation Council 1999, *Urban Air Quality*, media release, <http//www.qccqld.org.au/big.htm>, accessed 2002.

Rabinow, P. ed. 1991, *The Foucault Reader*, Penguin, London.

Rae, M. 1991, 'No, Australians won't have to live in caves', *Australian Quarterly*, vol. 63, no. 4, pp. 383–93.

RCEP (Royal Commission on Environmental Pollution) 1971, *First Report*, HMSO, London.

Reilly, W. 1990a, 'The green thumb of capitalism: The environmental benefits of sustainable growth', *Policy Review*, Fall, pp. 16–21.

——1990b, 'A vision for EPA's future', *EPA Journal*, vol. 16, no. 5, September/October, pp. 4–7.

Reuters News Service 2003, *Planet Ark Archive*, <http://www.planetark.org/searchhome.cfm>, accessed 2004.

——2004, 'Negligence led to deadly China gas leak', *Planet Ark*, 5 January, <http://www.planetark.com/dailynewsstory.cfm/newsid/23313/story.htm>, accessed 2004.

Richards, J., Glegg, G. & Cullinane, S. 2000, 'Environmental regulation: Industry and the marine environment', *Journal of Environmental Management*, vol. 58, pp. 119–34.

Richardson, G. 1994, *Whatever It Takes*, Bantam, Sydney.

Richman, L. 1992, 'Bringing reason to regulation', *Fortune*, vol. 126, no. 8, 19 October, pp. 94–6.

Rio Earth Summit 1992, *Agenda 21*, United Nations, <http://www.un.org/esa/sustdev/agenda21.htm>, accessed 1996.

Rio+5 1997, *Resolution Adopted by the General Assembly*, United Nations, <http://www.un.org/documents/ga/res/spec/aress19–2.htm>, accessed 1997.

Rio+10 2002a, *Report of the World Summit on Sustainable Development*, Johannesburg, South Africa, 26 August–4 September, United Nations, <http://www.johannesburgsummit.org/html/documents/summit_docs/131302_wssd_report_reissued.pdf>, accessed 2002.

——2002b, *UN Johannesburg Summit Press Release*, United Nations, <http://www.johannesburgsummit.org/html/whats_new/feature_story 39.htm>, accessed 2002.

RMIT (Royal Melbourne Institute of Technology) Centre for Design 1994, *Job Description for Project Coordinator—EcoReDesign*, Royal Melbourne Institute of Technology, Melbourne.

Roddick, A. 1991, *Body and Soul*, Ebury Press, London.

—— 2000, *Business as Unusual*, Thorsons, London.

Rose, H. 2000, 'Risk, trust and scepticism in the age of the new genetics' in *The Risk Society and Beyond: Critical Issues for Social Theory*, eds B. Adam, U. Beck & J. Van Loon, Sage, London, pp. 63–77.

Rosenbaum, W. 1991, *Environmental Politics and Policy*, Congressional Quarterly, Washington DC.

Rowell, A. 1994, *Shell-Shocked: The Environmental and Social Costs of Living with Shell in Nigeria*, Greenpeace, <http://www.greenpeace.org/~comms/ken/over.html>, accessed 1997.

Ruckelshaus, W. 1993, *US EPA Oral History Interview—1: William D. Ruck-elshaus*, US EPA History Program, Washington DC.

Rustow, D. 1990, 'Democracy: A global revolution?', *Foreign Affairs*, vol. 69, no. 4, pp. 75–91.

Rutherford, P. 1994, 'The administration of life: Ecological discourse as "intellectual machinery of government"', *Australian Journal of Communication*, vol. 23, no. 3, pp. 40–55.

Rutherford, P. & Fowler, R. 1992, 'The federal EPA: States vs. Commonwealth', *Chain Reaction*, vol. 65, March, pp. 18–22.

Schang, E. 2003, 'Top Danish environmentalist rejects fraud charges', *Planet Ark*, Reuters, 13 January, <http://www.planetark.org/dailynewsstory.cfm?newsid=19383andnewsdate=13-Jan–2003>, accessed 2003.

Schneider, S. 2002, 'Global warming: Neglecting the complexities', *Scientific American*, vol. 286, no. 1, pp. 62–5.

Schrecker, T. 1990, 'Resisting environmental regulation: The cryptic pattern of business–government relations' in *Managing Leviathan: Environmental Politics and the Administrative State*, eds R. Paehlke & D. Torgerson, Belhaven Press, London, pp. 165–99.

Schwartz, P. & Randall, D. 2003, *An Abrupt Climate Change Scenario and its Implications for United States National Security*, US Department of Defence, Washington DC, <http://www.ems.org/climate/pentagon_climatechange.pdf>, accessed 2004.

Scott, A. 2000, 'Risk society or angst society?' in *The Risk Society and Beyond: Critical Issues for Social Theory*, eds B. Adam, U. Beck & J. Van Loon, Sage, London, pp. 33–46.

Selcraig, B. 1997, 'What you don't know can hurt you', *Sierra*, January/February, pp. 38–43, 94–5.

Shapiro, M. 1990, 'Toxic substances policy' in *Public Policies for Environmental Protection*, ed. P. Portney, Resources for the Future, Washington DC, pp. 197–226.

Shiva, V. 2000, 'The historic significance of Seattle', *Synthesis/Regeneration*, vol. 22, Spring, <http://www.greens.org/s-r/22/22–18.html>, accessed 2000.

Simberloff, D. 2002, 'The environment: Skewed skepticism', *American Scientist*, vol. 90, no. 2, March–April, pp. 184–7.

Simon, J. & Kahn, H. 1984, *The Resourceful Earth*, Blackwell, New York.

Simons, L. 1998, 'Indonesia's plague of fire', *National Geographic*, vol. 194, no. 2, August.

Slagle, B. 1995, 'New developments in environmental policy', *Business Council Bulletin*, October/November, pp. 10–12.

Smith, J. 2001, 'Cyber subversion in the information economy', *Dissent*, vol. 48, no. 2, pp. 48–52.

Smith, R. 2001, 'The implementation of EIA in Britain' in *European Union Environmental Policy and New Forms of Governance*, eds H. Heinelt, T. Malek, R. Smith & A. Toller, Ashgate, Aldershot, pp. 167–84.

Society of Chemical Industry UK 1994, 'Campaigners scorn pollution inventory', *Chemistry and Industry*, vol. 18, September, p. 704.

Soskice, D. 1992, *Reconciling Markets and Institutions: The German Apprenticeship System*, Institute of Economic Statistics, Oxford University, Oxford.

Starr, C. 1969, 'Social benefit versus technological risk: What is our society willing to pay for safety?', *Science*, vol. 195, pp. 1232–8.

Stigler, G. 1971, 'The theory of economic regulation', *Bell Journal of Economics and Management Science*, vol. 2, no. 1, Spring, pp. 3–21.

Stratford, E. 1994, 'Disciplining the feminine, the home and nature in three Australian public health histories', *Australian Journal of Communication*, vol. 21, no. 3, pp. 56–71.

Streets, S. & Di Carlo, A. 1999, 'Australia's first national environmental protection measures: Are we advancing, retreating or simply marking time?', *Environmental and Planning Law Journal*, vol. 16, no. 1, pp. 25–60.

Sullivan, R. 1999, 'The national environment protection measure for the National Pollution Inventory: Legal, technical and policy issues', *Environmental and Planning Law Journal*, vol. 16, no. 5, pp. 365–75.

Sunday Tasmanian, The 1992, 'How you voted', 2 February, p. 6.

Suzuki, D. 1990, *Inventing the Future*, Allen & Unwin, Sydney.

Suzuki, D. & Dressel, H. 2002, *Good News for a Change: Hope for a Troubled Planet*, Allen & Unwin, Sydney.

Symmonds, M. 2000, 'Government and the Internet: Digital democracy', *The Economist*, vol. 355, no. 8176, pp. 31–4.

Taberner, J. 1999, 'Environmental law—disclosure and privilege', *Australian Company Secretary*, November, pp. 469–72.

Thomas, I. 1996, *Environmental Impact Assessment in Australia: Theory and Practice*, Federation Press, Sydney.

Thompson, E. 1980, 'The "Washminster" mutation' in *Responsible Government in Australia*, eds P. Weller & D. Jaensch, Drummond and the Australasian Political Studies Association, Victoria, pp. 32–40.

Thompson, J. 1995, 'Sustainability, justice and market relations' in *Markets, The State and the Environment*, ed. R. Eckersley, Macmillan, Melbourne, pp. 275–93.

Thompson, M., Rayner, S. & Ney, S. 1998a, 'Risk and governance Part I: The discourses of climate change', *Government and Opposition*, vol. 33, no. 2, pp. 139–66.

——1998b, 'Risk and governance Part II: Policy in a complex and plurally perceived world', *Government and Opposition*, vol. 33, no. 3, pp. 330–54.

Tomaney, J. 2000, 'End of the Empire State? New Labour and Devolution in the United Kingdom', *International Journal of Urban and Regional Research*, vol. 24, no. 3, pp. 675–88.

Toyne, P. 1994, *The Reluctant Nation: Environment, Law and Politics in Australia*, ABC Books, Sydney.

Train, R. 1993, *US EPA Oral History Interview—2: Russell E. Train*, EPA Oral History Program, Washington DC.

Tribe, D. 2003, 'Harsh blow for green Luddites', *The Australian*, 26 December, p. 9.

Tyson, L. & Kenen, P. eds 1980, *The Impact of International Disturbances on the Soviet Union and Eastern Europe*, Peramgon Press, USA.

UK Department of Environment, Food and Rural Affairs 2002, *Expenditure by Industry on Environment Protection*, HMSO, London, <http://www.defra.gov.uk/environment/statistics/envsurvey/expn2000/index.htm>, accessed 2003.

UK Department of Trade and Industry 1991, *Cleaner Technology in the UK: Final Report by PA Consulting Group*, HMSO, London.

UK EA (United Kingdom Environment Agency) 1997, *Corporate Plan Summary 1997/98*, HMSO, London.

——2000, *Pollution Inventory—Background*, <http://www.146.101.4.38/wiyby/html/b_isr.htm>, accessed 2001.

——2001, *New Pollution Inventory Shows Significant Reduction in Key Pollutants*, <http://www.environment-agency.gov.uk//modules/MOD44.876.html>, accessed 2001.

——2002, *Annual Report and Accounts 2001/02: Planning for a Sustainable Future*, HMSO, London.

UK Government 1990, *This Common Inheritance: Britain's Environmental Strategy*, HMSO, London.

—— 1994, *Sustainable Development: The UK Strategy*, HMSO, London.

——1999, *A Better Quality of Life: A Strategy for Sustainable Development in the UK*, HMSO, London.

——2002, *Achieving a Better Quality of Life: Review of Progress Towards Sustainable Development—Government Annual Report 2002*, HMSO, London.

UK Local Government Management Board 1997, *Local Agenda 21 in the UK: The First 5 Years*, HMSO, London.

UK Office of Statistics 1998, *Britain 1999: The Official Yearbook of the United Kingdom*, HMSO, London.

UK Sustainable Development Commission 2003, *Agenda 2003: Where Next for Sustainable Development?*, HMSO, London.

UNCED (United Nations Conference on Environment and Development) 1992, *Agenda 21*, <http://www.erin.gov.au/portfolio/esd/nsesd/Agenda21.html>, accessed 1996.

Underwood, J. 1993, 'Going green for profit', *EPA Journal*, vol. 19, no. 3, pp. 9–13.

UNEP (United Nations Environment Program) 1990, *Global Outlook 2000*, United Nations, New York.

——2002, *Global Environment Outlook 3*, Earthscan, <http://www.unep.org/geo/geo3/english/index.htm>, accessed 2003.

US Department of Commerce, Economic Affairs Office of Business Analysis 1985, *The US Primary Iron and Steel Industry Since 1958*, US Government Printing Office, Washington DC.

US Department of State 1972, *Safeguarding Our World Environment: The UN Conference on the Human Environment, Stockholm, June 1972*, US Government Printing Office, Washington DC.

US EPA (United States Environmental Protection Agency) 1990, *A Preliminary Analysis of the Public Costs of Environmental Protection: 1981–2000*, EPA Office of Administration and Resources Management, Washington DC.

——1993, *Sustainable Development and the Environmental Protection Agency: Report to Congress*, Policy Planning and Evaluation, Washington DC.

——1994a, *Creating a US Environmental Protection Agency That Works Better and Costs Less: Phase I Report, National Performance Review*, US EPA, Washington DC.

——1994b, *The New Generation of Environmental Protection: EPA's Five-Year Strategic Plan*, Office of the Administrator, Washington DC.

——1995a, *The U.S. EPA's 25th Anniversary Report: 1970–1995*, <http://www.epa.gov/25year/>, accessed 1997.

——1995b, *Guide to Environmental Issues*, US EPA, Washington DC.

——1997, *Managing for Better Environmental Results*, US EPA, Washington DC, <http://www.epa.gov/reinvent/annual/>, accessed 1997.

——2000, *Toxics Release Inventory*, US EPA, Washington DC, <http://www.epa.gov/tri>, accessed 2000.

——2001, *TRI Releases 1988–1998*, US EPA, Washington DC, <http://www.epa.gov/tri/tri98/data/sum8898c1.pdf>, accessed 2001.

——2002, *Fiscal Year 2001 Annual Report*, US EPA, Washington DC, <http://www.epa-gov/ocfo/finstatement/2001ar/Zoolar.htm>, accessed 2003.

——2004, *Summary of the EPA's Budget FY 2004*, US EPA, Washington DC, <http://www.epa.gov/ocfo/budget/2004/2004bib.pdf>, accessed 2004.

US Government 1991, 'Environmental Protection Agency' in *Federal Government Directory*, US Government Printing Office, Washington DC.

——1992, *US Actions for a Better Environment: A Sustained Commitment: Response to the Rio Earth Summit*, Washington DC.

US House of Representatives Committee on Energy and Commerce— Subcommittee on Oversight and Investigations, Together with Minority Views 1984, *Investigation of the Environmental Protection Agency: Report on the President's Claim of Executive Privilege Over EPA Documents, Abuses in the Superfund Program and Other Matters*, US Government Printing Office, Washington DC.

Van Berkel, R. 2000, 'Cleaner production in Australia: Revolutionary strategy or incremental tool?', *Australian Journal of Environmental Management*, vol. 7, no. 3, September, pp. 132–46.

Van Loon, J. 2000, 'Virtual risks in an age of cybernetic reproduction' in *The Risk Society and Beyond: Critical Issues for Social Theory*, eds B. Adam, U. Beck & J. Van Loon, Sage, London, pp. 165–82.

Vidal, J. 1997, 'World turning blind eye to catastrophe', *Guardian Weekly*, vol. 156, no. 5, 2 February, p. 1.

Vogel, D. & Kun, V. 1987, 'The comparative study of environmental policy: A review of the literature' in *Comparative Policy Research: Learning from Experience*, eds M. Dierkes, H. Weiler & A. Antal, Gower, Aldershot, pp. 99–170.

Wagman, R. ed. 1995, *The World Almanac of US Politics*, 1995–97 edn, World Almanac Books, New Jersey.

Walker, K. & Crowley, K. 1999, *Australian Environmental Policy 2. Studies in Decline and Devolution*, University of New South Wales Press, Sydney.

Warren, K. 1997, *Ecofeminism: Women, Culture, Nature*, Indiana University Press, Bloomington.

Waud, R., Hocking, A., Maxwell, P. & Bonnici, J. 1989, *Economics*, Australian edn, Harper and Row, Sydney.

WCED (World Commission on Environment and Development) 1990, *Our Common Future*, Australian edn, Oxford University Press, Melbourne.

Weale, A. 1998, 'The politics of ecological modernization' in *Debating the Earth*, eds J. Dryzek & D. Schlosberg, Oxford University Press, Oxford, pp. 301–18.

West Australian Government 1994, *The Proposed National Environment Protection Council (NEPC): Analysis and Criticisms of the Concept by the Government of Western Australia*, Perth.

Weston, J. 1997, 'EIA in the UK' in *Planning and Environmental Impact Assessment in Practice*, ed. J. Weston, Longman, London, pp. 1–25.

Wilhelm, A. 1999, 'Virtual sounding boards: How deliberative is online political discussion?' in *Digital Democracy: Discourse and Decision Making in the Information Age*, eds B. Hague & B. Loader, Routledge, London, pp. 154–76.

Williams, D. 1993, *The Guardian: EPA's Formative Years, 1970–1973*, US EPA, Washington DC.

Williams, P. 1997, *The Victory: The Inside Story of the Takeover of Australia*, Allen & Unwin, Sydney.

Williams, R. 1977, 'Government response to man-made hazards', *Government and Opposition*, vol. 12, no. 1, pp. 3–19.

Wise, J. 1992, 'Partnership for environmental technology education', paper presented to the Second Semi-Annual Resource Instructor Conference, 21 February, Las Vegas.

Wolf, C. 1979, 'A theory of non-market failures', *Public Interest*, vol. 55, Spring, pp. 114–33.

Yearley, S. & Forrester, J. 2000, 'Shell, a sure target for global environmental campaigning?' in *Global Social Movements*, eds R. Cohen & S. Rai, The Athlone Press, London, pp. 134–45.

Zarsky, L. 1990, 'The green market', *Australian Left Review*, vol. 124, December, pp. 12–17.

Zysman, J. 1994, 'How institutions create historically rooted trajectories of growth', *Industrial and Corporate Change*, vol. 3, no. 1, pp. 243–83.

Index